Seasons of Refreshing

Also by the Author

Charles Grandison Finney, 1792–1875:
    Revivalist and Reformer

Issues in American Christianity:
    Primary Sources with Introductions

Ingredients of the Christian Faith:
    Teachings of the Bible in Plain Language

The Spiritual Awakeners: American Revivalists
    from Solomon Stoddard to Dwight L. Moody

Seasons of Refreshing

Evangelism and Revivals in America

Keith J. Hardman

Foreword by Luis Palau

Wipf & Stock
PUBLISHERS
Eugene, Oregon

Wipf and Stock Publishers
199 W 8th Ave, Suite 3
Eugene, OR 97401

Seasons of Refreshing
Evangelism and Revivals in America
By Hardman, Keith J.
Copyright©1994 Hardman, Keith J.
ISBN: 1-59752-512-X
Publication date 3/1/2006
Previously published by Baker Books, 1994

Cover: A Methodist camp meeting held near Wilmington, Delaware, in 1853
(Courtesy of the Billy Graham Center Museum)

To my wife, Jean

.

Contents

$\mathcal{F}$oreword

Keith J. Hardman's *Seasons of Refreshing* has stimulated me—and I'm sure will stimulate all its readers—to a renewed passion for evangelism and revival in America in our day.

As this book shows, the history of America is closely tied to the history of evangelism and revivals, from long before the Declaration of Independence to our own day:

Two and one-half centuries ago, colonial America experienced its first spiritual awakening under the preaching of Jonathan Edwards and other great preachers. A second awakening followed two generations later.

One and one-half centuries ago, Charles Finney spontaneously moved out by the Holy Spirit. He had a great mind but little theological training. As he promoted revival of the heart he also awakened the conscience of America to social issues from slavery and habit-forming vices to the need for a sanctified family. His influence on society touched the nation before, during, and after its greatest time of national crisis, the Civil War.

One hundred years ago D. L. Moody and others preserved the spirit of the nation by the proclamation of the gospel to great masses across the land. Those crusades unquestionably encouraged the nation to look upward and pull together after the Civil War in response to the pressures of urbanization and industrialization.

At the beginning of the twentieth century R. A. Torrey, John Wilbur Chapman, and Billy Sunday were God's instruments to keep biblical doctrines and the concept of conversion and sanctification before the nation.

Between the two World Wars—during the Roaring Twenties and the Great Depression—Christians unfortunately engaged in conflict and severe confrontations with one another more than they sought to make a national impact through the preaching of the gospel. The outbreak of World War II, however, set off a new explosion that the noted historian of evangelism and revivals, J. Edwin Orr, called the mid-century revival. Allied troops were evangelized, the National Association of Evangelicals was organized, a great push was made into radio, the number of Christian colleges and seminaries with a strong biblical base swelled, tens of thousands of college and university students were converted, a movement of lay men and women responded to the need for day-to-day evangelism and discipling, and such influential magazines as *Christianity Today* kept the movement informed, homogenous, and on course.

That mid-century revival seemed to come to a shocking halt, however, as a consequence of the Vietnam War and its aftermath. After years of shying away from political and social action, converted Christians—upon seeing the national decay—rightly turned their attention toward Washington, D.C., and its power to change the nation politically. They also turned to Dallas, Los Angeles, New York City, and other cities of power for media influence.

Two major currents emerged: (1) powerful political action, and (2) heavy involvement in electronic media. These currents have definitely left their mark on the heart and psyche of American Christianity in the 1990s.

Fifty years after the mid-century revival, however, a reevaluation is taking place. Despite the excellent socio-political involvement, which was imperative, frustration has set in. The nation has not been fundamentally restored to the extent that the evangelical crusade envisaged. Witness:

- rampant corruption
- family disintegration
- violence in the streets
- outward professions of faith without a salt-and-light effect on society
- biblical illiteracy
- church membership presumably at 40 percent but regular attendance at less than 20 percent

Such disturbing trends have provoked evangelical leaders and thinkers to reevaluate where America stands spiritually and morally in its national leadership, the state of the church, the void of God-honoring programming in the secular media, and the paganization of the younger generation because of the exclusion of God from the schools. Decay has set in internally, as during the days of Israel and Judah of old. Scanning the daily newspapers and newscasts reveals a nation morally rotting and on a slippery slope to judgment and destruction at an accelerated pace.

We have once again seen that without conversion there is no vital change in the hearts of men and women. Repentance, faith in Jesus Christ as the crucified and resurrected Son of God, obedience to Christ's words and commands, and the expectation of his second coming are the only steps upward to change and renewal for any nation. Only as Jesus Christ indwells millions of Americans by his Holy Spirit can a nation find the peace and wholeness that Christian (and even secular) activists dream of securing.

In this book Hardman directly and indirectly calls upon us, through his perceptive historical analysis, to join forces in the Body of Christ, to support one another, to speak well of one another, and to work together to reevangelize this nation in our day.

All of us who love Jesus Christ want to see a mighty and fresh evangelistic explosion in our generation. By faith we can imagine seeing in our time the rescued lives, the sanctified young people, the flourishing families, and the revitalized inner cities. Hardman reminds us that it has happened in our history before; it should happen again in our time.

History will some day tell if we rose to the occasion in the name of God Almighty, using the Word of God authoritatively in this generation to lovingly reach out to friend and foe alike with the saving gospel of Jesus Christ.

Luis Palau, president
Luis Palau Evangelistic Association

$\mathcal{P}$reface

This volume owes its existence to a number of good people who have taught, guided, or otherwise inspired me, and to whom I am greatly indebted. I first became interested in awakenings during graduate work at Princeton Seminary, Columbia University, and the University of Pennsylvania. Since those delightful days my interest in the entire field has continued to grow. One of my mentors in this was a foremost authority on revivals, J. Edwin Orr, whose seminars at Oxford University I attended with much profit.

I deeply appreciate the help given by the staff at Baker Book House, where there is a large number of highly talented people. Special thanks are extended to Paul R. Ingram, an editor of great skill who also has a firm grasp of church history and helped me avoid many errors. Thanks also to Wells Turner who guided the book through the later stages of editing. Jack Johnson is a fine design editor who turns out magnificent art work under the skilled supervision of Dwight Baker and Dan Malda. Dan Van't Kerkhoff, Jim Weaver, and Maria denBoer are editors who have been most helpful and supportive. To all of them I extend my sincere appreciation.

The Billy Graham Center Museum, on the campus of Wheaton College, houses a fine collection of photographs related to awakenings and evangelism. Wendy McDowell, the assistant curator, has provided a number of illustrations for this volume, and I am very grateful for all her help.

Many colleagues in the academic world have provided aid and insight. Particularly helpful were librarians at Princeton University, the Presbyterian Historical Society, Haverford College, Yale University, Oberlin College, the University of Pennsylvania, Princeton Theological Seminary, Ursinus College, Columbia University, and the Historical Society of Pennsylvania. For a number of years the interest of many of my students has also heightened my own interest in prominent leaders and awakenings. I appreciate lively student curiosity.

In dedicating this volume to my wife, Jean, I attempt to express in a small measure my gratitude to her. She is always of incalculable help in many ways.

*I*ntroduction

The Evangel

E*vangel* comes from a Greek term in the New Testament meaning "glad tidings" or "good news." In the Christian context the words *evangelism, evangelical,* and *evangelist* all have to do with the spreading of the gospel of Christ's salvation. *Gospel* comes from the Anglo-Saxon tongue and also means "good tidings."

The concept of *evangelism*—spreading the good news concerning the coming of the Savior, the kingdom of God, and salvation—was indelibly stamped on the Christian faith by Jesus Christ, in statement after statement recorded in the New Testament. His Great Commission of Matthew 28:18–20 is a ringing command meant for all Christians

Martin Luther declares, "Here I Stand. I can do no other," before the Diet of Worms.

throughout time: "All authority in heaven and on earth has been given to me. Therefore go and make disciples of all nations, baptizing them in the name of the Father and of the Son and of the Holy Spirit." Similarly in Mark 16:15–16 Jesus directed, "Go into all the world and preach the good news to all creation. Whoever believes and is baptized will be saved, but whoever does not believe will be condemned." (See also Matthew 11:28–30; 16:24–28; Luke 19:9–10; John 7:37; and other texts throughout the Gospels.)

Evangelism. Awakening. Revival. In the minds of most Western Christians such words evoke a personal image, whether shaped by a television evangelist, a childhood tent meeting experience, or a neighborhood visitation program. With the varied definitions and emotional responses that have grown up around these terms, no wonder there is some confusion. By looking at the history of mass evangelism, and at several major periods when a refreshing wind of grace seemed to blow across whole communities and nations, this book will attempt to clear away some mystification by addressing these key questions:

- Are there connections between evangelism practiced on a large scale—directed to reach multitudes of people—and powerful workings of the Spirit of God, usually called "awakenings"?
- Is mass evangelism mere emotional manipulation, or has God made available to his people an empowering spiritual connection that particularly energized the church in the 1740s, the early 1800s, and the 1850s?
- Who on today's scene follows in the line of such extraordinary works of divine grace?
- How can Christians today practice biblical evangelism in a blatantly secular culture?
- What can believers do today, individually and corporately, to bring revival to a church and society?
- Will there be more great awakenings of Christianity around the world?

The words *revival* or *awakening* may be defined as *the restoration of God's people after a period of indifference and decline.* There are two main thrusts: (1) the conversion or salvation of a number of unbelievers, and (2) the reestablishment of biblical truth, so that the church is built up and empowered for the work of God in a lost and dying world. The principle of revival is scriptural (see, for example, Ps. 85:6; 138:7; Isa. 57:15; Hab. 3:2). Revivals came often to the Israel of Old Testament times, notably under Josiah (2 Kings 22–23), in Zerubbabel's day (Ezra 5–6), and under Nehemiah (Nehemiah 8–9, 13). In the New Testament the awakening that came upon God's people at Pentecost (Acts 2) became an inaugurating paradigm for the Holy Spirit's work of awakening. This first great period (Acts 4:23–27) prepared the infant church for subsequent fierce persecutions. The eminent preacher D. Martyn Lloyd-Jones has written:

> I am profoundly convinced that the greatest need in the world today is revival in the Church of God. Yet alas! The whole idea of revival seems to have become strange to so many Christian people. There are some who even seem to resent the very idea, and actually speak and write against it. Such an attitude is due to both a serious misunderstanding of the Scriptures, and to a woeful ignorance of the history of the Church. Anything therefore that can instruct God's people in this matter is very welcome.[1]

16

Awakening in its regenerative sense cannot be divorced from the larger concept of *evangelism*—spreading the Christian message with the goal that unbelievers will convert to Christianity. Evangelism is bearing the gospel ("good news") of salvation from sin in Jesus Christ and God's free grace and love. It involves three basic steps: (1) explaining to a person his or her need of a Savior; (2) encouraging the person to make a personal declaration of trust in Christ and his atoning work on the cross; and (3) bringing the new Christian into a fellowship of believers where spiritual growth may occur. Those engaged in *mass evangelism*, as opposed to a one-on-one, individualized sharing of the gospel, work through these three steps with a large number of people at one time, perhaps in organized meetings. Teaching, preaching, and witnessing communicate the following basic points:

1. *We are all sinners.* "For all have sinned and fall short of the glory of God" (Rom. 3:23). *Sinner* is a biblical term that refers to the corruption of imperfect, "fallen" human beings that makes them unacceptable on their own before a holy, ethically righteous God. While popular Christianity has come to avoid such biblical terms as *lost in sin*, *hell*, *saved*, and *born again*, these are the concepts of historic evangelism.

2. *We are all spiritually lost.* "For the Son of Man came to seek and to save what was lost" (Luke 19:10). Since a holy God cannot have fellowship with evil, and humans are evil, a great gulf separates them. They are without hope, for their sins qualify them only for eternal separation from a perfect, ethically righteous God.

3. *We cannot save ourselves from the just wrath of this holy God.* "For it is by grace you have been saved, through faith . . . not by works, so that no one can boast" (Eph. 2:8–9). Historic evangelism rejects the idea of self-salvation through meritorious works.

4. *Jesus alone, through his death and resurrection, is able to save and connect us to God.* "Come to me, all you who are weary and burdened, and I will give you rest," Jesus said (Matt. 11:28). "For there is no other name under heaven given to men by which we must be saved" (Acts 4:12). In today's climate of extreme tolerance many believe that all roads lead to heaven, and Jesus stands on a par with Buddha. The Bible, however, stresses that only one from outside humanity (God) could have become sin in our place, taking onto himself the punishment we deserved. Jesus is both God and human, and his death made a way for peace with God.

5. *God will forgive, cleanse, and renew a person who confesses his sins and receives Christ as Savior and Lord.* "If we confess our sins, he [God] is faithful and just and will forgive us our sins and purify

us from all unrighteousness" (1 John 1:9). God is more ready to for-give than humans are to be forgiven. It was out of love that Jesus came to earth to die in our place, for:

> There was no other good enough
> To pay the price of sin;
> He only could unlock the gate
> Of heaven, and let us in.[2]

6. *The saved person experiences complete forgiveness, is led toward maturity in faith through the Holy Spirit, and has assurance of life after physical death in the presence of God.* "But if Christ is in you, your body is dead because of sin, yet your spirit is alive because of righteousness" (Rom. 8:10). A glorious future hope fills one who confesses sins, accepts Christ as Savior, and thereby becomes accept-able and holy before God. Salvation is expressed in the person's life through growing trust in God and love for God and others.

Great awakenings and mass evangelism, as described in this book, are only the most noticeable means of introducing people to salvation in Christ and to the church. The primary story of Christianity involves people in fervent prayer and one-on-one witness. The Book of Acts, which shares God's working in the history of the early church, recounts Peter's stirring sermon to the crowd on the Day of Pentecost, but is no less con-cerned with accounts of individual conversions.

With this in mind, it should be made clear that this book is not about the broader ministry of evangelism in its many forms. If the North Ameri-can churches had to rely on mass evangelism and the organized "campaign" as the major means of proclaiming the gospel and inviting people to enter into the Christian life, they would be in trouble. Churches lead people to Christ in a number of ways, from educational and social ministries to para-church outreach agencies. However, in American history the spiritual awak-enings and ministries of great evangelists receive special attention.

The Church Aflame

After Jesus' resurrection, the theme that salvation is only through faith in Christ was immediately taken up by Peter and the other apostles. Peter's sermon on the Day of Pentecost ended with his call, "Repent and be bap-tized, every one of you, in the name of Jesus Christ so that your sins may be forgiven" (Acts 2:38). On that day, through Peter's challenging evan-gelism, three thousand were saved and added to the infant church (Acts

2:41). Later, when Paul was converted, his message was the same: "We tell you the good news. . . . My brothers, I want you to know that through Jesus the forgiveness of sins is proclaimed to you" (Acts 13:32, 38).

The early church flourished and spread around the Mediterranean seacoast from its base in Jerusalem as long as it adhered to the practice of evangelism. By A.D. 65, when the apostle Paul was martyred, Christians and churches had extended throughout Asia Minor, Greece, and as far as Rome. By 177 there were churches all over Southern Europe. In Lyon, France, the presbyter Irenaeus wrote, "The Father has revealed the Son to this end, that he may be displayed to all through the Son, and that those who believe in him and are justified may be received into immortality and eternal refreshment."[3] ·

Eventually, evangelistic zeal was quenched. In 476 the Roman Empire fell, and the Middle Ages approached. Lands that had been brought under the sway of Christianity began to fall before the armies of Islam. Mohammed, founder of the Islamic religion, died in 632, but the conquest he had planned was carried out by the Caliphs Omar and Othman. Damascus fell before Islam in 635, Jerusalem and Antioch in 638, and the Persian kingdom in 641. By the latter seventh century all of North Africa was conquered, while Arab forces pushed into the Indus Valley and the outer reaches of China. By 711 the Muslim armies crossed the strait of Gibraltar into Spain, bringing the Visigothic monarchy to a close, and swept forward into France. All Europe stood paralyzed; was Christianity and all they loved about to be eradicated? In one last desperate stand, Charles Martel in 732 commanded the Franks at the great battle between Poitiers and Tours in Gaul. Knowing full well that the European forces had to win or be wiped out, Martel and the Franks were victorious, and the Muslim advance into Europe was halted. However, many lands previously Christian were already in Muslim control, and Christianity was largely wiped out there.

Corrupting practices and ideas attached themselves to the medieval church. In the late Middle Ages, increasingly sharp criticism was directed against the wealthy Roman Church and the arrogance of the monks in particular. Two men accelerated the process of fermentation and stood at the forefront of efforts to bring the evangel back into the church by reestablishing the Bible as the authority.

John Wycliffe (1328?–1384), a professor at Oxford University, taught that the Scriptures are the only law of the church. The church is not centered in the pope and cardinals. It is the whole company of the elect, and its certain head is Christ. Convinced that the Bible is the Word of God, Wycliffe proceeded between 1382 and 1384 to translate it from the Latin Vulgate into English. The circulation of Wycliffe's translation was large. It had a great impact on England, helping to prepare the way for the Reformation.

John Huss (1373?–1415), a professor at the University of Prague, became intimately acquainted with Wycliffe's writings. He soon gained an immense popular following through his fiery sermons, in which he condemned many of the medieval church's doctrines. For this he was called before the Council of Constance, and in 1415 he was condemned and burned at the stake. As with Wycliffe, Huss left behind a movement with enmity toward the Roman church and a passion for making biblical teachings available to all.

A Renewed World Vision

After these and other forerunners prepared the way, Martin Luther (1483–1546), an Augustinian monk and professor at the University of Wittenberg in Germany, posted ninety-five theses or issues he wished to debate, on the castle church door on October 31, 1517. "Not an organizer or politician," writes Williston Walker, "he moved men by the power of a profound religious faith, resulting in unshakable trust in God, and in direct, immediate and personal relations to Him, which brought a confident salvation that left no room for the elaborate hierarchical and sacramental structures of the Middle Ages."[4] Martin Luther is one of the few humans, Walker continues, whose work profoundly altered the history of the world. At first Luther was chiefly angered by the church's sale of indulgences (payments to secure the release of the dead from purgatory), but after 1517 he condemned more medieval practices and sought to replace them with truly biblical concepts. Evangelism, whether personal or for the masses, was not part of his program. Rather, he thought of purifying and revitalizing the church, bringing it back to its biblical foundations.

It remained for John Calvin (1509–1564), a second-generation reformer, to put the Christian church back on the track of evangelism. Born in Noyon, France, Calvin was the son of a notary. Although we know little of Calvin's conversion, he had frequent contacts with people of Reformation tendencies during his days as a student at the University of Paris and at Orleans. As a young man with considerable ability and a reputation for learning, he became one of the leaders of the Protestant movement at the Sorbonne in Paris. By November 1533 he was forced to leave Paris, and for the next three years he had to be continually on the move in France, Italy, and Switzerland to avoid persecution or arrest.

In 1536 Calvin published in Basel a slim volume of seven chapters that profoundly affected the course of history. *Institutes of the Christian Religion* was prefaced by a letter to the king of France defending the Protestants. A summary of the Christian faith, this work soon became popular among Protestants as an able exposition and a forthright apology for the doctrines. By its final 1559 revision it was five times its original size.

*Humanist scholar John Calvin was the unlikely
evangelist God used to shake the world
from Geneva, Switzerland.*

On a one-night stopover in Geneva, Switzerland, during the summer of 1536, Calvin was visited by Guillaume Farel (1489–1565), a preacher of flaming zeal who had introduced reform into that city. Farel was determined to enlist Calvin, while Calvin's intention was to be a retiring scholar and writer, avoiding the limelight. The interview was both dramatic and historically momentous. "If you refuse to devote yourself with us to the work," Farel thundered, "God will condemn you." Calvin later testified that he, twenty-seven years old, had been terrified and shaken by the older man's dreadful threat and felt as if God had laid his hand upon him.

After a number of difficult years, Calvin's work met with success. In 1556 John Knox wrote that Geneva was "the most perfect school of Christ that ever was in the earth since the days of the Apostles. In other places, I confess Christ to be truly preached; but manners and religions to be so sincerely reformed, I have not yet seen in any other place." In bringing back to the Christian church the biblical concept of evangelism, Calvin began with great emphasis on the sovereignty of God. While

Luther found the center of his theology in the problem of salvation, Calvin looked primarily to the glory and majesty of God as his focal point. Luther had the concept of love as the basis of his idea of God, while with Calvin it was that of power and sovereignty. Luther also made the witness of the Holy Spirit the chief criterion by which to distinguish saved people, God's elect believers, from the unsaved. Calvin added emphasis on the righteousness and moral activity of the believer as evidence of salvation, for good works and a righteous life cannot come as other than the fruit of the Holy Spirit's indwelling. Luther saw Christians primarily as vessels of the Holy Spirit, a great step forward. Calvin saw Christians as tools by which God's will is fulfilled. Therefore the whole panorama of this existence is not for the benefit of humans, but ultimately for the glory of the Almighty.[5] As Calvin wrote:

> We admit, that when God reconciles us to himself by the intervention of the righteousness of Christ, and bestowing upon us the free pardon of sins regards us as righteous, his goodness is at the same time conjoined with mercy, so that he dwells in us by means of his Holy Spirit, by whose agency the lusts of our flesh are every day more and more mortified, while that we ourselves are sanctified; that is, consecrated to the Lord for true purity of life, our hearts being trained to the obedience of the law. It thus becomes our leading desire to obey his will, and in all things advance his glory only.[6]

When this system of thought was made explicit by Calvin, especially in *Institutes of the Christian Religion,* it had an enormous impact upon the world, and many throughout Europe soon professed to be his disciples. John T. McNeill writes:

> The *Institutes* became for three centuries the essential textbook of theology in the Reformed churches. It remains for the historian the readiest key to the thought of the Reformation, and for the theologian a still invigorating treatise. . . . All that follows in this book, and indeed all modern Western history, would have been unrecognizably different without the perpetual play of Calvin's influence. His vigorous and orderly affirmation of an evangelical faith secured the Protestant cause against forces that might otherwise have destroyed it.[7]

Among the many who came to study under Calvin at Geneva were a number from the British Isles. The English congregation in Geneva was led by John Knox, William Whittingham, Christopher Goodman, and Anthony Gilby, and it fostered a desire to see Calvin's system of faith and worship begun in England and Scotland. These men, together with Miles Coverdale, translated the Geneva Bible in 1560, which was used widely for two generations. The friendship of Calvin toward the English and Scottish exiles is well attested, and he had a number of other contacts with their home-

Geneva at the time of Calvin

land. In June 1548 Calvin dedicated to the Protector Edward Seymour, duke of Somerset (ca. 1506–1552) his *Commentary on I Timothy,* and a few months later he sent Somerset a long letter of advice on the essentials of a complete reform of the church in England, in worship, preaching, and discipline. A close confidant of Calvin, Nicholas des Gallars, made a visit to England in 1551 and reported to Calvin that his letters to Somerset and the boy king, Edward VI, had been very favorably received. Even with the death of sixteen-year-old King Edward VI in 1553 and the succession of Mary, who was Roman Catholic, Calvin's influence in England did not cease, and in Scotland it grew strong under John Knox (1514?–1572). Knox had made several visits to Geneva to study under Calvin, became a convinced Presbyterian, and was asked to return to Scotland by its Protestant lords in May 1559, where he headed the forces to reform that nation.

This world vision introduced into the church by Calvinism was eventually taken up by those in other traditions. English and American awakening and mass evangelism movements were strongly influenced by Arminian Methodism, which was a descendant of Moravian Pietism.

Yet even the Methodists owed some debt to Calvinism's influence on the Church of England. Charles Wesley particularly was influenced by the Calvinistic vision of a sovereign-God-directed and Holy Spirit-empowered church that Christ had unleashed on the world. The Puritans were directly influenced by Calvinism. And if one wanders through the great names of Western evangelism, most have ties to Calvinist thought, from the Puritans, Jonathan Edwards, and George Whitefield, to Charles Spurgeon and Billy Graham. Even Charles Finney, though he forcefully rejected the teachings, was nurtured under a Calvinist preacher.

The United States and Great Britain were truly the parents of mass evangelism. Many Christians in these two nations took seriously Proverbs 29:18 and Psalm 33:12, "Blessed is the nation whose God is the Lord." Evangelical movements around the world and the great awakenings in America raised up solid Christians to expand the witness of, and provide native leaders for, national churches.

Epitaph for the Evangel?

Edwards. Whitefield. Timothy Dwight. Finney. Dwight L. Moody. Billy Sunday. Graham. These are among the most honored names in American religious history. All were evangelists, in that one of their great concerns was to win people to Christ. Is their time over? Some writers would have everyone think so. "The emotional manipulation of the revival meeting," "sawdust trail primitivism," "hysterical fanaticism," "slaughterhouse religion," and worse epithets have been hurled at evangelism in the twentieth century. Evangelism as practiced since Pentecost in Acts 2, and the conservative Christianity that promotes it, long have been described as relics of an outmoded and humorous brand of Christianity that has been mercifully embalmed.

"Fifty years ago most learned interpreters of American religion expected revivalists, fundamentalists, and Pentecostals simply to wither and die," historian Nathan O. Hatch writes:

> It was thought that these remnants of a bygone era, these expressions of old-fashioned orthodoxy and overt supernaturalism, could not hope to keep pace with the modern world. . . . What neither scholars nor denominational leaders counted on was the persistence of revivalistic Bible Christianity among ordinary American churchgoers and the furious organizational counteroffensive launched by those who spoke for them. . . . Their unexpected achievements have surprised, and often flustered, outside observers.[8]

It is amusing to read the diatribal predictions of half a century ago by liberals and modernists against "pietists" and "fundamentalists." Their favorite target was the revival meeting, a type of evangelism. "Through the last century," wrote the former dean of Harvard Divinity School in 1946, "the revival kept something of its original sincerity, but like all usages, hardened into custom, it became standardized and was eventually stage-managed. [Billy Sunday] represents the final degeneration of what had been one of our major religious institutions. . . . We are tired of religious revivals as we have known them in the last half century. Their theology was often incredible . . . their mechanism too obvious, too well oiled."[9]

In 1930 it appeared such a eulogy over an expired evangelistic movement might be true. There was no apparent successor to Moody, Finney, and Edwards. But mass evangelism did not disappear. Instead, it has grown to unprecedented proportions. Mass evangelism is a world phenomenon. Millions of people in other nations responded in record-breaking ways in evangelistic crusades. While keeping many of their crusades within the United States, Graham, Luis Palau, Ralph Bell, Akbar Haqq, and others managed to maintain a global perspective, recognizing the phenomenal opportunities in Eastern Europe, Africa, and Latin America to bring modern evangelicalism to places where it had never existed.

This change to a global ministry accelerated after World War II. Career missionaries residing in one place for years were no longer the chief means of converting non-Christians. Now field missionaries were greatly assisted by Christian radio and TV broadcasts that penetrated inaccessible places, by print and mail ministries, and by famous evangelists who came with organizational teams to set up complex campaigns, huge rallies, and TV and radio hook-ups connecting audiences in distant cities to the central meetings.

In the late twentieth century a new and more dynamic phase had been entered, stimulated by religious, technological, and historical developments. On November 9, 1989, came what may be one of history's most far-reaching and dramatic events—the end of the Berlin Wall, symbolizing the collapse of Eastern European Communism. In the spring of 1989, Hungary and Czechoslovakia opened their borders. Graham, who had been holding meetings in Moscow since 1982, now found that Russia placed no restrictions on his work. With complete freedom, Graham took his "School of Evangelism" to Moscow on July 15, 1991, inviting 4,902 Christian leaders to attend the five-day seminars. Graham met privately with Boris Yeltsin, president of the Russian Republic, and Mikhail Gorbachev, president of the Soviet Union, to discuss the new freedoms and moral and spiritual issues. Another massive crusade in Moscow, interlinked by closed-circuit TV with dozens of other cities, occurred in October 1992.

Above: *A raised pulpit was sufficient for John Calvin to reach the people of Geneva who gathered in St. Peter's Cathedral.*
Below: *On Sept. 22, 1991, Billy Graham spoke on John 3:16 to 250,000 New Yorkers, his largest audience ever in North America. He has spoken to more than 1 million in Seoul, Korea. (Billy Graham Evangelistic Association)*

*In Essen, Germany, hundreds gather before the platform to make
commitments at Luis Palau's "Pro Christ '93" rally.
(Luis Palau Evangelistic Association)*

Palau was holding evangelistic meetings in Russia, Hungary, Romania, Czechoslovakia, and Bulgaria. In 1989 at the Olympic Stadium in Leningrad (now St. Petersburg), 50 percent of the audience at one meeting responded to the invitation to accept Christ, demonstrating a vast spiritual hunger among the people. The next year 46,100 made decisions in three Romanian cities in Palau's meetings. On June 4, 1991, Palau invited the crowd of 10,500 in the stadium at Constanta, Romania, to come down to the platform if they would accept Christ. More than 8,100 walked down, making a public declaration of faith—*nearly 80 percent of the audience!* Then Palau went to Sofia, Bulgaria, and 5,900 of the 16,200 who attended three meetings made decisions for Christ. That 36 percent response set a record for an entire Palau crusade.

Are Christians overly captivated by such numbers? Have we forgotten Zechariah 4:6: " 'Not by might nor by power, but by my Spirit,' says the LORD Almighty"? Palau has responded:

27

> I wholeheartedly believe in one-on-one evangelism. I practice it, I teach it. But it can only be a complement to the greater movement of God within a nation. You can prepare the groundwork, but eventually it's necessary to move the masses, sway public opinion, influence the thought patterns of the media. A nation will not be changed by timid methods. . . . As I see it, we're in a last surge of evangelism, in which many hundreds of thousands of new Christians are being added to the fold every day. Just look how many millions have been converted in just the last fifty years! There are more Christians now, in total number and in percentage of the total world population, than ever before in history.[10]

There are many encouraging signs regarding the impact of evangelism. One-third of all Americans identify themselves as "born-again" Christians. The percentage is even higher among adults of the "baby boom generation." Much of this identification is superficial. Biblical illiteracy is rampant and the lifestyle of many Christians differs little from that of unbelievers. Still, these people at least belong to churches and support evangelical agendas to some extent. This means, based on past spiritual awakenings and revivals, that the groundwork is laid for another great awakening in America, should the Holy Spirit so move and cause Christians to pray earnestly for it.

Nor has evangelical energy been turned only inwardly, to the nation. U.S. evangelicals virtually monopolize the field of foreign missions. Sixty years ago evangelical mission boards sent out 40 percent of all American missionaries. Today they send over 90 percent, while the number of missionaries sponsored by mainline Protestant denominations has declined dramatically. Wycliffe Bible Translators alone has more missionaries overseas today than do the American mainline denominations combined.

Evangelism and the Dying-Church Stereotype

This brings into question the popular myth that Christianity is dying, at least in the West. One who follows current events might fear the worst. In the United States Supreme Court a series of decisions over several decades has seemed prejudicial toward men and women of faith in general and Christians in particular. A bitterly divisive debate over the intent of the First Amendment to the Constitution and its "no establishment" clause has twisted the founding fathers' desire not to have an established religion into a modern desire not to have any religious influence in public life. Evangelical Christians seem surrounded by a nation whose institutions and general worldview have turned to secular humanism. The communications media remain belligerent toward Christians and their values, highlighting negative stories and ignoring complimentary or positive accounts. On television, when religion is mentioned at all, it is portrayed stereotypically as anachronistic, defunct, problem-ridden, or the enemy of freedom, progress, and pleasure. Rarely in movies are clergy shown as well-balanced human beings and churches as valuable, involved, contributing institutions. Distinctions are seldom clear between Bible-believing evangelicals and radical cultists. The onslaught of stereotypes against Judeo-Christian values seems most pronounced outside the media in the larger "entertainment" industry, academia, and politics. One powerful television network owner calls all Christians "losers," and the media gleefully smear "televangelists" (and occasionally all pastors) with the paint of Jim Bakker and Jimmie Swaggart.

Such portrayals take their toll. Fred Barnes, writing in *New Republic*, referred to religion as "the blind spot of American journalism." He noted that studies offered evidence that journalists are much less likely to believe in God or to attend religious services than is the public at large. This dichotomy between the media and the citizenry keeps recurring in polling data. A 1985 *Los Angeles Times* poll showed that, while 74 percent of the American public favored allowing prayer in public schools, only 25 percent of American reporters felt that way.

In an editorial, the *Philadelphia Inquirer* admitted the problem:

A Gallup poll in 1989 found that 69 percent of Americans were members of a church or synagogue, and that 43 percent had attended services that week. These numbers have remained virtually constant since Gallup started asking the questions in the 1930s. Another Gallup poll showed that 95 percent of Americans said they believed in God, 85 percent prayed regularly, and 71 percent believed in life after death. . . . What does it mean? I'm not sure. It has been my feeling, unproven and perhaps unprovable, that America's recent epoch of malaise has been related to the fact that certain segments of society, notably the press, academe and the entertainment industry, have gotten fundamentally out of sync with the society's underlying moral and spiritual underpinnings.[11]

Protestantism has suffered as the butt of attacks and ridicule since H. L. Mencken's day. Roman Catholicism, formerly sacrosanct, is frequently derided. Statistics on the loss of members and any drop in annual contributions in mainline Protestant denominations, and the decline in candidates for the Roman Catholic priesthood, are reported with evident satisfaction. The *Wall Street Journal*, in an article on April 9, 1993, noted that calling an argument "religious" has become tantamount to dismissing it. Christianity does not get good press.

But are these portrayals accurate? Hardly. According to *Christianity Today*:

Christianity is still the world's top religion, and faith is growing. Some say that the golden age of Christianity is over and that the growth of the Christian faith is being usurped by Islam and other beliefs. But Christianity is not only the world's fastest-growing religion, it is actually growing faster than the world's population, according to the Lausanne Statistics Task Force.[12]

Excellent statistical summaries have been compiled by the Lausanne Task Force and others. The most massive project culminated in the *World Christian Encyclopedia*, edited by David B. Barrett and published by Oxford University Press. *World Christian Encyclopedia* carefully distinguishes between committed Christians and those who live in nations where Christianity is far and away the majority religion, and thus all citizens are considered "nominal Christians." Barrett and the demographers who assisted him calculated that in 1998 the world population would be approximately 5.9 billion people. Of this number, approximately 1.79 billion (31 percent) could be considered at least nominally Christian.[13]

The Lausanne Statistics Task Force, headed by Barrett, estimates that 14.7 percent of the world's population can be classified as "committed, Bible-believing Christians," or evangelicals. This ratio has been rising at an impressive rate, due largely to what has happened in the Third World in recent decades. It is estimated that as recently as 1900 only 3.7 percent of the world population was composed of evangelicals (1 in 27). In 1950 approximately 4.8 percent were evangelicals (1 in 21). Then dramatic changes occurred. By 1980 the number of evangelicals had soared to 9.1 percent of the world population (1 in 11), and currently it is about 14.7 percent (1 in 6.8). The task force researchers concluded that the evangelical movement is growing three times faster than the world's population.[14]

The influence and impact on the world of these committed people has expanded phenomenally. Since 1900, Christianity has been accepted as the religion of developing countries in the Third World, Africa in particular. Among other contributing factors to this increase in influence are the developments of print ministries and television and radio evangelism worldwide. By 1994 the total monthly audience listening regularly to Christian radio and TV programs had climbed to a staggering 1.4 billion, or 26 percent of the world's population.

Neither Triumphalism nor Despair

With such impressive statistics, concerned Christians need to avoid the pitfall of triumphalism. These statistics do not indicate that the battle has largely been won. However, surveys that show Christian success that contradicts the dying-church stereotype are often labeled superficial and triumphalist. That is itself a superficial reading of the situation. Phenomenal growth or numerical success do not necessarily indicate spiritual depth, but neither do they signify terminal illness. The organized, institutional church is not equivalent to the kingdom of God. Numbers may indicate outward success and popularity, but Christians should always be mindful that the Lord does not operate through the great wind nor the powerful earthquake nor the fire, but in "the still, small voice" of 1 Kings 19:12.

The mainstay of the evangelical movement continues to be, as over the centuries, the conversion to Christ of the individual—*evangelism*. As long as evangelicals in America and other nations continue to expand, presumably so will mass evangelism on a worldwide scale. The evangelical resurgence of the last half-century has unintentionally chipped away at the influence and power of the institutional church, transferring much interest and money to parachurch agencies. Still, evangelism from whatever source has increased U.S. church membership by 10 percent in the last half of the twentieth century, despite a simultaneous decline in membership in mainline Protestant denominations. Half of the increase is due to Roman Catholic growth, but this tapered off greatly in the 1980s. The other half is the direct result of the expanding number of evangelicals in the nation.

As long as such trends continue, it bodes well for continued efforts in mass evangelism. The writer and theologian Os Guiness said, "Our generation is in a shopping mood for answers." Across the world, there are unprecedented opportunities for planting the gospel and bringing people to the cross—for hope, for peace, for joy, for purpose in life.

The Beginnings
of Modern Mass Evangelism

Puritanism began as a movement within the English church during the reign of Queen Elizabeth I—its general aim to implement a full Calvinistic reformation. After the Protestant Elizabeth ascended to the throne in 1558, English exiles in the Rhineland and Switzerland had great hope for the English church. They were disappointed with the Elizabethan Settlement in 1559, however, feeling that too many relics of Roman Catholicism were retained. Along with their friends in Parliament they pressed for further reformation according to the Word of God and the example of the best Reformed churches like Geneva. The name *Puritan* was given to them, since they wanted to purify the church of all customs, vestments, and ceremonies inherited from the medieval church.

A leader of the Puritan movement, Thomas Cartwright (1535–1603) was appointed professor of divinity at Cambridge University in 1569. He

*The Puritans give thanks for a safe voyage upon landing
on the shores of the New World. They undertook their "errand
in the wilderness" with evangelistic expectations of showing the world
what God could do with a people who fully obeyed him.
(From an engraving in the author's collection)*

began to demand of Parliament that a presbyterian system of church government replace the episcopal system in England. By 1582 a sizable group
advocated "reformation without tarrying for anie," a phrase coined by
Robert Browne, a popular Puritan leader.

During the reign of James I (1603–1625) the Puritans continued to grow
in power and numbers. The majority was content to stay within the
Church of England and work for reform. The archbishopric of Canterbury
was occupied over the years by such men as Thomas Cranmer (1489–1556),
Matthew Parker (1504–1575), Edmund Grindal (1519?–1583), John Whit-
gift (ca. 1530–1604), Richard Bancroft (1544–1610), and George Abbot
(1562–1633), men who were Calvinists and, to a degree, Puritans.

The coming of Charles I (1625–1649) to the English throne dimmed
the hopes of the Puritans to reform the church. William Laud

(1573–1645) was made archbishop of Canterbury in 1633, and began to harry them out of England in a campaign for strict conformity. Laud sought not only the use of the Anglican rituals but a shift from a Calvinistic to an Arminian interpretation of the creed, and introduced the doctrines that Christians can lose their salvation and that God's grace is not irresistible. This denied Calvinistic teachings important to the Puritans. Reaction against the Puritans set in, and many of them took this opportunity to sail to America. If England could not be made God's "elect nation," then perhaps in the New World a kind of theocracy, a Zion, could be set up in which society could be more righteous and truly Christian.

To the New World

During the 1620s and 1630s, the great Puritan migration to America took notable scholars, political leaders, and preachers who yearned to set up a new order in the wilderness. Their writings often expressed a conviction that God had preserved America as an unknown part of the world, revealing it to explorers in time for their settlement, a time when Britain no longer would be hospitable to their freedom and hopes. By 1640, when the "Long Parliament's" open rebellion against Charles and Laud removed the religious motive for migration to the New World, more than twenty thousand had reached Massachusetts. That hardly anyone came to that colony in the 1640s is the best evidence that the motive of the colonizers was overwhelmingly religious.[1]

The Old World was impoverished by the departure of the Puritans, but people of such faith and character were required to lay the foundations for a new nation on the bleak shores of New England. Such a concentration of educated people—graduates of Oxford and Cambridge universities—in a new settlement is unparalleled throughout history. The Puritans possessed profound convictions drawn from the pattern of the nation of Israel in the Old Testament, convictions that, if necessary, they were willing to die for. Their principles enabled them to put aside their ancestral traditions and comforts to engage in the uncertainty and hardships of a pioneer enterprise. To do this they had to be people of intense moral earnestness and great love for God. Willing to accept great sacrifices, they began their "errand in the wilderness" for the glory of God and the extension of Christ's kingdom.

The Puritans who founded New England, standing firmly in the tradition of John Calvin, entertained no illusions about the true nature of man. Human nature was at its core thoroughly sinful and fallen, and only the love and grace of God manifested in the vicarious atonement of Christ on the cross could redeem human beings. A utopian society was impossible on this earth, and all the fine hopes of John Winthrop (1588–1649), William Bradford (1589?–1657), and William Brewster (1567–1644) could not make a paradise in the wilderness. As Bradford recounted,

> But hear I cannot but stay and make a pause, and stand half amased at this poore peoples presente condition; and so I thinke will the reader too, when he well considers the same. Being thus passed the vast ocean, and a sea of troubles before in their preparation (as may be remembered by that which wente before), they had now no freinds to wellcome them, nor inns to entertaine or refresh their weatherbeaten bodys, no houses or much less townes to repaire too, to seeke for succoure. . . . These savage barbarians, when they mette with them (as after will appeare) were readier to fill their sids full of arrows then otherwise. And for the season it was winter, and they that know the winters of that cuntrie know them to be sharp and violent, and subjects to cruell and fierce stormes, deangerous to travill to known places, much more to serch an unknown coast. Besides, what could they see but a hidious and desolate wildernes, full of wild beasts and willd men? and what multituds ther might be of them they knew not. . . . What could now sustaine them but the spirite of God and his grace? May not and ought not the children of these fathers rightly say: Our faithers were Englishmen which came over this great ocean, and were ready to perish in this willdernes; but they cried unto the Lord, and he heard their voyce, and looked on their adversitie, etc. Let them therefore praise the Lord, because he is good, and his mercies endure for ever.[2]

Errand into the Wilderness

The Puritans reasoned that Satan would be on the attack in New England as he was in the Old World. Some people were not regenerate, and the first formal statement of faith adopted in New England, the Cambridge Platform (1648), emphasized that conversion preceded church membership.

> The Doors of the Churches of Christ upon Earth, do not by God's appointment stand so wide open, that all sorts of People, good or bad, may freely enter therein at their pleasure, but such as are admitted thereto, as Members, ought to be examined and tried first, whether they be fit and meet to be received into Church Society, or not. . . . The Officers are charged with the keeping of the Doors of the Church, and therefore are in a special manner to make Tryal of the fitness of such who enter. . . .
> The things which are requisite to be found in all Church Members, are repentance from Sin, and Faith in Jesus Christ. . . .

The weakest measure of Faith is to be accepted in those that desire to be admitted into the Church, because weak Christians, if sincere, have the substance of that Faith, Repentence and Holiness which is required in Church-Members, and such have most need of the Ordinances for their Confirmation and growth in Grace.[3]

With this strict insistence upon conversion and the constant reminders in Puritan society of Christian sacraments and symbols, it was inevitable that the second and third generations would present problems. If they were unable to fulfill such requirements of membership, could their children, at least, be baptized? The problem grew out of the federal or covenant theology of the Puritans, according to which church membership included both the covenanting adults and children. However, on reaching the age of discretion, the children were required to make their own confession of personal conversion, if they were to attain full communicant status. With the decline of religious zeal in the second and third generations, an increasing number of parents could not qualify for communicant status, and were termed "half-way covenanters." But if they had never made a profession of faith, could their children receive baptism? The Synod of 1646–48, which produced the Cambridge Platform, postponed decisive action on the question. Controversy continued at a high pitch until 1662, when another synod decided that the children of half-way covenanters should be baptized. Many feared that this would lead to further laxity, and such was the result, as the clergy continued to lose prestige and power despite enlarged congregations.

Zion's Departing Glory

From the 1660s the clergy of New England frequently arraigned the laity for "declension" from the earnestness of their fathers. As embodied in the formula of the *jeremiad*, a sermon of lament and pleading for repentance, New England's lamentations for its departed glory were accompanied by warnings of God's judgments on a backslidden people. Since the jeremiad appears so frequently in the pulpit arsenal of Puritan preachers from this time through the Great Awakening, it is certain the pastors were genuinely frightened and were not merely demonstrating verbal pyrotechnics. Samuel Torrey, pastor of the church in Weymouth, in 1683 bewailed the evils of the day before the general court of the Massachusetts Colony:

That there hath been a vital Decay, a Decay upon the very Vitals of Religion, by a deep Declension in the Life, & Power of it; that there is already a great Death upon Religion, little more left than a Name to live; that the Things which remain are ready to die; and that we are in great Danger of dying together with it: This is one of the most awakening, and humbling Considerations of our present State and Condition. . . . Consider we then how much it is dying respecting the very Being of it, by the general Failure of the Work of Conversion; whereby only it is that Religion is propagated, continued, and upheld in Being among any People. As Converting-Work doth cease, so Religion doth die away; though more insensibly, yet most irrecoverably. How much Religion is dying in the very Hearts of sincere Christians, by their Declensions in Grace, Holiness, and the Power of Godliness.[4]

Increase Mather (1639–1723), pastor of the Second Church of Boston, declared in 1677, "There never was a generation that did so perfectly shake off the dust of Babylon . . . as the first generation of Christians that came to this land for the Gospel's sake."[5] Against that claim, any posterity would be hard pressed to excel, and in the next year Mather addressed his contemporaries' failures, as he saw them:

> Prayer is needful on this Account, in that Conversions are become rare in this Age of the World. . . . In the last Age, in the Days of our Fathers, in other Parts of the World, scarce a Sermon preached but some evidently converted, and sometimes Hundreds in a Sermon. Which of us can say we have seen the like? Clear, sound Conversions are not frequent in some Congregations. The Body of the rising Generation is a poor, perishing, unconverted, and (except the Lord pour down his Spirit) an undone Generation. Many that are Profane, Drunkards, Swearers, Lascivious, Scoffers at the Power of Godliness, Despisers of those that are good, Disobedient. Others that are only civil, and outwardly conformed to good Order, by Reason of their Education, but never knew what the New Birth means.[6]

In 1679 the decline in spirituality was sufficiently pronounced to warrant calling a *Reforming Synod*. A series of calamities, including King Philip's War against a confederation of tribes, the outbreak of smallpox, a major fire in Boston, and the enmity of James II, persuaded Increase Mather and other prominent ministers that "God hath a Controversy with his New-England People." Addressing itself to the "necessity of reformation," the synod produced a gigantic jeremiad in thirteen major sections, giving a detailed indictment of the sins of the "Holy Commonwealth": (1) the visible decay of godliness among Christians; (2) pride in spiritual matters and in dress; (3) neglect of the church and its ordinances; (4) profanity and irreverent behavior; (5) sabbath-breaking; (6) the decline of spirituality in the family; (7) "Sinful Heats and Hatreds," "unrighteous Censures, Back-bitings, hearing and telling Tales"; (8) intemperance and drunkenness; (9) "want of Truth"; (10) worldliness and idolatry; (11) obstinance to reformation; (12) selfishness and lack of concern for others and the colony; and (13) impenitence and unbelief.[7]

Despite this massive condemnation and diagnosis of societal ills, the decline continued, and Increase Mather saw no improvement through the rest of his long life, as he bemoaned in 1721:

> I am now in the eighty third Year of my Age: and having had an Opportunity to converse with the first Planters of this Country, and having been for sixty five Years a Preacher of the Gospel; I cannot but be in the Disposition of those ancient Men who had seen the Foundation of the first House, and wept with a loud Voice to see what a Change the Work of the Temple had upon it. . . . I complain there is a grievous Decay of Piety in the Land . . . and the very Interest of New-England seems to be changed from a religious to a worldly one. Oh! that my Head were Waters, and mine Eyes a Fountain of Tears.[8]

Revival in the British Isles

The Puritans remembered that specific revivals had occurred since the Reformation, particularly in the British Isles. There had been an awakening at the Scottish General Assembly of 1596 under the preaching of Bruce of Edinburgh. Among the best known of the awakenings was the so-called Stewarton Sickness, which lasted for several years beginning in 1625. It was connected with the ministry of David Dickson, the son of a wealthy merchant of Glasgow, who was born about 1583.

After receiving the degree of Master of Arts from the University of Glasgow, Dickson became the professor of philosophy at that school for eight years. In 1618 he was ordained minister to the town of Irvine, where he labored till 1642. His ministry was one of the most successful in Scotland at that time.

> Crowds, under spiritual concern, came from all the parishes round about Irvine, and many settled in the neighborhood, to enjoy his ministrations. Thus encouraged, Mr. Dickson began a weekly lecture on the Mondays, being the market-day in Irvine, when the town was thronged with people from the country. The people from the parish of Stewarton, especially, availed themselves of this privilege, to which they were strongly encouraged by their own minister. The impression produced upon them was very extraordinary. In a large hall within the manse there would often be assembled upwards of a hundred persons, under deep impressions of religion, waiting to converse with the minister, whose public discourses had led them to discover the exceeding sinfulness of sin, and to cry, "What shall I do to be saved?" And it was by means of these week-day discourses and meetings that the famous Stewarton revival, or the "Stewarton sickness," as it was derisively called, began, and spread afterwards from house to house for many miles along the valley in Ayrshire. . . .
>
> The impulse given by this revival continued from 1625 to 1630, when it was followed by a similar effusion of the influences of the Spirit in another

part of the country. This took place at the Kirk of Shotts. And here also it is observable that the honour of originating the revival was reserved not to the minister of the parish, but to one of those faithful servants who suffered for their nonconformity to the innovations of the time. . . . An immense concourse of people gathered from all parts to attend the dispensation of the ordinance, which was fixed for Sabbath the 20th of June 1630. Among the ministers invited on this occasion . . . were the noble and venerable champion, Robert Bruce of Kinnard, who was still able to preach with his wonted majesty and authority, and John Livingstone, chaplain to the countess of Wigton.[9]

Livingstone was at this time twenty-seven years of age, and left this record of the occasion:

> The only day in all my life wherein I found most of the presence of God in preaching was on a Monday after the communion, preaching in the church-yard of Shotts, June 21, 1630. The night before I had been with some Christians, who spent the night in prayer and conference. When I was alone in the fields, about eight or nine of the clock in the morning, before we were to go to sermon, there came such a misgiving of spirit upon me, considering my unworthiness and weakness, and the multitude and expectation of the people, that I was consulting with myself to have stolen away somewhere and declined that day's preaching, but that I thought I durst not so far distrust God, and so went to sermon, and got good assistance about an hour and a half upon the points which I had meditated upon. . . . And in the end, offering to close with some words of exhortation, I was led on about an hour's time, in a strain of exhortation and warning, with such liberty and melting of heart, as I never had the like in public all my lifetime.[10]

In gratitude, the Church of Scotland for over two centuries thereafter commemorated the day following that communion as a day of public thanksgiving. "To this sermon, under the blessing of God, no less than five hundred people ascribed their conversion. . . . From this, and other well-attested instances, it appears that the revival on this occasion was not characterized by those excesses which have brought discredit on similar scenes in our own country and elsewhere."[11]

Stoddard—A Voice in the Wilderness

Solomon Stoddard (1643–1729), pastor of the church at Northampton, Massachusetts, from 1669 until his death, would not accept defeat at the hands of increasing worldliness. The measures he proposed to recultivate a vital spiritual tone became normative for much of American Protestantism. Since he was the dominant pastor in the Connecticut River Valley and an imperious figure among both clergy and laity, he was able to impose his hopes and methods on that frontier, where an evangelistic approach might be more successful than in sophisticated Boston.

As Stoddard often wrote, he was an evangelical, a soul-winner, and he harbored an intense desire to reach the unconverted. His labors were crowned with much success, as his grandson, Jonathan Edwards, related: "And as he was eminent and renowned for his gifts and grace: so he was blessed, from the beginning, with extraordinary success in his ministry, in the conversion of many souls. He had five harvests, as he called them. . . . In each of them, I have heard my grandfather say, the greater part of the young people in the town seemed to be mainly concerned for their eternal salvation."[12]

Stoddard derived the idea of "harvests," or revivals, from the history of the Christian church, which had experienced awakenings over the centuries. The Puritans, ever zealous students of Scripture, saw in such texts as Psalm 85:6 ("Wilt thou not revive us again: that thy people may rejoice in thee?"KJV) injunctions to pray for the renewing of the people of God. The absence of revivals, as in Mather's experience, was cause for great distress and searching of the soul. With other Christians, Puritans looked to the outpouring of the Holy Spirit at Pentecost (Acts 2:1–47) as the paradigm to be emulated. At the time of the Reformation (which was regarded as one great reviving of the church) Calvin had written concerning Peter's sermon at Pentecost based on Joel 2:28–32:

> Wherefore, that which Peter bringeth . . . [was] that the Jews might know that the Church could by no other means be restored, which was then decayed, but by being renewed by the Spirit of God. Again, because the repairing of the Church should be like unto a new world, therefore Peter saith that it shall be in the last days. And surely this was a common and familiar thing among the Jews, that all those great promises concerning the blessed and well-ordered state of the Church should not be fulfilled until Christ, by his coming, should restore all things.[13]

Puritan ecclesiology demanded that revivals recur periodically if the church was to prosper. But it was Stoddard who first brought awakenings to the churches of the New World. The scene of Stoddard's ministrations, the First Church of Northampton, Massachusetts, was founded in 1661. Its first pastor was Eleazer Mather, brother of Increase, and by 1669 he found that he needed assistance. Stoddard, the son of a wealthy Boston merchant, had graduated from Harvard in 1662, and he accepted the call to be Mather's assistant. Soon Mather died. Stoddard then followed the common practice of marrying his predecessor's widow (making him Increase Mather's brother-in-law), and began an extremely influential pastorate lasting nearly sixty years.

Following the views of J. R. Trumbull[14] and Perry Miller,[15] many scholars have accepted the idea that "after 1700 [Stoddard] dominated the

Connecticut Valley down to New Haven" and that his wishes and practices generally prevailed in these churches.[16] One practice of Stoddard's was open communion, based on his view that all those who were over the age of fourteen years could be admitted to church membership and the Lord's Supper if they were morally respectable and possessed a sound understanding of Christian doctrine. However, several other churches in this area had practiced open communion before Stoddard came to Northampton. Therefore, on the evidence of the Connecticut Valley's ecclesiastical records that indicate the opposition of a number of the clergy and laity, Paul R. Lucas has cautioned against the assumption that Stoddard's domination was complete.[17]

His power over his own church, however, is undeniable. At first, rather naturally, his congregation balked at the autocracy and gave him the nickname "Pope Stoddard" in resentment. Later, however, it was used increasingly in love, for "in his last years they were with him to a man."[18] He began by abandoning the half-way covenant at Northampton, and opening the sacrament to all who would partake. Although other churches had open communion, particularly in Connecticut, this was still viewed as a contravention of the "New England way" and a startling departure, especially in Boston. Stoddard defended it by saying that only God knew who was truly regenerate, and that taking communion was a "converting ordinance." His reasoning was transparent: As an influential pastor he could, by welcoming half-way covenanters to the sacrament, have some sway over them and in time bring about their conversion. Through powerful preaching, such control over the consciences of many might conceivably bring about mass conversions and revivals. According to Stoddard, all "visible saints" who were "not scandalous," and who "have knowledge to examine themselves and discern the Lords Body" should be encouraged to attend preaching and partake of communion, even though they could not profess a definite experience of saving grace. To Stoddard, the concept of "visible saints" meant all persons who make "a serious profession of the true Religion, together with those that do descend from them, till rejected by God."[19]

"Harvests" in the New World

Perry Miller has remarked that by this action of throwing open the communion to all who were not scandalous Stoddard "identified the visible church no longer with the Communion of the saints, but with the town meeting."[20] In response to the strong preaching and pastoral methods of Stoddard, five awakenings (or "harvests" as he called them) in 1679, 1683, 1696, 1712, and 1718 converted souls in numbers probably unequaled elsewhere in New England before the Great Awakening. Thus

Stoddard could claim to speak with authority about the ways of divine grace, and particularly about the ways in which the clergy could assist the Almighty in bringing revivals.

In cosmopolitan Boston, however, awakenings eluded the clergy, and their jeremiads mounted in intensity. In 1687 Stoddard completed his first book, the massive *Safety of Appearing at the Day of Judgment,* and asked his brother-in-law Increase to write a preface for it saying, "it may be a few words from your selfe may gain it the greater acceptance." But since Mather had been nettled for years by Stoddard's independence of Boston's leadership and his successes in contrast to Mather's problems, he refused to write such a preface. Mather had originally opposed the half-way covenant, but he became one of its supporters by the late 1670s. Out of his anger at Stoddard's innovations, he engaged in a pamphlet controversy with the "Pope" of Northampton for the next thirty years. The following selection is representative.

> In Mr. Stoddard's Sermon on Exodus xii. 47, 48. lately published, there are many Passages which have given Offence to the Churches in New England, as being contrary to the Doctrine which they have learned from the Scriptures, and from those blessed Servants of the Lord, who were the Instruments in the Hand of Christ in building Sanctuaries for His Name, in this part of the Earth. But there are Especially two Heterodox Assertions therein; One is, That Sanctification is not a necessary quali-fication to Partaking in the Lord's Supper. The other is, That the Lord's Supper is a Converting Ordinance; Consequently, That Persons who know themselves to be in an Unregenerate Estate, may & ought to approach unto the Holy Table of the Lord, whilest they remain in their Sins. . . .
>
> But Mr. S. has the strangest Notion that ever was heard of in the World. For his assertion is, The Saints by calling are to be accepted of the Church, whether they be converted or no. But did you ever hear of Unconverted Saints by calling before? Had he said, Visible Saints, and Seemingly Called, but not Really and Inwardly such in the sight of God, may be acceptable by the Church, he would have affirmed, that which no body will contra-dict; but as he expresseth it, his Notion is *Contradictio in ad jecto,* a noto-rious Contradiction of itself. Certainly, so far as men are Sanctified, they are Converted. If they are called to be Saints, they are called out of their Worldly, and so out of their Natural Unconverted Estate, John 15.19.[21]

Whatever might have been the tendencies of these practices in Mather's eyes, Stoddard did not mean to play down conversion, nor to deprecate the founders and their theology. "Men are wont to make a great noise," Stoddard complained (with the attacks of Increase obviously in mind), "that we are bringing in of Innovations, and depart from the Old Way: But it is beyond me to find out wherein the iniquity does lye. We may see cause to alter some practices of our Fathers, without despising of them, without priding our selves in our own Wisdom, without Apostacy. . . ."[22] How could he be the one, with his stalwart evangelism, who was open to the charge of bringing declension? Rather, Stoddard believed, it was the clergy of eastern Massachusetts—those who looked only to the defense of traditionalism and had no answers for the dilemmas of the day—who had allowed their people to backslide until conversions were few and problems many. Stoddard advocated more powerful attacks on the false security of the people. But how could such assaults on the conscience be made if the people were neglecting the churches. Must not they be brought in—unconverted—to hear powerful and convicting preaching?

Practicing What He Preached

Stoddard emerged from his debates with the Mathers and others as a man of great power and confidence who was so convinced of the rightness of his cause that he held off all attackers for decades. Miller has called him "a magnificent individual."

> He appears to our eyes as the herald of a new century and a new land, the eighteenth against the seventeenth, the West against the East. He was the first great "revivalist" in New England. . . . His sermons were outstanding in his day for the decision with which he swept away the paraphernalia of theology and logic, to arouse men to becoming partakers of the divine nature, and he was the first minister in New England openly to advocate the preaching of Hell-fire and brimstone in order to frighten men into conversion.[23]

The method Stoddard advocated for other pastors to copy in their own ministries was a carefully-worked elaboration of skeletal concepts first presented in *The Safety of Appearing at the Day of Judgment*: The gospel of Christ's love and forgiveness was the only means to conversion. Before conversion, every sinner had to undergo certain preparatory stages, although those stages had no salvific power in themselves. Such preparations were similar to the Puritan "convictions," in which a "law work" based on the paradigm of the Old Testament legal dispensation manifested the sinner's helplessness and need. This instruction in helplessness prepared the sinner for introduction to the saving grace of Christ. Preparations, said Stoddard, came in the two stages of humiliation and contrition. If the person was in attendance at the ordinances of the church—communion, preaching, the Word—he would be helped toward the moment when grace would enter.

Since the faithful pastor played such a large part in the conversion of sinners, Stoddard frequently warned his colleagues that theirs was an awesome responsibility. In their public and private dealings with people, he advised:

43

Men should be solemnly Warned against all evil Carriages; and if this be omitted, it gives great increase of Sin in the Land. . . . Faithful Preaching would be beneficial in two ways; one way as it would cut off occasions of anger, and prevent those sins, that bring down the Wrath of God on the Land; we should enjoy much more Publick Prosperity: The other is, that it would deliver men from those Vicious Practises that are a great hindrance to Conversion.[24]

He would deal plainly with his colleagues in the ministry, said Stoddard; it was *their* fault that conversions were so few. Some preaching actually hardens men in their sins, because it does not make the way of salvation clear, and therefore sinners do not strive for it, thinking it very difficult or uncertain. "In some Towns godly men are very thin sown. Most of the People are in as bad a condition as if they had never heard the Gospel."[25] The preacher's job is not easy or popular, and men will initially hate the proclamation of the gospel, as it condemns their sins. But after conversion, they will be greatly blessed, and thankful.

Hence many men that make an high Profession, lead Unsanctified Lives. . . . They are not dealt Roundly with; and they believe they are in a good Estate, and Conscience suffers them to Live after a Corrupt Manner. . . . If they were rebuked Sharply, that might be a means to make them Sound in the Faith, Tit.1.13. It might make them not only to Reform, but lay a better Foundation for Eternal Life.[26]

Faithful Shepherd

How was this preaching to be done? Sermons were to be given without notes. Stoddard was famous for preaching without a manuscript before him. This did not mean a message might be given extemporaneously; Stoddard's well-organized sermons show great preparation. He had developed the practice of mastering the manuscript before entering the pulpit and delivering it from memory, or at least giving a close approximation to the original.

The reading of Sermons is a dull way of Preaching. Sermons when Read are not delivered with Authority and in an affecting way. It is Prophecied of Christ, Mic. 5.4. He shall stand and feed in the Strength of the Lord, in the Majesty of the Name of the Lord his God. When Sermons are delivered without Notes, the looks and gesture of the Minister, is a great means to command Attention and stir up Affection. Men are apt to be Drowsy in hearing the word, and the Liveliness of the Preacher is a means to stir up the Attention of the Hearers, and beget suitable Affection in them. Sermons that are Read are not delivered with Authority, they savour of the Sermons of the Scribes, Mat. 7.29. Experience shows that Sermons Read are not so Profitable as others. It may be Argued, that it is harder to remember Rhetorical Sermons, than meer Rational Discourses; but it may be Answered, that it is far more Profitable to Preach in the Demonstration of the Spirit, than with the enticing Words of mans wisdom.[27]

44

And what should be the content of these closely-reasoned, well-prepared, and actively presented discourses? Stoddard was very precise at this point: It was little wonder conversions were so few, with the mass of unsound doctrine that was coming from pulpits. That, combined with the dull, listless homilies that currently afflicted New England, was a sure recipe for decline, causing sinners to grow colder and farther from God.

> If any be taught that frequently men are ignorant of the Time of their Conversion, that is not good Preaching. . . . Men are frequently at a loss whether their Conversion were true or not; but surely men that are Converted must take some notice of the Time when God made a Change in them: Conversion is a great change, from darkness to light, from death to life. . . . Conversion is the greatest change that men undergo in this world, surely it falls under Observation.[28]

Here was another result of weak and faulty preaching: insufficient stress had been placed on sanctification, so New Englanders did not know that a decisive alteration in a person's life was expected after conversion. Some preachers put so little emphasis upon this doctrinal complement to justification that many congregations did not even understand the importance of a changed life. In addition:

> If any be taught that Humiliation is not necessary before Faith, that is not good Preaching. Such Doctrine has been taught privately and publickly, and is a means to make some men mistake their condition, and think themselves happy when they are miserable. . . . Men must be led into the Understanding of the badness of their Hearts and the strictness of the Law, before they will be convinced of the Preciousness of Christ.[29]

This humbling is standard Puritan doctrine, the idea that the humbled sinner is the prepared sinner. This work of illumination is strictly an operation of the Spirit, whereby the truth in Christ of the soul's lost condition and its great need is presented so that pride is crushed, and the soul elevates the riches of Christ's salvation to its proper place, esteeming it above all else. Stoddard also called this spiritual light by the terms *spiritual conviction*, *spiritual knowledge*, and *spiritual sight*. It must be contrasted to the *common illumination* that the reason of the natural man may receive.

And what of damnation? Stoddard continued,

> When Men don't Preach much about the danger of Damnation, there is want of good Preaching. Some Ministers preach much about Moral Duties and the blessed Estate of godly Men, but don't seek to awaken Sinners and make them sensible of their Danger; they cry for Reformation: These things are very needful in their places to be spoken unto; but if Sinners don't hear often of Judgment and Damnation, few will be Converted. Many men are in a deep Sleep and flatter themselves as if there were no Hell, or at least that God will not deal so harshly with them as to Damn them. Psal. 36.2.

45

. . . Ministers must give them no rest in such a condition: They must pull them as Brands out of the burnings. . . . Ministers are faulty when they speak to them with gentleness, as Eli rebuked his Sons. Christ Jesus often warned them of the danger of Damnation: Mat. 5.29.30.[30]

New Era of Evangelism

Stoddard thus inaugurated a new era of evangelism. To him, proper preaching rejected delicate homilies calculated not to offend sensitive souls, nor did even the jeremiads of New England's clergy qualify. Such tirades were general threats and whimperings and cajolings that did little good, for they were not poised as a dart aimed at the foul and dissimulating human heart. Stoddard's formula for keeping the church voluntaristic and full was to preach the terrors of the law, to offer to the populace open communion, to preach in the plain style, to balance the terrors of the law with the love of the new birth, and then to combine all of this with strict church discipline. He admitted that people were more concerned with their salvation at certain seasons than at others, that "piety is not natural to a people, and so they do not hold it long," but he held forth to other pastors this proper combination of fear and hope as the method for bringing new concern for salvation.

Good preaching is doctrinal preaching, Stoddard insisted, and the proper beginning is with the sovereignty of God and the lostness of people. "If men be thoroughly scared with the danger of Damnation, they will readily improve their possibility, and not stand for assurance of Success."[31] Preaching must be modified accordingly, to aim at conviction and decision. Currently, many are asleep in a perishing state, and the general run of preaching is entirely ineffective to alert them to their danger.

They are so hardnd, that talking moderately to them . . . takes no more impression on them, than on the Seats of the Meeting house. . . . Gods way is to bless suitable Means. . . . Some Ministers affect Rhetorical strains of Speech, as if they were making an Oration in the Schools; this may tickle the Fancies of Men, and scratch Itching Ears; but we have Mens Consciences to deal with. . . . We are not sent into the Pulpit to shew our Wit and Eloquence, but to set the Consciences of Men on fire; not to nourish the vain humours of People, but to lance and wound the Consciences of Men.[32]

This brought Stoddard to his theology of revival. It is actually developed in numerous works, and all, except the massive *Safety of Appearing at the Day of Judgment,* are later writings giving the mature reflections of his last years. Miller has called these works, including *The Presence of Christ with the Ministers of the Gospel* (1718), *A Treatise Concerning Conversion* (1719), and *The Defects of Preachers Revealed* (1724) "as searching investigations of the religious psychology as any published in New England."[33]

Like Trees in Winter

Stoddard begins his magnum opus, *The Safety of Appearing,* by stating that God's wisdom is always inscrutable; he deals with humans in ways unknown to any mortal. People are generally hardened in this day, and "God does sometimes withdraw from his own children the sensible quickenings of his Spirit."[34] While the Spirit of God is never wholly withdrawn in times when God's dealings with humans are less than at other periods, people at such times are dull and senseless, and a stoniness takes over their hearts. We must learn from this that the church of God is subject to great fluctuations. Sometimes the church flourishes, and at other times it languishes. It is the same with individuals; at times they are greatly concerned with the progress of the gospel. "And at other times they are in a slumbering Condition; they are like sick Men that are unfit for Service, like Trees in Winter."[35] But in times of diligence to spiritual things, people try to take the kingdom of heaven with violence, honoring God and their profession of faith, their lights shining before the world. Thus, when the church is in a diminished condition, we must not conclude that it will always be so. These things are in God's hand, and flourishing times will certainly return.[36]

During flourishing times and diminished times, both ministers and church people have responsibilities. It is the pastor's duty at all times to remind his flock of the dangers of being outside Christ, of sudden death, the great span of eternity, and the awful misery of hell.

The people's responsibility is always to be faithful. God constantly builds up his saints to live a life of faith, to depend upon God according to his Word. "He does in his Providences put them upon that; he takes away other Props that they may lean upon the Promise more."[37] The people of God are to live by faith and not to depend upon signs. At times God's people have put more trust in signs than in their faith in the infallible testimony of God. Signs are occasionally given by God, but often no signs are given; "when God denies signs there is a sufficient foundation for Faith."[38] This is what God delights at, to see his people resting firmly upon acts of faith.

Then, when both preachers and laity are faithful to their duties, revival will eventually come. Here Stoddard explained what an awakening would be like, in his experience.

Q: How is it with a People when Religion is revived?
A: 1. *Saints are quickened.* It contributes much to the flourishing of Religion, when Righteous men flourish in Holiness, as it is foretold, Psal. 92.12. ... There be times of Temptation, when godly Men are in a flourishing Condition, Math. 25.5. While the Bridegroom tarried, they all slumbered and slept. They grew worldly, and Proud, and Formal, and don't maintain much of the Life of Godliness. And there be times when their Hearts are lifted up

in the ways of God. . . . When their Souls are in a prosperous Condition, and they are in gracious Frames of Spirit, going on from Strength to Strength. Sometimes they run the Ways of God's Commandments, because God enlarges their Hearts. . . . This mightily increaseth Holiness among a People.

2. *Sinners are Converted.* God makes the Gospel at times to be very Powerful. So it was in the Primitive times, Rom. 15.29. . . . The Gospel was written to the End that Men might believe and be saved. Joh. 20.21. And it is preached for that End; and sometimes God gives great Success to it. . . . There is a mighty Change wrought in a little Time: They that were Dead, are made Alive, and they that were Lost are Found. The Gospel is made a savour of Life to many. Some times there is a great Complaint for want of this. Psal. 12.1. . . . At other Times the Number of Saints is greatly multiplied. Acts 9.31. . . .

3. *Many that are not Converted, do become more Religious.* When Israel went out of Egypt, there was a mixt Multitude that went with them. So when God is pleased to Convert a Number, there be many others that have a common Work of the Spirit on their Hearts: they are affected with their Condition, Reform their evil Manners, and engage in Religious Duties, and attain to considerable Zeal, are full of Religious Affections. When God works savingly upon some, it is frequent that others have common Illuminations, whereby great Reformation is wrought, and the Reputation of Religion advanced, and People are disposed to keep the external Covenant.[39]

Stoddard's Importance

Solomon Stoddard confronted the theological problems of America with new answers that pointed toward effective evangelism. He also introduced what was to become the paramount question in the theology of revivals: *To what extent can clergy and laity be partners with the Almighty in the bringing of awakenings?* During his lifetime, while he explored the possibilities of his theology, the clergy of eastern Massachusetts despaired over declining church membership and relied on a sterile ecclesiology that had nothing new to contribute except the ideology of the jeremiad and the system of covenants. They lamented declension, deplored the scarcity of converts, threatened divine wrath, attempted to improve the baptismal covenant and urged owning of the covenant in order to baptize a few more. And the decline continued.

The Old-World theology of revivals, and also that of eastern Massachusetts, was that awakenings would come in the Lord's good time. They were unpredictable, and preachers had no control over their arrival. While Stoddard gave lip service to this ("There are some special Seasons wherein God doth in a remarkable Manner revive Religion among his People"),[40] his entire approach assumed that clergy and laity could assist in the bringing of revival, and his method was the first to delineate the

48

steps necessary to cooperate with God in this. He urged the acceptance of the following as a proven methodology of revival:

- the preaching of damnation
- the teaching that only God knows who is regenerate anyway, so all should respond to the gospel invitation
- the requirement of humbling as the sinner examines his life and passes through the successive stages of preparation
- the preaching of spiritual illumination and the germ of faith implanted by the Holy Spirit
- the subsequent ability of the sinner to respond in faith to the gospel
- the shattering experience of conversion as a dateable event upon which some assurance of salvation could be erected[41]

Although later evangelists in America would differ from Stoddard at points, generally this pattern was followed.

Stoddard would have made a large contribution had he done no more than assail the despair many felt in assuming that they were not of the elect. He taught that election cannot be known for sure in this life, and therefore everyone should respond to the gospel as if he or she were of the elect. Stoddard's modification required that people have more scope in working out their salvation than Calvinist theologians had traditionally allowed.

Previously it was thought by many to be absurd to persuade people to seek salvation if they were as lost and helpless as Calvinism seemed to decree. Stoddard resolved the apparent contradiction between Calvinist theory and his evangelistic practice by insisting on the unknowability of it all. He clung tenaciously to the scriptural picture of total inability before God, but at the same time Stoddard developed concepts of "undertaking," "holy violence," "coming," and "choosing," by explaining in great detail exactly what his hearers and readers could do in the stages leading to regeneration. He rationalized this "contradiction" between theology and practice by arguing that humans are free only to prepare themselves to receive God's grace, but that the actual granting of grace is entirely in God's power. This was precisely the breakthrough that mass evangelism needed, and it was to be followed by his grandson Jonathan Edwards, by Jonathan Dickinson, and by every other evangelist of consequence in the Great Awakening.

$\mathcal{F}$relinghuysen:
Pietist Evangelist

T he Dutch Reformed churches of New Jersey and New York were in a disturbed condition in the year 1723. It was all traceable to the pastor of the four small churches around Raritan, New Jersey— the Reverend Theodore Jacob Frelinghuysen.

When three members of those churches came to see the Rev. Bernard Freeman of the Dutch Reformed church of Long Island on March 12 of that year, he ushered them into this home. Immediately the three, Pieter DuMont, Simon Wyckoff, and Hendrick Vroom, began to complain bitterly about what Frelinghuysen was doing. Their first charge was that he did not teach correct doctrine. But Freeman countered by saying Frelinghuysen had been abundantly certified as orthodox by the Synod of Emberland in Holland, and also by the Classis of Amsterdam. Fur-

In 1719 the young pastor Theodore J. Frelinghuysen left the Netherlands for a new and difficult life in colonial America. (From an engraving in the author's collection)

thermore, Freeman said, he knew Frelinghuysen well and was certain their claim was untrue. In the ensuing argument all of the men became increasingly angry. DuMont stated that Frelinghuysen had taught from the pulpit that no one in the congregation had exhibited true sorrow for sin. Freeman answered that that was not heresy nor soul-destroying doctrine. After a long exchange, Pastor Freeman leveled his finger at the three and charged them with showing a spirit of hatred and revenge. If their pastor erred they must draw up a list of grievances and present it to their church board. If they did not, they would be regarded as creators of schism. Then he told them to leave his house. Freeman believed that he had done what was best in the growing dispute over the unusual ministry of Frelinghuysen.[1]

51

Early Influences

In the Middle Colonies of America the first evangelist of great importance was this thirty-one-year-old firebrand over whom few could be
neutral. Frelinghuysen was born in Westphalia, Germany, in 1692 and
had received his early education from his parents. He studied at the
University of Lingen in Holland from 1711 to 1717. At the urging of a
professor, he became as proficient in the Dutch language as he was in
German.

Throughout his youth Frelinghuysen absorbed the influences of the
movement known as *Pietism,* which at that time was revitalizing many
of the churches in Germany and Holland. Pietism can be described as
orthodox Christianity that emphasizes "a heart warm toward God" rather
than doctrine. Pietists demanded new birth through faith in Christ but
taught that denominational differences were less important than the
oneness of believers in Christ. True faith was shown, not so much in
knowledge, as in deeds of love to one's neighbor. Doctrinal disputes
were to be avoided.

German Pietism sprang up within the Lutheran churches through the
teachings of Philipp Jakob Spener (1635–1705) and August Hermann
Francke (1663–1727), who stressed the importance of Bible study, the
spiritual life, devotional literature, and practical teaching. In Holland,
Pietism was influenced more by Calvinism or Reformed theology as found
in English Puritanism. This Reformed Pietism was becoming strong in
many churches during Frelinghuysen's youth.

All aspects of Pietism shared a crucial expectation that those destined
for eternal life undergo a definite conversion arrived at after an experience of conviction of sin and repentance. Formalism in religion, with its
outward piety and perfunctory ritual, was assailed by the Pietists so forcefully that their opponents denounced Pietist ideas as heretical. In turn,
clergymen who opposed Pietists were sometimes denounced as unconverted. Frelinghuysen absorbed all these influences during his formative years and reflected them through the rest of his life.[2]

Frelinghuysen was ordained in 1717 and, after holding several posts,
was approached by recruiters looking for a young minister to go to the
demanding field of New Jersey. They were searching for a man of excellent qualifications and great dedication because work in America was
difficult, and pastors had to minister to far-flung congregations.
Frelinghuysen expressed a willingness to go and landed in New York in
January 1720. Almost immediately he offended such powerful men as
Domine Boel and Domine DuBois, the pastors of the Dutch Reformed
congregation in New York, with his animated preaching and prayers and
his omission of the Lord's Prayer.

The stolid Dutch farmers and burghers of Raritan, New Jersey, welcomed their new pastor on January 31, 1720. They must have been entirely unprepared for the sermon he preached on his first Sunday in the four small churches he was to serve. To those complacent congregations he declared that people seeking eternal life must first undergo an agonizing conviction of their sinful condition. Such people are lost and damned while still in their natural state and totally unable to achieve their deliverance or redemption by any natural means. The process of regeneration then leads to a period when sinners fall into great despondency over their spiritual condition, freely confess their sins, and condemn and abhor themselves. Eventually they begin to yearn for the righteousness of Christ. If the regeneration process is completed they place their hopes on Christ, thus coming out of their spiritual experience in a condition of grace and regeneration.

The Demands of Salvation

Frelinghuysen said that only one who has been through such a conversion can possess salvation. Moral and upright people who have not had this experience, but who are proud and self-righteous, have no hope for eternal life.[3] As he declared in an early sermon,

> What think ye my hearers? Are ye poor, contrite in spirit, and those who tremble at the Word of God? If you have given your earnest attention, you have been able to learn how it is with you in this respect. Calmly ask yourselves in the presence of the all-seeing God:
> 1. Am I spiritually poor? Have I a sensible knowledge of my sad and condemned state? Do I feel that in myself I am so guilty, impure, and evil—so alienated from God, and the life of God—so wretched, poor, miserable, blind, naked, and unable to deliver myself, or do aught towards my deliverance, that I must perish if I remain thus?
> 2. Have I through a sense of my spiritual need, and desperate state, become distressed, concerned, and at a loss? Do I accuse, condemn, and loathe myself? Am I anxious to know how I may be delivered from so sad a condition? . . .
> 3. Am I contrite in spirit through a painful sense of sin? Do my sins oppress me? Are they burdensome? Do I experience in my inmost soul sorrow for sin, proceeding from love to God and true excellence, and from hatred and aversion to sin, in its shamefulness, loathsomeness, and deformity; and because committed against so holy, good, and righteous a God; together with a purpose of heart henceforth to live according to the will of God? . . .
> I know, indeed, that you will be unwilling to believe that you have no right to come to the Lord's table, although you clearly perceive that you are not of

53

the number of the poor, contrite in spirit, and such as tremble at the word of God; but, I also know, (you may believe it or not,) that according to the word of God, you have no right; and that if you do, you will seal your condemnation. Oh! that you saw how necessary is such frame of mind!—that no one can be found in favor with God, unless he be poor, and contrite in spirit.[4]

The Dutch farmers of his congregations did not find such teaching unacceptable in itself, but obviously their new minister regarded many of them as unsaved, pharisaical, and self-righteous. William Demarest, Frelinghuysen's translator, says that "great laxity of manners prevailed through the churches, naturally associated with neglect on the part of the rulers, and great tenacity with regard to their abstract church rights on the part of the members—that while horse-racing, gambling, dissipation, and rudeness of various kinds, were common, the sanctuary was attended at convenience, and religion consisted of the mere formal pursuit of the routine of duty."[5]

Some of the Dutch burghers in the churches around Raritan, outraged that Frelinghuysen considered them unregenerate and had excluded some of them from the sacrament, pleaded their case to the New York ministers Boel and DuBois. Several attempts were made in May 1720 to confer together, but nothing came of it.

Attacks and Counterattacks

Frelinghuysen was as angered by the charges made against him as the burghers were by his actions. When he published three sermons in June 1721, he added this preface defending himself:

> For if you be not a stranger in our New-Netherlands Jerusalem, you are aware that I have been slanderously charged as a schismatic, and a teacher of false doctrines. That I am thus accused is too manifest to require proof. You will allow it that it were the duty of those who thus accuse me, to establish what they say, either by word of mouth or by pen; but since hitherto this has not been done, let no one imagine that it is here my intention to vindicate myself. The trifling stories, the notorious falsehoods, that are circulated concerning me, and are by some so greedily received are not deserving of mention much less of refutation. It is true, there is much said of my manner in relation to the Lord's Supper, but that I teach nothing else concerning this ordinance, but what has in every age been taught by the Reformed Church, can, in the following discourses, be readily discussed by any impartial person. . . .
>
> . . . I have written nothing that is inconsistent with the rule of faith, and the genuine doctrines of the Reformed Church; for I have followed

54

the steps of numerous orthodox, faithful, and godly men, whose writings I have also employed, since I felt unable to make any improvement upon them. June 15, 1721.[6]

In 1723, the leaders of the opposition sought advice and encouragement from Bernard Freeman of the Long Island church in the interview reported at the beginning of this chapter, but Freeman saw them as troublemakers and rebuked them, telling them to plead their case before their consistory. The opposition then turned for further advice to Boel, stating that Frelinghuysen was unorthodox in his belief in a personal conversion, in his administration of the communion, and in his criticism of other clergymen. But the members of Frelinghuysen's churches who agreed with their minister challenged these separatists in a letter to the church authorities back in Holland:

> We . . . lay to heart the evil report which is dogging our minister, that he teaches false doctrine. And although Mr. Boel, and his brother, the lawyer, have not been appointed as Popes and Bishops over us, yet you correspond and consult with the said gentlemen, because they assert that our minister teaches false doctrine; yet they, in three years' time, have not been able to prove this, and, indeed, never will be able. . . . Your course tends only to discord and mutiny in church and civil life. . . . Our pastor has shown himself to be an active and earnest antagonist against the evil lives of many persons. He has exhorted them out of the Word of God and warned them in the name of God, that the wrath of God and eternal damnation are abiding upon them; and that unless they repent, they are bringing everlasting punishment upon themselves.[7]

The faithful members of Frelinghuysen's congregations felt that the separatists had resisted the straightforward teachings of the Word of God and their lawful pastor. "Hatred, envy, anger, revenge, calumny, falsehood, ignorance, and irreligion prevail among the members of your [seceded] Congregation."[8] The members who opposed Frelinghuysen were ordered by the consistory to present their charges against the pastor. If they failed to do so they would face charges leading to excommunication.

"Keys of the Kingdom"

The opposition refused to come before the consistory, and Frelinghuysen then moved to excommunicate the leaders, Wyckoff, Hayman, Vroom, and DuMont, in September 1723. Many times Frelinghuysen had explained to the church the discipline allowed by the Scriptures, as in this sermon on Matthew 16:19, where Christ speaks of the keys of the kingdom.

Thus Peter employed this key against Simon, the sorcerer (Acts 8:21–23) and Paul in relation to Elymas. And that it may have greater effect, it is associated with a denunciation of the divine curse upon a sinner (I Cor. 16:22). . . .

He sadly mistakes, who regards this opening and shutting of the kingdom of heaven by the preachers of the gospel as vain, and without force, since it is to be recognized as the voice of God, and not merely of man. . . .

In this work of exclusion are comprised four steps:

1. Admonition, warning, reproof, either in private, or (if this be not regarded) in the presence of consistory.

2. To forbid them the table of the Lord.

3. To propose to the congregation those who proceed in their erroneous and wicked course; that it may be known that the keys of the kingdom of heaven are used; that the erring may be prayed for, and made ashamed, and turn to the Lord; and this must be done first, with the withholding of the name, and upon continuance in obstinacy, with an announcement of it; that a deeper impression may be made, both upon the offender and the congregation. All this proving ineffectual, we are conducted to the

4. And last step. The offender is cut off—he is interdicted all fellowship with the Church, and no longer recognized as a brother or sister; but regarded as a heathen and publican. This is the Apostle's command, 1 Cor. 5:13: "Put away from among yourselves that wicked person."

. . . The end and object of the ban is not any corporeal infliction, but,

1. To render ashamed, and bring to reflection. (2 Thess. 3:14.)

2. That being led to regard the exercise of authority towards him as an indication of the displeasure of the Lord Jesus, the offender may turn from his evil ways. (1 Cor. 5:5.)

3. To cause others to fear divine inflictions.[9]

Still determined to undermine Frelinghuysen, the leaders of the opposition published a *Complaint Against Frelinghuysen* in 1725. This was not only a reply to the consistory's citations of 1723, but also a complaint about Frelinghuysen's assumption of the authority to discipline members. It was signed by sixty-nine people, which gives some measure of the opposition in his congregations.

The split in the Raritan congregations continued until 1733, when the articles of peace submitted by the Classis of Amsterdam were received by Frelinghuysen's consistory and the complainants. These articles stipulated that the complainants should return to their congregation and accept Frelinghuysen, and that the consistory, which had backed him, should reinstate those who had been excommunicated and drop the matter.[10] It is interesting that his two New York opponents, Boel and Du Bois, who previously united against Frelinghuysen, split at this point. Domine Boel continued his opposition to revivals, while his senior colleague, Domine Du Bois, began a movement to join with those gathering around Frelinghuysen in a desire for independence from the Classis of Amsterdam.[11]

Dutch Reformed Awakening

Meanwhile, under Frelinghuysen's vibrant preaching and close pastoral care, the members of his four churches were becoming a "very different people." His congregations increased, and there were conversions among people who were new to the Dutch Reformed churches. The subjects of Frelinghuysen's revival had all experienced such a conversion as had never before been insisted upon in these areas—a severe spiritual conflict ending in an attachment to Christ as Savior and Lord, and a determination to make the attainment of their highest moral ideals the dominating purpose of their lives.

Since the Great Awakening, historians have connected these events with the effect Frelinghuysen had through his preaching, which converted many in the Raritan area and drove away those who were obstinately unregenerate. This evaluation has the best of credentials. On November 20, 1739, shortly after arriving in the Middle Colonies, George Whitefield preached near Raritan and recorded in his *Journals,*

> Among others who came to hear the Word, were several ministers, whom the Lord has been pleased to honour, in making them instruments of bringing many sons to glory. One was a Dutch Calvinistic minister, named Freeling Housen, pastor of a congregation about four miles from New Brunswick. He is a worthy old soldier of Jesus Christ, and was the beginner of the great work which I trust the Lord is carrying on in these parts. He had been strongly opposed by his carnal brethren.[12]

Jonathan Edwards gave Frelinghuysen immediate recognition when he included in his *Faithful Narrative of the Surprising Work of God,*

> But this shower of divine blessing has been yet more extensive: there was no small degree of it in some parts of the Jerseys; as I was informed when I was at New York. . . . Especially the Rev. William Tennent, a minister who seemed to have such things at heart, told me of a very great awakening of many in a place called the Mountains, under the ministry of one Mr. Cross; and of a very considerable revival of religion in another place under the ministry of his brother the Rev. Gilbert Tennent; and also at another place, under the ministry of a very pious young gentleman, a Dutch minister, whose name as I remember was Freelinghousa.[13]

Presbyterian Stirrings and the Tennents

Beginning with Frelinghuysen's work, a network of emerging evangelistic activity in the Middle Colonies shifted to Presbyterian auspices. William Tennent, Sr., was an eminent colonial educator and head of a very capable family. He was born in 1673 of a Scottish family and married in 1702 in County Down, Ireland, to Catherine Kennedy, the daughter of Gilbert Kennedy, a prominent Presbyterian clergyman.

Gilbert Tennent, the eldest son of William and Catherine, was born on February 5, 1703. He was baptized by the Reverend Alexander Bruce, minister of Vinnecash, near Gilbert's birthplace in County Armagh, Ireland. With this strong Presbyterian background it is strange that William Tennent entered the Church of Ireland as a deacon in July 1704 and was ordained a priest two years later. The rest of William's children were baptized in the Anglican Church: William, Jr., born in 1705; John in 1706; Eleanor in 1708; and Charles in 1711.

In 1718 William Tennent decided to come to America and was admitted into membership in the Presbyterian Church, giving a list of scruples in which he dissented from the Church of Ireland.[14] After spending several years as minister at Bedford, New York, in 1727 he moved to Neshaminy, Bucks County, Pennsylvania, to minister to that congregation.[15] By that time immigrants from Ireland had begun to arrive in large numbers, and many were settling in the rural areas around Philadelphia. Clergy for churches were in short supply, so Tennent decided to train men for the ministry. No better man could have been found for this; an excellent scholar and teacher, he was without equal in the Presbyterian Church as an educator. At that time there were three colleges in America: Harvard, founded in 1636 in Cambridge, Massachusetts; William and Mary, founded in 1693 in Williamsburg, Virginia, and Yale, founded in 1701 in New Haven, Connecticut. It was difficult for many who wished to be educated, especially future ministers, to travel to distant colleges, and Tennent filled a real need for a college in Pennsylvania. In the rural area of Neshaminy a building was erected for his "Log College," and by 1734 four young ministers were admitted into the denomination who had been trained by Tennent. Those were his three sons, Gilbert, John, and William, Jr., and Samuel Blair.[16]

Gilbert Tennent began at an early age to study for the ministry under his father's direction. At one point he became so discouraged about his qualifications that he turned to the study of medicine instead. At the age of fifteen, while crossing the Atlantic, Gilbert was converted after a period of "convictions" and "law work." His was a classic Puritan conversion.

Gilbert's training under his father at the "Log College" must have been thorough, because he was licensed by the Presbytery of Philadelphia in 1725 and, having attended Yale College for some time, he received a master of arts degree in the same year. In 1726 Gilbert was ordained by the presbytery to gather a new church in New Brunswick, New Jersey. At first Frelinghuysen opposed Tennent's appointment to begin a church,[17] but Tennent's enthusiastic dedication soon commended him to the Reformed pastor, and the two became friends. Tennent was impressed by the effects of Frelinghuysen's evangelistic preaching. The Reformed pastor then wrote Tennent an encouraging letter urging him to give "to every man his portion in due season, through the divine blessing."[18] Tennent must have learned a great deal from Frelinghuysen's methods, but the basic evangelicalism of the Tennent family had already committed Gilbert to the Puritan concept of conversion.[19] The increasing cooperation of the two pastors became a matter of concern to the Classis of Amsterdam. From then on one chief complaint against Frelinghuysen and others in the Raritan area was that he allowed Tennent to preach in the churches, especially the church on Staten Island. The Dutch ministers answered by defending the orthodoxy of Tennent and the Presbyterians in general, arguing for religious tolerance and assuring the classis that the congregations of those churches requested Tennent's preaching.[20]

Gilbert Tennent later described his beginning in the ministry:

> The labours of the Reverend Mr. Frelinghousa,[21] a Dutch Calvinist Minister, were much bless'd to the People of New Brunswick and Places adjacent, especially about the Time of his coming among them. . . . When I came there, which was about seven years after, I had the Pleasure of seeing much of the Fruits of his Ministry. . . . This together with a kind Letter which he sent me respecting the Necessity of dividing the Word aright . . . excited me to greater Earnestness in ministerial Labours. I began to be very much distress'd about my want of Success. . . . It pleased God to afflict me about that Time with Sickness, by which I had affective views of Eternity. I was then exceedingly grieved that I had done so little for God, and was very desirous to live one half Year more if it was his Will. . . . The Petition God was pleased to grant manifold, and enable me to keep my Resolution in some Measure. . . . I found many Adversaries . . . which thro' divine Goodness did not discourage me in my Work. I did then preach much upon Original Sin, Repentance, the Nature and Necessity of Conversion, in a close examinatory and distinguishing Way; labouring in the mean Time to sound the Trumpet of God's Judgments, and alarm the Secure by the Terrors of the Lord. . . . While I lived in the place aforesaid, I don't remember that there was any great ingathering of Souls at any one Time; but thro' Mercy there were pretty frequent Gleanings of a few here and there, which in the whole were a considerable Number. . . . But at Staten Island one of the Places where I statedly laboured, there was . . . a more general Concern about the Affairs of Salvation, which hopefully issued in the Conversion of a pretty many.[22]

Results of Frelinghuysen's Ministry

Since the Great Awakening, it has been customary to recognize Frelinghuysen not only as a distinct source of the Great Awakening,[23] which he undoubtedly was, but also as the leader of an earlier revival throughout the Raritan Valley. Yet, little about Frelinghuysen's work is known. Gilbert Tennent, as close as he was to the situation, gave few details. And it is almost incredible that the voluminous material in the *Ecclesiastical Records* [of the] *State of New York* on many areas of Frelinghuysen's ministry does not supply evidence that large numbers were being converted. It does substantiate the existence of the revival spirit that Frelinghuysen had created, which prepared for what was to come.

We only know for sure that in 1726, the year of Tennent's letter, seven new communicants were added to the twenty already in the Raritan church. Forty-four were converted and joined that congregation during Frelinghuysen's entire ministry of twenty-eight years there.[24] On the other hand, it is manifest that his approach to congregational discipline made membership difficult to attain, although there is no evidence that he forbade it to those he was convinced were regenerate. But perhaps the extent of his awakening should not be judged by the number of new converts. It may be that Frelinghuysen was so strict in admitting into church membership even those recently converted, that the numbers were deliberately kept low. At any rate, historian Charles Maxson's statement exceeds the evidence in claiming that "In some years, particularly in 1726, the ingathering was so great proportionately as to give a foregleam of the time when Whitefield should come flaming through the country."[25] The available evidence suggests that, in addition to Frelinghuysen's searching exhortations preparing the heart of New Jersey for what was to come under Tennent and Whitefield, there was a minor awakening under his ministry during the 1720s, although statistically its results were small.

Answers to Colonial Problems

Other aspects of Frelinghuysen's ministry may be described with certainty. First, Frelinghuysen was among the first to answer problems confronting the churches of the colonies. Through his strict church discipline and his demand for a conversion experience, he undergirded the authority of the clergy and strengthened the power of the churches on the American frontier. The surprising result of Frelinghuysen's "tyranny" over his members was that so many responded positively to this rigid authority. It took him many years to do so, but he enlisted a responsible church membership that did not stoop to contemporary lay indifference.

A second answer to problems of that day rested in his development of private devotional meetings similar to the Pietists' *Collegia Pietatis,* or small conventicles. To strengthen the zeal of the converted, Frelinghuysen organized private meetings open only to his converts, but in 1745 they were changed to public meetings.

Third, he developed the transformation of his *voorlesers* into lay preachers. During his frequent absences from his congregations he appointed one or two elders to conduct the services. This grew into having them preach, as they developed their gifts. Henry Melchior Muhlenberg later developed a similar tactic in his Lutheran churches, and the rise of lay preaching was to become a sore issue during the Great Awakening.

In addition, beyond question Frelinghuysen aided in the general expectation and receptivity to the Great Awakening when it came. Much of this was through his sermons, which were widely distributed among the Dutch-speaking populace.

Because of these crucial influences upon other Presbyterian and Reformed clergymen, Frelinghuysen deserves to be remembered as an important herald, if not the father, of the Great Awakening.[26] Whatever the size of his awakening, his contributions to the restructuring of a ministry concerned with and organized for revival, and to the disciplining of the churches involved, assure Frelinghuysen a place among those inculcating this ecclesiology in the American church.

*E*dwards:
America's Greatest Theologian

From his early youth Jonathan Edwards had the inclinations of a scholar. He believed his abilities might best be cultivated in an academic environment or in small parishes where he would have time for his studies. However, for much of his career that was not to be. As a well-published writer and pastor of a large and important church, Edwards made a major contribution to the Great Awakening and to evangelistic theory in general. These monuments to his genius aside, Sydney Ahlstrom has stated that "his largest claim to remembrance stems from words on freedom, sin, virtue, and God's purposes which were put to paper in remote frontier villages. His chief contribution is an enduring intellectual and spiritual reality, a monumental reconstruction of strict Reformed orthodoxy which is remembered for its exegetical insight, its literary power, and its philosophical grandeur."[1]

Windsor, Connecticut, birthplace
of Jonathan Edwards
(From an engraving in the author's collection)

With this bent toward a retiring, studious life, Edwards faced a problem in 1727: he had received a call to a large and important church. And it was not a call he could easily refuse, for he was invited to become assistant pastor to his own grandfather, Solomon Stoddard, at Northampton, Massachusetts. Not only would the call involve Edwards in pastoral work, but it also meant that, should the 84-year-old Stoddard soon become incapacitated or die, the entire responsibility would be thrown onto him.

Edwards dutifully assumed his new responsibilities in February 1727, and his grandfather lived two more years. After that, Edwards was the sole pastor in Northampton, a town of great importance in western Massachusetts. The church's theological stature was due entirely to Stoddard. For sixty years Northampton parishioners had heard the powerful evangelistic preaching of this domineering yet widely-loved personal-

The Northampton, Massachusetts, parsonage on King Street where Edwards lived
(From an engraving in the author's collection)

ity, who had influenced a wide area. The origins of the Great Awakening can be traced back to the Connecticut revivals of 1721 and the largest awakenings in New England before the general revival—those conducted under Stoddard in 1679, 1683, 1696, 1712, and 1718. Thus Edwards succeeded to one of New England's most influential pulpits, where evangelism and revivals had been a crucial part of the vitality of the church. In addition, Edwards was born into the evangelical tradition of the Connecticut River Valley and had the blessing of belonging to a family already distinguished for its integrity of life and intellectual attainments.

The Early Years

Jonathan Edwards was born on October 5, 1703, at Windsor, Connecticut. His father, the Reverend Timothy Edwards, was the beloved pastor of the town over a ministry of sixty years. Jonathan was the only son, and he had ten sisters. He early showed great precocity and interest in the spiritual life. While still a child he acquired the elements of scriptural knowledge and underwent several profound spiritual experiences. At fourteen he read John Locke's *Essay Concerning Human Understanding*, a book newly come to America and understood by few adults at the time. He was enrolled at Yale College before he was thirteen, and graduated four years later at the head of his class. After two short pastorates he returned to Yale as a tutor and took his master of arts degree in 1724.

At the Northampton church, Edwards secluded himself in his study for thirteen hours a day. In the pulpit he read closely reasoned sermons from a semi-legible manuscript, giving him a reputation as a scholar but hardly a revival preacher. He soon became quite distressed by the "licentiousness" of the townspeople, who had lapsed into the degeneracy of the times. "Many of them [were] very much addicted to night-walking, and frequenting the tavern, and lewd practices. . . . It was their manner very frequently to get together in conventions of both sexes, for mirth and jollity, which they called frollics; and they would often spend the greater part of the night in them."[2]

In addition, many of them were "indecent in their carriage at meeting," and "very insensible of the things of religion." He also complained that Arminian principles, including the doctrine of human ability, were partly responsible for the complacency.

After he became pastor, Edwards tried to bring back to his parishioners a concern for their souls, and in 1734 he succeeded. The awakening was caused by a series of solidly biblical sermons. At first no effects were visible, but in December of 1734, as Edwards informs us, "the Spirit of God began extraordinarily to set in, and wonderfully to work among us; and there were, very suddenly, one after another, five or six persons who were to all appearances savingly converted, and some of them wrought upon in a very remarkable manner."[3] His *Faithful Narrative of the Surprising Work of God* was an attempt to objectively report what happened, and Edwards attributed all to the work of the Almighty among the townspeople: "This work of God, as it was carried on, and the number of true saints multiplied, soon made a glorious alteration in the town; so that in the spring and summer following, anno 1735, the town seemed to be full of the presence of God; it was never so full of love, nor of joy, and yet so full of distress, as it was then. There were remarkable tokens of God's presence in almost every house. It was a time of joy in families on account of salvation being brought unto them."[4]

The Fire Falls

To Edwards' evident joy, his first harvest lasted well over a year and equaled anything Stoddard had seen in over sixty years of ministry. No available evidence suggests that Edwards used any methods that his grandfather had not developed. Perhaps his success was due to the touch of a younger but equally skilled hand with a fresh approach. At any rate, his *Faithful Narrative* reports that the town was completely enveloped in spiritual concern:

More than 300 souls were savingly brought home to Christ, in this town, in the space of half a year, and about the same number of males as females. By what I have heard Mr. Stoddard say, this was far from what has been usual in years past; for he observed that in his time, many more women were converted than men. . . . I hope that by far the greater part of persons in this town, above sixteen years of age, are such as have the saving knowledge of Jesus Christ. By what I have heard I suppose it is so in some other places; particularly at Sutherland and South Hadley.[5]

Evidence that Edwards had also received the mantle of Stoddard's leadership among the Connecticut River Valley's churches is seen in the spread of the revival to several other towns. Windsor, East Windsor (where Edwards' father was minister), Suffield, Deerfield, Hadley, and the Connecticut towns of Lebanon, Coventry, Durham, Mansfield, and others felt the flames of revival.

Eventually the excitement passed, and we may imagine that the young evangelist, then thirty-two years of age, was well pleased with the blessing of God on his ministry. When revival came to the Valley in 1735, and then most of New England in 1740, he might easily have been caught up in the activities associated with evangelists who try to spread themselves and their work over impossibly wide areas. Jonathan Edwards was not that sort. Having thought out the proper theological formulas, he did his duty within his own parish, let other clergy follow suit if they chose, and let the Spirit guide the movement. Edwards traveled a bit in the Hampshire Valley and as far as Boston defending the cause, but he was sedentary in comparison with other revivalists. If revival was the work of God, he argued, then God must carry it to its proper ends. The Almighty needed no puny men to further his designs. In observing the ways of God, Edwards declared:

God has also seemed to have gone out of his usual way, in the quickness of his work, and the swift progress his Spirit has made in his operations on the hearts of many. It is wonderful that persons should be so suddenly, and yet so greatly changed. . . . God's work has also appeared very extraordinary in the degrees of his influences; in the degrees both of awakening and conviction, and also of saving light, love, and joy, that many have experienced. It has also been very extraordinary in the extent of it, and its being so swiftly propagated from town to town. In former times of the pouring out of the Spirit of God on this town, though in some of them it was very remarkable, yet it reached no further than this town: the neighbouring towns all around continuing unmoved.[6]

In one sermon Edwards addressed the inhabitants of Northampton:

It seems, by God's providence, as though God had yet an elect number amongst old sinners in this place, that perhaps he is now about to bring

66

in. It looks as though there were some that long lived under Mr. Stoddard's ministry, that God has not utterly cast off, though they stood it out under such great means as they then enjoyed. It is the more likely that God is now about finishing with them, one way or another, for their having been so long the subjects of such extraordinary means. You have seen former times of the pouring out of God's Spirit upon the town, when others were taken and you left, others were called out of darkness into marvellous light, and were brought into a glorious and happy state, and you saw not good when good came. How dark will your circumstances appear, if you shall also stand it out through this opportunity, and still be left behind![7]

Allowing the Spirit to Lead

Such cool and studied detachment was typical of Edwards' attitude. He refused to identify himself as chief source or exponent of revivalistic activities, not so much out of modesty as out of his belief that people are mere means for God's designs. Edwards desired to disclaim leadership of the awakening and took few active measures to further it himself. Rather, he published as accurate an account as he could make—the *Faithful Narrative*—and let God use that if he saw fit. It was only natural that, if forced to identify with any party that argued over the awakening's more spectacular and excessive phases during the early 1740s, he went with the moderates. He distrusted human nature too much to be pulled to any extreme. The moderates who agreed with Edwards were those who saw that the result of the revivals was good, for many had been helped or quickened, and therefore they accepted it as valid. Although Edwards and the moderates did not condone emotional display or ally with enthusiasts, neither would they oppose them.

The only important thing to Edwards, in the end, was that God was working in the movement. Who is qualified to judge, if there be evidence that God is deriving glory from a work? As he wrote in 1742 in *Some Thoughts Concerning the Present Revival of Religion in New England:*

> Indeed God has not taken that course, nor made use of those means, to begin and carry on this great work, which men in their wisdom would have thought most advisable, if he had asked their counsel; but quite the contrary. But it appears to me that the great God has wrought like himself, in the manner of his carrying on this work; so as very much to shew his own glory, exalt his own sovereignty, power, and all-sufficiency. He has poured contempt on all that human strength, wisdom, prudence, and sufficiency, which men have been wont to trust, and to glory in; so as greatly to cross, rebuke, and chastise the pride and other corruptions of men.[8]

Jonathan Edwards' first work on revival, *A Divine and Supernatural Light, Immediately Imparted to the Soul by the Spirit of God, Shown to be both a Scriptural, and Rational Doctrine,* was published in Boston in 1734. In some ways it may be regarded as a charter for the Great Awakening it heralded, for it lays down two aspects of a revival thereafter adhered to, though in ways Edwards did not foresee.

> I proceed now . . . to show how this Light is immediately given by God, and not obtained by natural means. And here, 'tis not intended that the natural faculties are not made use of in it. . . . They are the subject in such a manner, that they are not merely passive, but active in it; the acts and exercises of man's understanding are concerned and made use of in it. God in letting this Light into the soul, deals with man according to his nature, or as a rational creature, and makes use of his human faculties.[9]

If this statement had been read by those who later opposed the Awakening, they would have had to admit that this was the general doctrine of New England and that they had no real quarrel with Edwards. And if it had been read and properly understood by those who later caused complaints, excesses probably would not have occurred. The movement begun by Edwards in the Connecticut Valley gradually declined, but it did much to prepare for the Great Awakening in New England that began in 1740. Its fame spread, and both John Wesley and George Whitefield knew of it through reading *Faithful Narrative.*

Whitefield's Arrival

Widespread awakening came to the Middle Colonies before it touched New England, due largely to the efforts of the Tennents and George Whitefield (pronounced Whit-field), the preeminent British evangelist. A young man of only twenty-four at the time, Whitefield arrived in Philadelphia on November 2, 1739, having brought revival to London and other cities. There had been stupendous successes where he preached in Britain, with audiences in the thousands, and his activities had been reported in American newspapers. He was immediately enlisted by William Tennent, Sr., and his son Gilbert, to aid the "New Light" pro-revival cause in the Middle Colonies. Whitefield willingly joined these Presbyterians. For them, and for the furtherance of the revival throughout the colonies, his coming was fortuitous. Nothing imaginable could have created more public interest than did Whitefield. He could unify such diverse groups as the Moravians, Presbyterians, Baptists, and Congregationalists.

*George Whitefield (Courtesy
of the Billy Graham Center Museum)*

Whitefield exceeded the Tennents' expectations; his success in Philadelphia was overwhelming, and he followed it with a preaching tour of New Jersey, fanning awakenings to greater intensity. After a journey to Georgia, Whitefield closed his second triumphant campaign in the Middle Colonies on May 13, 1740, with multitudes converted and the Great Awakening firmly established there.

After a summer in Georgia and Carolina, Whitefield sailed by sloop to Newport, Rhode Island, arriving on September 14. "Into an atmosphere electrified with expectancy and emotion Whitefield came, bristling, crackling, and thundering," Edwin Gaustad has written.[10] "The religious state of New England was most favorable to Whitefield's success," notes Joseph Tracy. "Local revivals were already in progress, and were multiplying. . . . He had been invited to come, by several of the most eminent ministers and laymen; his arrival had been for some time impatiently expected, and there was a general impression on men's minds, that his coming would be followed by a great revival of religion."[11]

After a few days of Whitefield's preaching in Boston, the *News-Letter* reported, "He preached in the forenoon at the South Church to a crowded audience, and in the afternoon to about 5000 people on the Common; and Lord's Day in the afternoon, having preached to a great number of people at the Old Brick Church, the house not being large enough to hold those that crowded to hear him, when the exercise was over, he went and preached in the field, to at least 8000 persons."[12] Rather than declining, the crowds increased in number. For over a month Whitefield held meetings in Boston, Roxbury, Marblehead, Newbury, Portsmouth, and as far north as York, Maine. On Sunday, October 12, his farewell sermon in Boston was heard by an estimated 30,000 people.

While in Boston Whitefield examined Harvard College and was chagrined at its low spiritual tone and the inroads made by secularism. He stayed three days in Northampton to compare methods with Edwards. Whitefield at this period was allowing his congregations to display some emotion in response to his preaching, and Edwards had dealt with the dynamic of emotion in his early work, *A Divine and Supernatural Light*. Estimates of the emotionalism vary greatly, depending upon whether or not the commentator was friendly to the Awakening. One critic, Charles Chauncy, charged Whitefield with inciting prayer, singing, exhorting, and so on. Another Boston minister, Benjamin Colman, said, "I do not remember any crying out, or falling down, or fainting, either under Mr. Whitefield's or Mr. Tennent's ministry, all the while they were in Boston, though many were in great concern of soul."[13]

After the mutual encouragement Edwards and Whitefield gave each other, Edwards renewed his efforts to bring back revival in his area. His most famous sermon, "Sinners in the Hands of an Angry God," was preached at Enfield, Connecticut, on July 8, 1741. Although it is a scathing denunciation of sinful humanity, Edwards did not intend for it to frighten his hearers, but rather for them to grasp its arguments and to be convinced without any show of emotion. Edwards' manner of preaching was far different from Whitefield's. "'Mr. Edwards in preaching,' remembered one of the townspeople, 'used no gestures, but looked straight forward; Gideon Clark said "he looked on the bell rope until he looked it off."'"[14]

The Open Door of Mercy

In his famous sermon, "Sinners in the Hands of an Angry God," Edwards portrayed hell as vividly as anyone has ever done:

> There is nothing that keeps wicked men at any one moment out of hell, but the mere pleasure of God. . . .

Jonathan Edwards (Yale University Art Gallery)

O sinner, consider the fearful danger you are in! It is a great furnace of wrath, a wide and bottomless pit, full of the fire of wrath that you are held over in the hand of that God whose wrath is provoked and incensed as much against you as against many of the damned in hell. You hang by a slender thread, with the flames of divine wrath flashing about it and ready every moment to singe it, and burn it asunder.[15]

Although Edwards has been pilloried greatly for such messages, Ahlstrom has observed, "Actually there are fewer than a dozen imprecatory sermons among the more than a thousand for which manuscripts are extant. This sermon's [*Sinners . . .*] popularity with anthologists indicates the journalistic level of interpretation by which Edwards has been victimized."[16] It might be added that such fear-inspiring sermons are, in reality, simply collections of Scripture passages—what the Bible has to say on the subject. Edwards is excoriated for bringing them together.

On another occasion, when Edwards was preaching to an uninterested congregation, a complete change came over the hearers, and before the sermon was ended the assembly seemed deeply impressed and bowed down with a great conviction of their sin and danger.

The Justice of God

Another sermon, similar to "Sinners in the Hands of an Angry God," is "The Justice of God in the Damnation of Sinners." This was delivered in the same unemotional way, without any desire to bring the congregation into hysteria, but rather to make them realize the horrors of a future without Christ. But what congregation, no matter how quiet the delivery, could sit through such a sermon unmoved? Whenever there was an emotional outcry—at some points there was so much weeping and crying to God for mercy that Edwards could not be heard—he stopped and requested quiet so he could continue. The premise of the sermon is based on the absolute sovereignty of God.

> It is meet that God should order all these things according to his own pleasure. By reason of his greatness and glory, by which he is infinitely above all, he is worthy to be sovereign, and that his pleasure should in all things take place. . . .
>
> In the improvement of this doctrine, I would chiefly direct myself to sinners who are afraid of damnation, in a use of conviction. This may be matter of conviction to you, that it would be just and righteous with God eternally to reject and destroy you. This is what you are in danger of. You who are a Christless sinner, are a poor condemned creature: God's wrath still abides upon you; and the sentence of condemnation lies upon you. You are in God's hands, and it is uncertain what he will do with you. You are afraid what will become of you. You are afraid that it will be your portion to suffer eternal burnings, and your fears are not without grounds; you have reason to tremble every moment. But be you never so much afraid of it, let eternal damnation be never so dreadful, yet it is just. God may nevertheless do it, and be righteous, and holy, and glorious.[17]

Edwards' hearers during the Awakening felt that he was a messenger from God to their souls. One man who heard Edwards deliver a sermon on the subject of the day of judgment, stated that "so vivid and solemn was the impression made on his mind, that he fully supposed that as soon as Mr. Edwards should close his discourse, the judges would descend and the final separation take place."[18]

Opposition Gathers

Until 1741, those furthering the Awakening had their way. Many ministers, at first cool to revivals, were later won over—not least because of the hordes of new church members the awakenings were sending their way. But in the pulpit of First Church of Boston was

Charles Chauncy
(Courtesy of the Billy Graham Center Museum)

Charles Chauncy, who had a strategic position and the ear of ecclesiastical authorities. He was "Old Light," dull, dreary, prosaic, pedantic, and a foe of the Great Awakening. He was unquestionably in the vanguard of New England's intellectual life, and his influence in later years would help to bring Arminianism, universalism, and unitarianism into the region. In 1742 he still claimed to be a Calvinist. His temperament gave his theology a rationalistic bent, and he firmly believed everyone else should be the same way.

Chauncy did not believe that reason opposed revelation, but rather that the Holy Spirit dealt with humans as reasonable creatures able to perceive and be persuaded of the truth by reason confirming revelation. He felt that the emotions must be kept under rational control or they would run headlong into enthusiasm.

In all of this, Chauncy maintained that Edwards and his followers were the innovators, and he called to his support the shades of John Winthrop, Thomas Shepard, and Increase and Cotton Mather, all Puritans of unquestionable orthodoxy.

In July 1742, a follower of Whitefield and Tennent, James Davenport, came to Boston to ride the crest of popularity resulting from their visits. Davenport was of unsound mind and an exhorter in the worst sense.

Immediately upon his arrival he made the rounds of Boston's ministers to inquire if they were converted. Usually he was tolerated. But he made the fatal mistake, with great consequence, of knocking on Chauncy's door with the same errand. Until then Chauncy's opposition had been mild. But at this he rose to a veritable fury of indignation against the Awakening, publishing a broadside of seven letters or sermons and his magnum opus, *Seasonable Thoughts on the State of Religion in New England*, all within three years.

To obtain first-hand information, Chauncy set out on an arduous three hundred-mile circuit throughout New England to observe the Awakening. The results of his investigations, the above mentioned *Seasonable Thoughts*, appeared in the early fall of 1743 in a huge octavo volume of 424 pages. Chauncy began by listing "bad things attending this work" and put the itinerant preaching of Whitefield, Tennent, and Davenport at the top of his list.

> And what is the [meaning] of this going into other men's parishes? Is it not obviously this? The settled pastors are men, not qualified for their office, or not faithful in the execution of it; they are either unfit to take the care of souls, or grossly negligent in their duty to them. . . . Moreover, what is the tendency of this practice, but confusion and disorder? If one pastor may neglect his own people to take care of others, who are already taken care of; and, it may be much better than he can take care of them: I say, if one pastor may do this, why not another, and another still, and so on, 'till there is no such thing as church order in the land?[19]

Whitefield returned to Boston late in 1744 and read Chauncy's many slurring references to him. The two antagonists chanced to meet on the street. Chauncy, taking the offensive, stated that he was sorry to see Whitefield return. The latter replied, "So is the devil!"

But the atmosphere of intensity and zeal could not last forever, just as Stoddard had predicted in his revival theology of forty years before as he delineated the comings and departures of the Spirit. Another "Testimony" from more than one hundred clergymen in four colonies came from the presses, extolling the benefits and blessings of the "late happy Revival." But "the extraordinary season" was over, having burned brightly for more than three years. Edwards had foreseen its decline in 1743 and published his last polemical work, *Some Thoughts Concerning the Present Revival of Religion in New England.*

Edwards, with his analytical ability and penetrating insights, then turned to ponder other workings of the Spirit. There was, he thought, much to be done and volumes to be written. So he began working on those intricate and fascinating books dealing with recondite matters of theology for which he would later become famous.

However, by the time the Awakening was over Edwards was meeting problems in his own parish. He was unhappy with the lax standards of church membership allowed by the half-way covenant and with his grandfather's principles on admission to communion, which were still in effect. He continued to insist that membership be composed only of those who had a genuine experience of conversion. Many opposed him. In 1748 when he proposed to deliver a series of sermons on the qualifications for admission to the Lord's Supper that would challenge Stoddard's ideas, he was not only forbidden but asked to resign. On July 1, 1750, he preached his farewell message, and its muted strength still conveys Edwards' eminence over the pettiness of those who could not begin to appreciate the best-known pastor in all of New England.

From among the offers from churches wishing to secure this distinguished pastor, Edwards accepted a call from the church at Stockbridge, Massachusetts. This small frontier congregation would demand less of a pastor than had the large Northampton church. At Stockbridge he composed his masterful work on *Freedom of the Will* in four and one-half months, and saw it published in 1754. By general agreement it is one of the finest treatments ever written on this difficult theme. His treatise on *Original Sin* was completed in 1757 and ranks as an exceptional exposition of the biblical doctrine of sin.

In 1757 the New School Presbyterian college in Princeton, New Jersey, suddenly needed a president. The corporation, wishing to avail themselves of Edwards' services, extended an invitation to him. After deliberation, he accepted. He arrived in New Jersey in January 1758 to take up the challenging duties of guiding the thriving college filled with pro-revivalist students. His first sermon at Princeton was on the subject of the unchangeableness of Christ. It produced so deep an impression upon the audience that, although it lasted two hours, the congregation was distressed that it was concluded so soon.

Edwards' Death

An epidemic of smallpox was then raging in the area, and it was thought that Edwards should be inoculated as a safeguard. At first the inoculation seemed successful, but a severe fever followed and Edwards died on March 22, 1758.

Jonathan Edwards, the classic Puritan preacher, standing in wig and gown behind his sacred desk before a stricken congregation, was an awesome ambassador of the heavenly powers as he spoke of the anger of a righteous God.

*W*hitefield:
Catalyst of Evangelism

G eorge Whitefield was born in Gloucester, England, on December 16, 1714, the youngest of seven children. His father owned the Bell Tavern, the building in which George was born. Previously his father had been a wine merchant. George was only two when his father died, and his mother was determined to give the boy every advantage her limited resources could provide. He attended the grammar school of St. Mary de Crypt, but when he was fifteen the tavern was failing, so he left school and "washed mops, cleaned rooms, and, in one word, became professed and common drawer for nigh a year and a half."[1]

Whitefield preaching in a field: "I thought it might be doing the service of my Creator, who had a mountain for his pulpit, and the heavens for his sounding-board." (Courtesy of the Billy Graham Center Museum)

The Gin Age

The Evangelical Revival, spearheaded by George Whitefield and John Wesley, far more than any other factor or combination of factors lifted the English-speaking world from a moral jungle, began the missionary advance of the nineteenth century, abolished slavery, and furthered every area of social reform. This dynamic tide of proclamation was instrumental in countless conversions and the restoration of decency and morality. It began in about 1736 and continued throughout the nineteenth century.

The entire English nation was oppressed by a crisis of morals and religion in the first half of the eighteenth century. Conditions had improved somewhat over the extreme licentiousness of the Restoration, but the engravings of artist William Hogarth (1697–1764) depict a physical and mental poverty and a moral depravity that poisoned life for all Britain's people. Crime was rampant. Harsh penalties and frequent death sentences proved slight deterrents. It has been called the "Gin Age," because the poor viewed drinking as their only amusement. Every fourth house in Holborn, London, was a gin-shop. Henry Fielding, a London magistrate in 1751, said gin was "the principle sustenance (if it may be so called) of more than 100,000 people in this metropolis."[2] The case of Judith Dufour, recorded in the Old Bailey *Session Papers* for February 1735, is similar to many that could be cited to show the cruel and destructive influence of the liquor traffic on multitudes. This woman took her small child to the workhouse, where it was given clothing. Leaving the workhouse, she strangled the child, threw the body in a ditch, sold the clothes for one shilling and four pence, and spent the money on gin, which she shared with a woman who had helped in the murder.

The London Bills of Mortality reveal that in the time before the Evangelical Awakening 74.5 percent of children of all classes died before their fifth birthday. A petition to Parliament in 1739 to create a foundlings hospital tells of the constant "murder of poor miserable infants," of the custom of exposing new-born babies "to perish in the streets," of the placing of foundlings with "wicked and barbarous nurses" who for a small sum allow them to "starve for want of due sustenance or care," and of the few who survive being turned "into the streets to beg or steal." Some were "blinded, or maimed and distorted in their limbs, in order to move pity," and thus become "fitter instruments of gain" to "vile, merciless wretches."[3]

Charles Wesley's journal indicates that when he preached in one jail, fifty-two felons were waiting to be hanged, including a child of ten. While the judicial theorist Sir William Blackstone (1723–1780) was extolling the glories of the "unmatched Constitution" of England, men, women, and children were being hanged for any of 160 violations. To pick a pocket of more than one shilling, to break a small tree, to snare a rabbit on an estate, or even to appear on a high road with a blackened face were all hanging offenses.

At the time its moral voice was needed, the Church of England had ceased to be an institution with authority. The economic historian Richard Henry Tawney has charged that the church of this period abandoned the task of leadership against debauched social conventions.[4] Few contemporary estimates have anything better to say of the clergy. Philosopher Sir Leslie Stephen characterized the sermons of the mid-1700s as "dull, duller, and dullest."[5] The free-thinking Henry St. John Bolingbroke (1678–1751) had sufficient grasp of Christian teaching to sneer at a group of clergy, "Let me seriously tell you that the greatest miracle in the world is the subsistence of Christianity and its continued preservation as a religion, when the preaching of it is committed to the care of such un-Christian men as you."[6] Blackstone visited the churches of London to hear every clergyman of note; he reported that "it would have been impossible for him to discover from what he heard whether its preacher was a follower of Confucius, of Mohammed, or of Christ."[7] Bishop J. C. Ryle said of the eighteenth century in England,

> There were some learned and conscientious bishops at this era, beyond question. . . . But even the best of them sadly misunderstood the requirements of the day they lived in. They could not see that, without the direct preaching of the essential doctrines of Christ's gospel, their labors were all in vain. And, as to the majority of the bishops, they were potent for negative evil, but impotent for positive good; mighty to repress overzealous attempts at evangelization, but weak to put in action any remedy for the evils of the age.[8]

In this low period, out of the unpromising environs of a tavern, came the young Whitefield. In 1732, at the age of seventeen, he had the opportunity to enter Oxford University where he secured the position of servitor in Pembroke College. With this benefit and the kindness of friends, he was able to conclude three years' residence at the college with an indebtedness of only twenty-four pounds.

The Holy Club

To his journal Whitefield confessed youthful secret sins, but also that he was becoming serious and concerned for his soul. He admitted to having an interest "in studying my Greek Testament, but was not yet convinced of the absolute unlawfulness of playing at cards, and of reading and seeing plays, though I began to have some scruples about it." He began to read Puritan writers and to shun youths who invited him to "join in their excess of riot."[9] He then came into contact with some students who had formed what was dubbed by mockers "the Holy Club" or "Methodists." John Wesley was leader of the group and older than Whitefield by eleven years; his brother Charles assisted him. Their search for holiness was spurred by their admission that, while they earnestly desired salvation, they were not sure how it might be attained. The members devoted themselves to a monastic, legalistic routine that brought upon them the ridicule of the rest of the Oxford community.

Such a search for salvation through self-denial and good works was actually common in the Church of England at the time. While redemption through simple belief was not denied from the pulpits, it was put in abeyance. A sincere seeker could only gather from the insipid harangues a watery morality leading to assurance of faith. In later years when Whitefield was attacked by his fellow clergy, it is understandable that he would remember their failure to provide spiritual direction in his time of need. He further charged that some clergy

> frequent play-houses, they go to horse-races, they go to balls and assemblies, they frequent taverns, and follow all the entertainments that the age affords. . . . But, my dear brethren, observe they always go disguised, the ministers are afraid of being seen in their gowns and cassocks; the reason thereof is plain, their consciences inform them, that it is not an example fit for the ministers of the gospel to set.[10]

While the Oxford "Methodists" groped for assurance of salvation, they did everything in their power to assist one another. One biographer finds few instances in all of history "of personal influence so perfectly mutual, so profound and far-reaching in their effects on the world at large as the shuttle-like impacts of these three men on one another. They form a triangle of constantly-interchanging forces. John captures Charles, Charles lays hold of Whitefield, Whitefield bursts into flame, and in turn, pioneers John and Charles into the greatest religious achievement of the century."[11] In one key example of mutual edification Charles Wesley gave Whitefield, who was as caught in legalism as the rest, Scougal's *Life of God in the Soul of Man*, which had a great impact on his nurture:

> Though I had fasted, watched and prayed, and received the Sacrament so long, yet I never knew what true religion was, till God sent me that excellent treatise by the hands of my never-to-be-forgotten friend. At my first reading it, I wondered what the author meant by saying, "That some falsely placed religion in going to church, doing hurt to no one, being constant in the duties of the closet, and now and then reaching out their hands to give alms to their poor neighbors." "Alas!" thought I, "if this be not true religion, what is?" God soon showed me; for in reading a few lines further, that "true religion was union of the soul with God, and Christ formed within us," a ray of Divine light was instantaneously darted in upon my soul, and from that moment, but not till then, did I know that I must be a new creature.[12]

During this time his tutors did not know whether to tolerate his actions or pack him off to home as a madman. His bodily punishment brought him to a sickbed, and for seven weeks he despaired. But, in stopping his self-mortification, God had a chance to speak to him. "Though weak, I often spent two hours in my evening retirements, and prayed over my

Greek Testament, and Bishop Hall's most excellent 'Contemplations.'"
Then he discovered the true grounds of a sinner's hope and justification.
"I found and felt in myself, that I was delivered from the burden that had
so heavily oppressed me. The spirit of mourning was taken from me, and
I knew what it was to rejoice in God my Saviour."[13]

Whitefield was the first of the Holy Club to experience conversion, but
the ascetic practices of the group still influenced him to continue his rituals. He ate cheap food, fasted often, and wore "a patched gown and dirty
shoes, and therefore looked upon myself as very humble."[14] Gradually the
confusion in his mind was cleared, and he left off his self-mortification.
Whitefield had arrived at a confidence of salvation by 1735 that John and
Charles would seek for three more years until their Aldersgate experience.

In 1736, shortly before his graduation from Oxford, Whitefield was
ordained by Bishop Martin Benson, who was greatly troubled by the
impotence of the church and the low tone of the age. Benson, bishop of
Gloucester, sensed George's talents and insisted on his ordination, waiv-
ing his own rule that twenty-three was the minimum age. When Whitefield preached his first sermon, a complaint was lodged with the bishop
that fifteen people had been driven mad. To this Benson replied that he
"wished that madness might not be forgotten before next Sunday."[15]

Whitefield's appearance and abilities even at the youthful age of twenty-
one were unusual. He was about average height, his manner graceful, his
features regular, his complexion fair. His eyes were small, lively, and dark
blue. One eye had a squint, brought on by the carelessness of a nurse during a childhood bout with measles. In contrast to this feature, his voice
was a gift of God. It was incredibly strong, yet Whitefield could modulate
it in a great variety of ways through the whole range of human emotions.

The Divine Dramatist

Great popularity descended on Whitefield even in his early twenties,
not only because of his own ability in speaking, but also because so few
others in England preached in such a vital way. Thousands came out of
curiosity or to criticize; but many became impressed, then inspired, then
convinced, then converted.

Between the summer of 1736 and Christmas 1737, Whitefield's preaching became enormously popular in London, Bristol, Gloucester, and Bath.
His own vivid accounts give a better idea of what happened than any
other description. Of his first appearance in London he recorded:

On Sunday, August 8th [1736], in the afternoon, I preached at Bishopsgate
Church, the largeness of which, and the congregation together, at first a lit-

tle dazed me; but, by adverting to God, and considering in whose Name I was about to speak, my mind was calmed, and I was enabled to preach with power. The effect was immediate and visible to all; for as I went up the stairs almost all seemed to sneer at me on account of my youth; but they soon grew serious and exceedingly attentive, and, after I came down, showed me great tokens of respect, blessed me as I passed along, and made great enquiry who I was. The question no one could answer, for I was quite a stranger.[16]

Similar responses attended his preaching everywhere he went.

On Sunday mornings, long before day, you might see streets filled with people going to church, with their lanthorns in their hands. . . . The tide of popularity now began to run very high. In a short time, I could no longer walk on foot as usual, but was constrained to go in a coach, from place to place, to avoid the hosannas of the multitude. . . . Not that all spoke well of me. No; as my popularity increased, opposition increased also. At first, many of the clergy were my hearers and admirers; but some soon grew angry, and complaints were made that the churches were so crowded.[17]

On October 14, 1735, the Wesley brothers sailed for Georgia, Britain's newest colony, to work among the colonists. They were still in the primitive spiritual state that Whitefield had outgrown at Oxford. Ritualism was their byword. They asked him to come to Georgia and share their labors, which he did, sailing from England on December 28, 1737. He acted sensibly by taking collections in England for the colonists' benefit, and using the money to buy clothing, he came to America. By then the Wesleys' austerity had caused the people to reject them, and they returned to England bitter, half aware that their inadequate religion was the cause of their problems. Whitefield met with no such rebuff. The colonists took to him instantly, and he began to minister to their needs and to found an orphanage for homeless children. The care of the Savannah orphanage was to become a great interest in his life, and ever afterward he took collections from congregations in England and America for its upkeep. Whitefield remained a few months and then set sail for home on September 9, 1738, with mixed feelings—reluctant to part from these new friends, but eager to take up his preaching ministry.

By 1738 the Wesleys had come into full assurance of their faith, and Whitefield rejoiced. Their similar experiences meant the association of the three might be even closer. But George was a Calvinist in theology, in conformity to the tone of the Anglican articles, while the Wesleys were influenced by several factors to become Arminians. This resulted in the Methodists' teaching that the Christian could attain sinless perfection in this life. Whitefield could not accept this teaching, and it remained a bone of contention that was overcome only by their Christian love and regard for each other.

Whitefield assaulted by a mob: "I thought of Stephen, and was in hopes, like him, to go off in this bloody triumph, to the immediate presence of my Master." (Courtesy of the Billy Graham Center Museum)

Marked Men

Increasingly, Whitefield met with opposition, which was to harass him for years. The Wesleys had become marked men for their propagation of "societies" modeled after the Moravians, and Whitefield's connection with them put a similar odium upon him. These were the formative months of Whitefield's ministry, for in them he developed all the evangelistic methods he later used. After his ordination he decided to preach to the church at large. This was interpreted as irregular by some,

83

Whitefield preaching to soldiers: "As many as were in debt came to David, and he became a captain over them." (Courtesy of the Billy Graham Center Museum)

wrong simply because it was done by Quakers and other sects. As he attempted to preach from church to church, he often found the clergy cool and the buildings closed to him. Joseph Tracy writes, "The clergy had begun to perceive that either his doctrine or theirs, concerning the new birth and the way of a sinner's justification before God, must fall."[18] Pamphlets attacked his doctrines of regeneration, and sermons were leveled against him from within his own Church of England. Predictably, all this had the opposite effect his opponents intended. "The opposition of the clergy increased the people's inclination to hear; and their crowding to hear increased the opposition of the clergy."[19] The idea of preaching in the open occurred to him, and on February 17, 1739, at Kingswood, near Bristol, he first attempted it. His gathering was composed of ignorant and tough coal miners who were the terror of the city.

"I thought," he said, "it might be doing the service of my Creator, who had a mountain for his pulpit and the heavens for his sounding-board, and who, when his Gospel was refused by the Jews, sent his servants into the highways and hedges." The news spread rapidly among the colliers, and his audience soon increased to twenty thousand. The gospel was indeed "good news" to them, for they had never heard preaching before. Tracy writes, "The first discovery of their being affected was, to see the white gutters made by their tears, which plentifully fell down their black cheeks, as they came out of their coal-pits. Hundreds and hundreds of them were soon brought under deep convictions, which, as the event proved, happily ended in sound and thorough conversion."[20]

After this initial success at field preaching, Whitefield (and in turn John Wesley) was convinced of its value and used it for the rest of his life. As instances of such dramatic conversions multiplied, Whitefield's fame increased throughout England and in America. His powerful voice could be heard unaided by crowds of ten thousand to thirty thousand. Whitefield drew incredible congregations throughout his entire ministry and was able to address them without difficulty. A mass of people this large, even standing tightly together, could cover at least six to eight acres. Obviously no building could hold them. Whitefield turned to open-air preaching, not only for the extra space, but also because many churches refused to lend him their pulpits. Bishop Ryle said of his speaking abilities,

> Unhesitatingly, I believe no living preacher ever possessed such a combination of excellences as Whitefield. Some, no doubt, have surpassed him in some of his gifts. . . . But, for a combination of pure doctrine, simple and lucid style, boldness and directness, earnestness and fervor, descriptiveness and picture-drawing, pathos and feeling—united with a perfect voice, perfect delivery and perfect command of words, Whitefield, I repeat, stands alone. No man, dead or alive, I believe, ever came alongside of him.[21]

This galvanizing preacher, who was the talk of England, rapidly broadened his contacts and found sympathy among the Dissenters. He met and exchanged views with Isaac Watts (1674–1748) and Philip Doddridge (1702–1751) and greatly impressed them. But his mind was preoccupied with the orphanage, and he sailed for the colonies again on August 14, 1739.[22]

The New World Beckons

Whitefield was no stranger to those in the Middle Colonies when he landed for the second time in the New World. Two years before, newspapers in Philadelphia and elsewhere had carried notices of his activi-

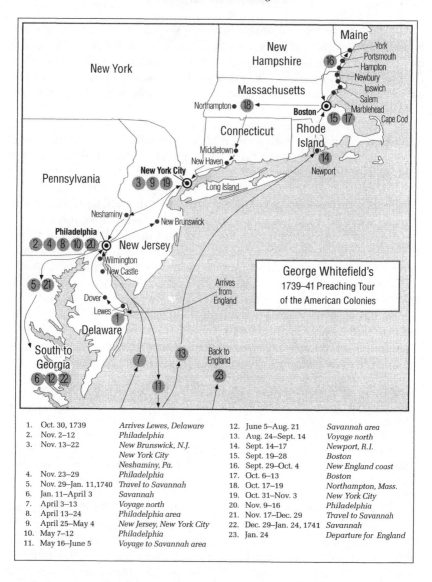

George Whitefield's
1739–41 Preaching Tour
of the American Colonies

1.	Oct. 30, 1739	*Arrives Lewes, Delaware*
2.	Nov. 2–12	*Philadelphia*
3.	Nov. 13–22	*New Brunswick, N.J.*
		New York City
		Neshaminy, Pa.
4.	Nov. 23–29	*Philadelphia*
5.	Nov. 29–Jan. 11,1740	*Travel to Savannah*
6.	Jan. 11–April 3	*Savannah*
7.	April 3–13	*Voyage north*
8.	April 13–24	*Philadelphia area*
9.	April 25–May 4	*New Jersey, New York City*
10.	May 7–12	*Philadelphia*
11.	May 16–June 5	*Voyage to Savannah area*

12.	June 5–Aug. 21	*Savannah area*
13.	Aug. 24–Sept. 14	*Voyage north*
14.	Sept. 14–17	*Newport, R.I.*
15.	Sept. 19–28	*Boston*
16.	Sept. 29–Oct. 4	*New England coast*
17.	Oct. 6–13	*Boston*
18.	Oct. 17–19	*Northampton, Mass.*
19.	Oct. 31–Nov. 3	*New York City*
20.	Nov. 9–16	*Philadelphia*
21.	Nov. 17–Dec. 29	*Travel to Savannah*
22.	Dec. 29–Jan. 24, 1741	*Savannah*
23.	Jan. 24	*Departure for England*

ties with Governor James Oglethorpe in Georgia toward the founding of the orphanage. Earlier in 1739 newspapers had reported on his revivals in England, his audiences in the thousands, the awful silence that fell upon his hearers, and how people climbed nearby trees to hear him. In mid-October they reported that Whitefield was returning to Georgia via Pennsylvania, and his arrival was imminent.

Source: Adapted from a map by Keith J. Hardman and A. Vinoy Laughner, *Christian History* 8, no. 3, issue 23, p. 17.

His only purpose in coming to Philadelphia was to gather supplies before continuing on to Georgia, but Whitefield was immediately invited to preach in the churches when he arrived there from Delaware on November 2. Whitefield had not planned a preaching tour through the colonies, and probably had not heard of the awakenings in Massachusetts and New Jersey.[23]

Whitefield's success in Philadelphia, however, was overwhelming. The Great Awakening had already spread to the town, largely as a result of the stirring preaching of William Tennent, Sr., and his sons, who were pastors of Presbyterian churches in Pennsylvania and New Jersey. Among many other acquaintances, Whitefield became a life-long friend of Benjamin Franklin, who described the evangelist's influence on the town:

> In 1739 arrived among us from Ireland the Reverend Mr. Whitefield, who had made himself remarkable there as an itinerant preacher. He was at first permitted to preach in some of our churches; but the clergy, taking a dislike to him, soon refus'd him their pulpits, and he was oblig'd to preach in the fields. The multitudes of all sects and denominations that attended his sermons were enormous, and it was a matter of speculation to me, who was one of the number, to observe the extraordinary influence of his oratory on his hearers, and how much they admir'd and respected him, notwithstanding his common abuse of them, by assuring them they were naturally half beasts and half devils. It was wonderful to see the change soon made in the manners of our inhabitants. From being thoughtless and indifferent about religion, it seem'd as if all the world were growing religious, so that one could not walk thro' the town in an evening without hearing psalms sung in different families of every street.[24]

Franklin wrote this account in his *Autobiography* years later, including some other well-known Whitefield stories. But his memory had dimmed a bit with regard to some details. Whitefield was, of course, not from Ireland, although he did minister there several times. Also, Franklin as a Deist was no authority on the churches in Philadelphia, and possibly was not aware that Whitefield preached from the Anglican pulpit throughout his visit, became friends with the Baptist and Presbyterian ministers, went to the Quaker meeting, and spoke outdoors from the courthouse steps to great crowds on Market Street because it had become difficult to fit the large congregations into the church buildings.

Awakening in the Middle Colonies

Leaving Philadelphia on November 12, he preached at Burlington, New Jersey, and then at Gilbert Tennent's church in New Brunswick,

Gilbert Tennent
(Courtesy of the Billy Graham Center Museum)

before reaching New York two days later. In New York Whitefield was denied the Anglican pulpit by the commissary, but Ebenezer Pemberton, a Presbyterian pastor, invited him to preach there, and he did so. Tracy writes: "Mr. Pemberton was a native of Boston, and too much of a Puritan to be frightened at Whitefield's doctrine of the new birth. As the house of worship could not hold all that desired to hear, Whitefield preached several times in the fields."[25] In addition, Gilbert Tennent, who had traveled with Whitefield to New York, preached in Whitefield's presence on their arrival in that city, and the Englishman was sincerely impressed: "I . . . never before heard such a searching sermon. He convinced me more and more that we can preach the Gospel of Christ no further than we have experienced the power of it in our own hearts. . . . He has learned experimentally to dissect the heart of a natural man. Hypocrites must either soon be converted or enraged at his preaching."[26]

The Log College of William Tennent, Sr., where evangelistic preaching was taught

Leaving New York, Gilbert Tennent took Whitefield on a tour of the Great Awakening in New Jersey and Pennsylvania, where probably the only clergyman Whitefield met who was not Presbyterian was the Dutch Reformed Theodore Frelinghuysen. Whitefield was much impressed:

Tuesday, Nov. 20. Reached here about six last night; and preached to-day, at noon, for near two hours, in worthy Mr. Tennent's meeting-house, to a large assembly gathered together from all parts; and amongst them, Mr. Tennent told me, was a great number of solid Christians. About three in the afternoon, I preached again; and, at seven, I baptised two children, and preached a third time. Among others who came to hear the Word, were several ministers, whom the Lord has been pleased to honour, in making them instruments of bringing many sons to glory. One was a Dutch Calvinistic minister, named Freeling Housen, pastor of a congregation about four miles from New Brunswick. He is a worthy old soldier of Jesus Christ, and was the beginner of the great work which I trust the Lord is carrying on in these parts. He has been strongly opposed by his carnal brethren, but God has appeared for him, in a surprising manner, and made him more than conqueror, through His love. He has long since learnt to fear him only, who can destroy both body and soul in hell.

Another was Mr. Cross, minister of a congregation of Barking Bridge, about twenty miles from Brunswick. He himself told me of many wonderful and sudden conversions that had been wrought by the Lord under his ministry. For some time, eight or nine used to come to him together, in deep distress of soul; and, I think, he said, three hundred of his congregation, which is not a very large one, were brought home to Christ. They are now looked upon as enthusiasts and madmen, and treated as such by those who know not God, and are ignorant of the hidden life of Jesus Christ in their hearts.[27]

These pages of Whitefield's *Journal* express his amazement and appreciation at the long-standing efforts of many such clergymen to bring revival. Suddenly he was conscious, as evidenced by these paragraphs, that what Solomon Stoddard and Jonathan Edwards had striven for and achieved in Northampton was not unique. Here in the Middle Colonies was a company of fellow evangelists, diligently working to bring about the Great Awakening. In addition, they welcomed him, and begged for his help. Not to cast his lot with them, however temporarily, would be a mistake. But Whitefield's mentor and guide, Gilbert Tennent, had more to show him. They too recognized the need for an educated ministry, even in a wilderness, and were struggling to fulfil it. Whitefield continued,

> Thursday, Nov. 22. Set out for Neshaminy (twenty miles distant from Trent Town), where old Mr. Tennent lives, and keeps his academy, and where I was to preach today, according to appointment. . . . It happens very providentially, that Mr. Tennent and his brethren are appointed to be a Presbytery by the Synod, so that they intend breeding up gracious youths, and sending them out into our Lord's vineyard. The place wherein the young men study now is, in contempt, called *the College*. It is a log-house, about twenty feet long, and nearly as many broad; and, to me, it seemed to resemble the school of the old prophets. That their habitations were mean, and that they sought not great things for themselves, is plain from that passage of Scripture, wherein we are told, that at the feast of the sons of the prophets, one of them put on the pot, whilst the others went forth to fetch some herbs out of the field. From this despised place, seven or eight worthy ministers of Jesus have lately been set forth; more are almost ready to be sent; and a foundation is now being laid for the instruction of many others.[28]

So the mutual appreciation of the revivalists and Whitefield grew increasingly through such incidents from the fall of 1739 to the following summer.

International Renown

In all, Whitefield crossed the Atlantic Ocean thirteen times to visit the colonies and his orphanage at Savannah. He traveled the length of the colonies, becoming the good friend of the great men of America— Franklin, Edwards, Gilbert Tennent, and others. His effect upon the

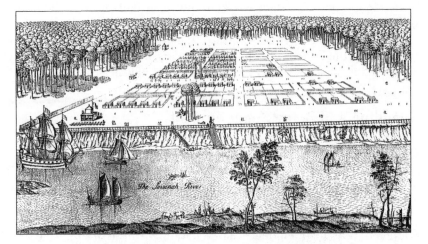

Shortly after James Oglethorpe founded Savannah, Georgia, George Whitefield
chose this frontier village as the site for his American orphanage.
(From an engraving in the author's collection)

colonies is fascinating to study. Franklin, then thirty-three but already a leading citizen of Philadelphia, and Whitefield, only twenty-five, became friends immediately. They talked of his plans for the orphanage, and Franklin suggested he move it to Philadelphia, then the largest city in America. Whitefield rejected this idea, however, so Franklin decided not to give him a penny toward it. But he had not counted on the power of Whitefield oratory:

> I happened soon afterwards to attend one of his sermons, in the course of which I perceived he intended to finish with a collection, and I silently resolved he should get nothing from me. I had in my pocket a handful of copper money, three or four silver dollars, and five in gold. As he proceeded I began to soften and concluded to give the copper. Another stroke of his oratory made me ashamed of that and determined me to give the silver, and he finished so admirably that I emptied my pocket into the collection dish, gold and all.[29]

In 1740 Franklin and other friends erected a hall in Philadelphia for Whitefield. After it had served his purposes it housed an academy, with Whitefield the inspirer and original trustee. Eventually the "Charity School" developed into the University of Pennsylvania. A similar demonstration of Whitefield's social concern and interest in education was his encouragement of William Tennent's Log College at Neshaminy, a few miles north of Philadelphia. This school was later moved to New Jersey and became Princeton University.

In 1740, when the Great Awakening was at its height in the Middle Colonies, Whitefield continued north, and his dynamic preaching brought the Great Awakening to New England. At Boston, Ipswich, Newbury, Hampton, Portsmouth, and other towns, he addressed throngs such as had not been seen before. Edwards welcomed him as a kindred spirit.

Spending and Being Spent for God

Only a few of the incidents that crowded Whitefield's life can be recounted. For thirty-four years, until his early death in 1770, his life was one uniform employment, incessantly preaching and comforting those under conviction. There was hardly a town of any size in England, Scotland, and Wales that he did not visit. When churches were opened to him, he preached as a priest of the Church of England; when churches were closed, he preached in a field. Always he had great effect. In one Whitsuntide week he preached in Moorfields, received a thousand letters from people inquiring about Christianity, and admitted to the Lord's Table 350 more. It has been estimated that in his lifetime he preached 18,000 times, and to more than 60 million people. Never, Ryle remarks, could it be so truly said that a man spent and was spent for God.

Many sermons of Whitefield's were famous, so it is difficult to select one as representative. The following excerpts show his evangelistic style, as well as the humor that could flash through. It is from a contemporary newspaper account describing the scene in Boston, Massachusetts:

After he had finished his prayer, he knelt a long time in profound silence; and so powerfully had it affected the most heartless of his audience, that a stillness like that of the tomb pervaded the whole house. Before he commenced his sermon, long, darkening columns crowded the bright sunny sky of the morning, and swept their dull shadows over the building, in fearful augury of the storm that was approaching.

"See that emblem of human life," said he, as he pointed to a flitting shadow. "It paused for a moment, and concealed the brightness of heaven from our view; but it is gone. And, where will you be, my hearers, when your lives have passed away like that dark cloud! Oh, dear friends, I see thousands sitting attentive with their eyes fixed on the poor unworthy preacher. In a few days we shall all meet at the judgment seat of Christ. We shall form part of that vast assembly which will gather before His throne. Every eye will behold the Judge. With a voice whose call you must abide, and answer He will inquire, whether on earth you strove to enter in at the strait gate; whether you were supremely devoted to God; whether your hearts were absorbed in Him. . . .

"O false and hollow Christians, of what avail will it be that you have done many things? That you have read much in the sacred Word? That you have made long prayers? That you have attended religious duties, and appeared holy in the eyes of men? What will all this be, if, instead of loving God supremely, you have been supposing you should exalt yourself in heaven by acts really polluted and unholy?

"O sinner! by all your hopes of happiness, I beseech you to repent. Let not the wrath of God be awakened! Let not the fires of eternity be kindled against you! See there!" said the impassioned preacher, pointing to a flash of lightning, "It is a glance from the angry eye of Jehovah! Hark!" continued he, raising a finger in listening attitude, as the thunder broke in a tremendous crash, "It was the voice of the Almighty as He passed by in His anger!"

As the sound died away Whitefield covered his face with his hands, and fell on his knees apparently lost in prayer. The storm passed rapidly by, and the sun, bursting forth, threw across the heavens the magnificent arch of peace. Rising and pointing to it the young preacher cried, "Look upon the rainbow, and praise Him who made it. Very beautiful it is in the brightness thereof. It compasseth the heaven about with glory and the hands of the Most High have bended it."[30]

Whitefield was asked to publish this sermon, and he replied that he would consent to it if the printer could manage to include, in addition to the words, the lightning, thunder, and rainbow which went with them!

Many of England's nobility were fascinated by Whitefield, and heard him frequently. Lady Huntingdon was one of his most loyal supporters. Philip Dormer Stanhope, Lord Chesterfield, another great admirer, declared, "Mr. Whitefield's eloquence is unrivalled, his zeal inexhaustible."

Once, the worldly Chesterfield attended a service where Whitefield compared the sinner to a blind beggar. Deserted by his dog, the blind man came up to a precipice. "But Whitefield so warmed with his subject, and unfolded it with such graphic power, that the whole audience was kept in breathless silence over the movements of the poor old man," one biographer tells us. Just as the beggar was about to fall to his destruction, the cynical Chesterfield could take no more. He leaped to his feet crying, "He is gone! He is gone!"[31]

Lord Bolingbroke was another who was greatly influenced by Whitefield, referring to him as "the most extraordinary man in our times. He has the most commanding eloquence I ever heard in any person; his abilities are very considerable; his zeal unquenchable; and his piety and excellence genuine—unquestionable. The bishops and inferior orders of the clergy are very angry with him, and endeavor to represent him as a

*John Wesley, with his brother Charles, was Whitefield's
life-long friend and inspiration, although they came
to disagree theologically. (From the author's collection)*

hypocrite, an enthusiast; but this is not astonishing—there is so little real goodness or honesty among them."[32]

His life was devoted and expended in that highest of pursuits—pointing souls to God. In that, Whitefield by human standards was fabulously successful. He, with his life-long friend John Wesley, brought much of the English-speaking world back from skepticism and immorality to its Christian inheritance. All Christendom benefited immeasurably from his labors. Ezra Stiles says of him:

> Whitefield was the first to essay open-air and field preaching, and the first to get into touch with and realize the potentialities of the Religious Societies of the period which undoubtedly contributed to the Methodist model. He was the first to see the necessity for and to appoint lay preachers and the first to perceive the possibilities of religious journalism. Finally, and perhaps most important of all, he saw very vividly the spiritual need of the wider world of his time, and pioneered the Methodist gospel in Scotland, Ireland, and the American colonies before Wesley had fairly got under way.[33]

This man provided the spark which set England on fire, and the inspiration for the Wesleys, who systematized his methods and reaped the benefits of the awakening Whitefield began.

94

Aftermath of the Great Awakening

The results of the Great Awakening were far-reaching. In New England, where the half-way covenant had vitiated the spirituality of the churches, the Great Awakening enabled the clergy to take up again the ideal of a regenerate congregation. In the Middle Colonies, where great numbers of rootless immigrants were flooding the area and the few churches and clergy were hopelessly inadequate to the task, the Great Awakening aroused laymen to concern, gave new faith to multitudes, developed a dedicated new generation of zealous preachers, and put the churches on a more solid base.

The first major result of the Awakening was the spiritual quickening of the churches of America. In the aggregate, the Congregational churches of New England received the greatest benefit from the revival. According to Ezra Stiles, president of Yale College, during the twenty years following 1740 "an augmentation of above 150 new churches has taken place, founded not on separations but on natural increase into new towns and parishes," bringing the total of Congregational churches to 530.[34] Historians have estimated that from 25,000 to 50,000 were added to the New England churches as converts of the revival. The population of New England in 1750 was approximately 340,000. Taking the lesser number of converts as a conservative estimate, more than 7 percent of the entire population of the New England colonies were received into the membership of the churches as a direct result of the Awakening.

In the Middle Colonies the increase in the New Light (pro-revival) Presbyterian churches was proportionally greater. From 1740 to 1760, the number of Presbyterian ministers in the American colonies increased from forty-five to more than a hundred. The churches multiplied with greater rapidity, and in 1760 there were more than forty churches without pastors in Pennsylvania and Delaware alone. Substantial gains were also made in the Southern colonies.

While the Baptists entertained some prejudices against the Awakening, they shared dramatically in its benefits. From 1740 to 1760, the number of Baptist churches in New England increased from twenty-one to seventy-nine. Some have credited this increase in part to accessions from separatist churches. The separatist additions were chiefly in Connecticut, however. As only eight new Baptist churches were reported in that colony, it is apparent that the increase from the separatists has been greatly overestimated. New churches were also formed in the South, and the foundations laid for the enormous growth experienced afterwards by the Baptists there.

95

Beyond statistical increases, the spiritual quickening of the churches was enhanced more by changes in theological atmosphere than by mere increases in membership.

> In the long run the influence of Jonathan Edwards and the unfinished edifice of his thought is the most enduring result of the New England Awakening. . . . Yet Edwards expounded a theological tradition that had deep popular roots; and its revival among the laity had important cultural results. A new and irrepressible expectancy entered the life of the churches. A national sense of intensified religious and moral resolution was born. Millennial hopes were kindled. The old spirit of the jeremiads was extinguished. Evangelicalism in a new key was abroad in the land, and its workings had a steady internal effect which was nowhere more apparent than in the Congregational churches. . . . Edwards's powerful witness and his development of a distinct school of theology would help to nurture these results. For a century his influence would put its stamp on New England preaching, keeping the concerns of the Awakening alive in the pulpit even as the excitement ebbed away.[35]

Missionary and Educational Endeavors

A second result of the revival was the impetus given to missionary and educational endeavors. The increased concern for missions in America reflected a similar spirit to that manifested wherever the Evangelical Awakening was found, both in Great Britain and Europe. Whitefield himself was a paradigm of what a missionary should be. In New England this concern manifested itself in efforts to reach the Native Americans. At Stonington, Connecticut, and Westerly, Rhode Island, most of the Native Americans who were reached by those ministries embraced Christianity.

Among the early converts of the revival at Norwich, Connecticut, was Samson Occum (1723–1792), a seventeen-year old Mohegan.[36] An ardent promoter of the Awakening, Eleazer Wheelock (1711–1779) of Lebanon, Connecticut, took Occum into his home to educate the obviously talented lad. Occum has traditionally been accorded the distinction of being America's first hymn writer of consequence. But since his authorship is open to question, and the first hymns attributed to him were not published until 1774, Samuel Davies (1723–1761) of Virginia is now usually given that honor. Davies' hymns appeared as parts of sermons as early as 1756.[37]

Wheelock had graduated from Yale in 1733 and became pastor of the second parish in Lebanon.In his first year there a revival broke out under Edwards' influence. In the early 1740s Wheelock devised a plan for educating Native Americans, who would then be sent out to evangelize their own people. He received from Colonel Joshua More the gift of a house

96

*In 1770, Eleazer Wheelock raised the first buildings for Dartmouth College,
which he planned as a school for Native American evangelists.
(Courtesy of the Billy Graham Center Museum)*

and school building at Lebanon for this purpose, and More's Charity
School opened in 1754. Funds were solicited from England, Scotland,
and the cities of America, and a trust was administered by a board whose
chairman was the earl of Dartmouth. The school was moved to Hanover,
New Hampshire, in 1769 and renamed Dartmouth College, opening its
doors to whites and Indians alike, and eventually graduating more than
forty New Light pastors.

The surge of intellectual and educational interest from the revival led to the founding of five colleges: Dartmouth, the University of Pennsylvania, Princeton, Rutgers, and Brown universities. Princeton University owes its origin to the Log College. Founded before 1730, by 1744 this institution had trained more than twenty young men, including the Tennent sons, Samuel Blair, John Rowland, Samuel Finley, William Robinson, and other influential preachers of the Awakening. In addition, the Log College inspired other academies to be founded by its graduates, such as the one begun by Blair in 1739 at Fagg's Manor in Chester County, Pennsylvania. Davies received his training at Fagg's Manor, and was considered an outstanding scholar. He was chosen to be president of Princeton in 1759. After Tennent's Log College at Neshaminy, Pennsylvania, was closed in about 1744, the work was taken up in 1746 by Jonathan Dickinson in his manse in Elizabethtown, New Jersey. Dickinson, like many clergymen of the time, had trained young men under his roof for years, and he was thought particularly suited to carry on the work in an expanded manner. He was elected the first president of the College of New Jersey (later Princeton University), and a charter was secured from Governor Jonathan Belcher of New Jersey, a noted friend of Dissenter causes. The transition from the less permanent facilities and one-man faculty of the log colleges to the permanence of a chartered and prestigious school was important at the time when the Awakening was feeding young men into the ministry. As an outgrowth of the Awakening, it was fitting that the College of New Jersey experienced revivals of its own in 1757 and 1762.[38]

Influence on Religious and Political Liberty

A third result of the Great Awakening was its influence upon religious and political liberty. In New England, except for Rhode Island, Congregationalism was established by law. In parts of the South, Anglicanism was the established denomination. The expansion of the newer denominations, particularly the Presbyterians and the Baptists, paved the way for tolerance of differing views and a broader concept of liberty of conscience. Competing denominations and rival sects existing side by side and openly propagating their differing tenets led to the introduction of guarantees of religious liberty to all, insofar as a group did not interfere with the peace of the state. With this tendency to diversity, a unifying influence was also at work. The ministry of Whitefield touched every area of the colonies and each sect, making the Awakening both the first intercolonial movement and an ecumenical endeavor of the churches in America. Without conflicting with denominational loyalty, his ministry emphasized a broader view of Christian fraternity that had been lacking.

Denominations could not, and in some cases did not wish to, give such a perspective to their people. Whitefield rendered to the churches of America a unique service in forcing the churches to work together in the Awakening. He made the clergy and laity understand that it was a work of God that superseded petty party differences. Rising above name and group, he enabled clergy and laity to apprehend the universal brotherhood in Christ that has come to mark American Christianity.

The Second Great
Awakening in the East

As a direct result of conversions made during the First Great Awakening, and in spite of demanding requirements for membership, the churches of New England added twenty thousand to fifty thousand new members.[1] Many more became convinced Christians in the Middle Colonies and in the South. Churches that supported the Awakening grew in strength. In New England particularly, Christian principles were again enthroned in common practice and in the general order.

Eventually the trough period Solomon Stoddard had described came to pass. The French and Indian War, which lasted from 1754 to 1763, brought changes that affected all Americans, especially in morals and religion. During this war, foreigners mingled extensively with the

*Ezra Stiles, president
of Yale College 1777–95
(Courtesy of the Billy Graham Center Museum)*

colonists for the first time. The colonial soldiers, who often lacked a deep understanding of Christian truth, easily imbibed new ideas and practices in an army composed of those they were taught to regard as their superiors. Many British officers and soldiers were Deists or atheists and tended to hold the colonists in disdain as unpolished bumpkins. The Americans, on the other hand, respected the British as coming from the "mother country," a place renowned for science, wisdom, and the arts. The British had engaging manners and practiced all the genteel vices that generally fascinate young people. When they returned home, the colonial soldiers had been influenced too deeply by the ideas and vices of the British to give them up easily.[2]

The Revolutionary War

As the Revolutionary War loomed in the early 1770s, faith and morals deteriorated further. While Americans fighting in the Revolution were not exposed to as many foreigners as in the French and Indian War, those they met were of far more dissolute character.[3] These were Frenchmen—disciples of Voltaire, Rousseau, Diderot, and others of the French Enlightenment—who were invariably atheists. The British infidel at this time usually showed some degree of reverence for God and admitted the possibility of an afterlife, but the French infidel despised the idea of God and vehemently denied any life beyond. In mannerisms, the French were like the British: urbane and self-assured. But they were more experienced at silencing arguments for morality with a sneer. In addition, they were the Americans' dear allies in the struggle against England; Americans owed them much for their magnanimous help in a time of tremendous need. "They perfectly knew," Timothy Dwight (1752–1817) observed, "how to insinuate the grossest sentiments in a delicate and inoffensive manner, to put arguments to flight with a sneer, to stifle conscience with a smile, and to overbear investigation by confronting it with the voice and authority of the great world."[4] Most of the American soldiers had never heard the divine origin of the Scriptures questioned, and they had no answers to even the simplest objections.

Peace with Great Britain was concluded in 1782, and more settled conditions began to prevail. Christian hopes that the foreign influences of atheism, Deism, and infidelity would lessen, however, were doomed to disappointment. Soon the prospect of the French Revolution arose, an event devastating in its cause and consequences. Since the Americans had just gone through a revolution of their own, they sympathized with those they supposed were aiming at the same desirable goals. Many assumed it would mean release from despotism and superstition for all Frenchmen. Americans were startled when the French Revolution began instead to produce horrors and evil consequences, including vicious leaders and successive massacres of innocent people.

Because the French were their own reporters in all this, the truth of the accounts was beyond question. To the women of the United States, the women of Paris appeared to be fiends incarnate. The guillotine curdled the blood of even the callous, and the murder of King Louis XVI awakened general disgust. Americans regarded the paganism of France and its violation of all moral principles as no less amazing than the accounts of its cruelties. Its gross immorality; brutal atheism in the proceedings of the national legislature; disregard for evidence, truth, and justice in the courts; ferocity in the behavior of its judges and juries; and savagery in the conduct of its new officials would have been unbelievable if it had not been reported by the French themselves.

For years prior to the Revolution, France had been going through the Enlightenment under the leadership of Voltaire, Rousseau, and the encyclopedists. The rallying cry was "Reason," which meant that the unaided human mind was the only authority, and should bow to no other. Many rejected Christian revelation, which they considered absurd, and looked upon the Bible as a collection of fairy tales at best, and at worst an evil book. In the name of Reason, the Roman Catholic Church was overthrown, its property confiscated and plundered, and its priests murdered by the hundreds. Under the supposed sway of liberated Reason, every house in France was prey to inspections by mobs coming to rob and destroy. In the cause of liberty, it was stated, the Bible and the vessels of the Mass were placed on an ass and marched through the cities to deride and ridicule them before throwing them on a bonfire. In the Jacobin Club of Paris, a formal comparison was made between the Savior Christ and the bloodthirsty Swiss revolutionary Jean-Paul Marat (1743–1793), and the latter was judged to be a greater benefactor to humankind. For the cause of liberty the Lord's Day was abolished and a week of ten days established.

The United States, a new nation anxious to take its place in the councils of the world, was particularly open to foreign influences and ideas at this time. France and other European nations were happy to oblige. The *Encyclopedia,* a vast number of volumes composed by Voltaire and other French infidels, the *Systeme de la Nature,* and Thomas Paine's *The Age of Reason,* were printed abroad in great quantities to be shipped to America, where they found many eager readers. An enormous edition of *The Age of Reason* was published in France and sent to America to be sold for a few cents per copy. Where it could not be sold it was given away. Paine's Deism and the ideas of the French encyclopedists were not closely reasoned arguments intended for scholars. They were designed, not to instruct or convince, but to amuse, baffle, and intrigue. They were addressed, not to educated people, but to the ignorant, the unthinking, and those already inclined to loose morals and a hatred of Christianity. In the name of reason these writers pandered to the weaknesses, passions, and prejudices of others.

Paine, Allen, and Palmer

The Deist and atheist writers who produced these works were industrious and bold. Their writings were sometimes clever, but when they came to the question of the authority of Scripture, they were incapable of understanding the nature of evidence. Today most of their reasonings are so palpably silly as to deserve no notice from any informed person. In *The Age of Reason,* Thomas Paine (1737–1809) attempted to use ridicule in denouncing the Bible:

> It is upon this plain narrative of facts, together with another case I am going to mention, that the Christian mythologists, calling themselves the Christian church, have erected their fable which, for absurdity and extravagance, is not exceeded by anything that is to be found in the mythology of the ancients. . . . Putting aside everything that might excite laughter by its absurdity, or detestation by its profaneness, and confining ourselves merely to an examination of the parts, it is impossible to conceive a story more derogatory to the Almighty, more inconsistent with his wisdom, more contradictory to his power than this story is.[5]

Responding in kind, the distinguished American Presbyterian Ashbel Green characterized Paine's *Age of Reason* as "a book in which the most contemptible ignorance, the grossest falsehood, the most vulgar buffoonery, the most unblushing impudence, and the most daring profaneness are united."[6]

Paine called Jesus a "virtuous reformer and revolutionist," and regarded him as a deluded but good man whose teachings were perverted by the apostle Paul and others. Voltaire (1694–1778), on the other hand, in his many attempts to disprove Scripture, aimed directly at Jesus as the chief deliberate deceiver. "Among the Jews," Voltaire declared, "there have always been men from the rabble who played at being prophets in order to distinguish themselves from the mob: here then is the one who made the most noise, and who was turned into a god."[7]

The anger of American churchmen at the coming of such books from across the seas to the New World turned to fury when pernicious volumes began to be published right at home. In 1784 Ethan Allen (1738–1789), the Revolutionary War hero who had captured Fort Ticonderoga from the British, issued *Reason the Only Oracle of Man* from a printer in Bennington, Vermont. Allen admitted in its preface that this long book of 477 pages was poorly written, but went on to assert that "the doctrine of the Trinity is destitute of foundation, and tends manifestly to superstition and idolatry." Regarding Christ's atonement Allen declares, "There could be no justice or goodness in one being's suffering for another, nor is it at all compatible with reason to suppose, that God was the contriver of such a propitiation."[8]

Elihu Palmer was an ardent admirer of Paine, calling him "one of the first and best of writers, and probably the most useful man that ever existed upon the face of the earth."[9] In 1802 Palmer, a defrocked Baptist clergyman who had been driven from his pulpit for preaching

104

against the deity of Christ, published the third popular book in this library of infidelity, *Principles of Nature.* In it he asserted: "The simple truth is, that their pretended Saviour is nothing more than an illegitimate Jew, and their hopes of salvation through him rest on no better foundation than that of fornication or adultery."[10] He called the Bible "a book, whose indecency and immorality shock all common sense and common honesty."[11]

These diatribes of Paine, Allen, Palmer, and others were widely discussed. Many of those who agreed with their ideas were gathered into the Democratic-Republican political party being formed under the leadership of Thomas Jefferson, an avowed Deist who had declared his doubts of Christian truth as early as 1781. Jefferson had been influenced strongly by the French *philosophes* during his years in France from 1783 to 1789. After his return he opposed the Christian ministry more intensely and adhered to Deism more firmly than before. Soon after his inauguration in 1801, President Jefferson wrote a very cordial letter to Paine in France, inviting him to return to America on board the naval sloop *Maryland* as the honored guest of the nation. All who had any doubts as to Jefferson's sentiments were convinced by this warm gesture, and when Paine arrived in Baltimore, newspapers of the land responded in fury. The *New York Evening Post,* and other papers, angry at Paine's anti-Christian militancy and his previous attacks on George Washington, resorted to wrathful versification:

TO TOM PAINE

Detested reptile! wherefore hast thou come
To add new evils to our groaning land?
To some wild desert let thy carcase roam,
Where nought can wither by thy blasting hand.

In the dark hour that brought thee to our shore,
The shade of Washington did awful scowl—
Hence, gloomy monster! curse mankind no more,
Thy person filthy as thy soul is foul.[12]

The outpouring of public opinion against Paine's coming was so strong that Jefferson was alarmed and regretted his connection with Paine's return. Still, many were swept into sympathy with the new ideas, especially during the visit of Citizen Edmond Genêt (1763–1834), representative of the revolutionary French Republic in 1793. "Jacobin" clubs, named after similar radical clubs in France, appeared everywhere before the insanities of the French Reign of Terror in 1793 and 1794 became well known in America. Concerning those who were swept into the vortex of infidelity, Dwight reflected:

Youths particularly, who had been liberally educated, and who with strong passions and feeble principles were votaries of sensuality and ambition, delighted with the prospect of unrestrained gratification and panting to be enrolled with men of fashion and splendor, became enamored of these new doctrines. . . . Striplings, scarcely fledged, suddenly found that the world had been involved in a general darkness through the long succession of preceding ages, and that the light of wisdom had but just begun to dawn upon the human race. . . . Men reluctantly conscious of their own inferiority of understanding rejoiced to see themselves without an effort become in a moment wiser than those who had spent life in laborious investigations.[13]

Unbelief at the Colleges

As might be expected, new ideas from Europe were welcomed by the college students. The colleges became a trial to godly people. Transylvania University in Kentucky, which had been founded by Presbyterians, was perhaps the most extreme example of a departure from its founding principles, as it was taken over by a faculty and student body who banished Christian teachings and instituted Deism. At Bowdoin College in Maine there was but one professed Christian in the student body in the 1790s. Bishop Meade of Virginia said, "Infidelity was rife in the state, and the College of William and Mary was regarded as the hot-bed of French politics and religion. I can truly say that then and for some years after in every educated young man in Virginia whom I met I expected to find a skeptic, if not an avowed unbeliever."[14]

Ashbel Green, who enrolled at Princeton in 1782, described a similar state of affairs in that college. "While I was a member of college, there were but two professors of religion among the students, and not more than five or six who scrupled the use of profane language in common conversation, and sometimes it was of a very shocking kind. To the influence of the American war succeeded that of the French revolution, still more pernicious, and I think more general."[15]

Lyman Beecher (1775–1863), in describing the condition of Yale College prior to the presidency of Dwight, said, "Before he came college was in a most ungodly state. The college church was almost extinct. Most of the students were skeptical, and rowdies were plenty. Wine and liquors were kept in many rooms; intemperance, profanity, gambling, and licentiousness were common. . . . That was the day of the infidelity of the Tom Paine school. Boys that dressed flax in the barn, as I used to, read Tom Paine and believed him . . . most of the class before me were infidels, and called each other Voltaire, Rousseau, D'Alembert, etc., etc."[16]

In addition to Jefferson, many prominent in public affairs and the councils of state embraced the new views. Washington, John Adams, and Patrick Henry were among those who had no sympathy for Deism and atheism, but infidelity was so arrogantly fashionable that sometimes they seemed to be in the minority. Jefferson's secretary of war, Henry Dearborn, was an avowed atheist and said of the churches of the land, "So long as these temples stand we cannot hope for good government." General Charles Lee was so violent in his opposition to Christianity that his will stipulated that he not be buried "in any church or church-yard, or within a mile of any Presbyterian or Anabaptist meeting-house."[17]

The perception of declining public morals and decency seemed so great that, during his presidency, John Adams set aside a national fast day for April 25, 1799, declaring in his proclamation, "The most precious interests of the people of the United States are still held in jeopardy by the hostile designs and insidious acts of a foreign nation, as well as by the dissemination among them of those principles, subversive of the foundation of all religious, moral, and social obligations, that have produced incalculable mischief and misery in other countries."[18] Here was official alarm from the highest level of government that European anarchy and immorality was subverting Americans.

Depressed Churches

The state of the churches was indeed very low. Along the eastern seaboard many were taking in almost no new members. Multitudes were leaving, lured by the opening frontier. Nearly 1 million people had deserted the East by 1800, seeking a new life and hoping for riches in the Ohio and Allegheny River valleys. This number greatly increased in the next few decades, as new states were formed from the rapid increase in the territory of the United States after 1803, the year of the acquisition of the Louisiana Purchase.

Seeing the people of Virginia leaving for an unchurched and unevangelized wilderness, in 1794 the Episcopal rector of Bath, Devereux Jarratt (1733–1801), wrote sadly, "The present time is marked by peculiar traits of impiety and such an almost universal inattention to the concerns of religion that very few will attend except on Sunday, to hear the word of the Lord. . . . The state of religion is gloomy and distressing; the church of Christ seems to be sunk very low."[19] Such a state was new for Jarratt, whose dynamic preaching had brought in great congregations. He had been influenced by fellow Anglican George Whitefield, and when Jarratt went to England for ordination he had met both Whitefield and John Wesley. Returning to Virginia he began an unusual ministry of vibrant evangelism and zealous preaching. His three churches became so crowded that he was compelled to hold services outside, following the Methodist pattern. He also followed their lead in meeting with earnest Christians in small groups, and when the Methodists came to Virginia, he had been of inestimable help to them. By 1794 everything had changed; the churches were again depressed, and many were leaving with hopes of finding rich land in Tennessee, Kentucky, and elsewhere.

For years the annual General Assembly of the Presbyterian Church in the U.S.A. issued pastoral letters to all their churches lamenting the decline of zeal and morals, but the pastoral letter of 1798 showed greater alarm than its predecessors:

> Dear Friends and Brethren: The aspect of divine providence, and the extraor-
> dinary situation of the world, at the present moment, indicate, that a solemn
> admonition by the ministers of religion and other church officers in Gen-
> eral Assembly convened, has become our indispensable duty.... A solemn
> crisis has arrived, in which we are called to the most serious contempla-
> tion of the moral causes which have produced it, and the measures which
> it becomes us to pursue.... Formality and deadness, not to say hypocrisy;
> a contempt for vital godliness, and the spirit of fervent piety; a desertion of
> the ordinances, or a cold and unprofitable attendance upon them, visibly
> pervade every part of the Church, and certain men have crept in amongst
> us, who have denied, or attempt to explain away the pure doctrines of the
> gospel; to introduce pernicious errors which were either not named, or
> named with abhorrence, but which have, within a few years since, been
> embraced by deluded multitudes. The Lord's day is horribly profaned, and
> family religion and instruction lamentably neglected.... God hath a con-
> troversy with us—Let us prostrate ourselves before him! Let the deepest
> humiliation and the sincerest repentance mark our sense of national sins;
> and let us not forget, at the same time, the personal sins of each individual,
> that have contributed to increase the mighty mass of corruption.[20]

Outpourings of the Spirit

Only one year later, the Presbyterian General Assembly's annual pastoral letter called to the attention of its churches that, while there was
still much vice and immorality,

> amidst this generally unfavourable aspect, there are several particular cir-
> cumstances peculiarly comforting and encouraging.... We have heard
> from different parts the glad tidings of the outpourings of the Spirit, and
> of times of refreshing from the presence of the Lord. We have heard from
> several parts of our church, and elsewhere, of the late hopeful conversion
> of many. From the east, from the west, and from the south, have these joy-
> ful tidings reached our ears.[21]

Still greater joy was expressed by the General Assemblies of 1800 and 1801.

What was happening? It was not a revulsion from the horrors of the French Revolution or disgust at the scurrilities of the Deist and atheist writers that was calling the nation back from the brink of infidelity. Rather, God was moving again in convicting power.

Renewal began in the West: Kentucky, Tennessee, Ohio, and western Pennsylvania. The Presbyterian General Assembly reported in 1800, "The success of the missionary labours is greatly on the increase. God is shaking the valley of dry bones on the frontiers, a spiritual resurrection is taking place there."[22] But the East soon felt similar movings of God. "Thus," as E. H. Gillett has described, "the century which was just closing, and which had threatened to close with dark and dismal prospects, was destined to leave behind it a brighter record. A new era had dawned upon the Church—an era of revivals."[23]

Although a new era was indeed dawning in which awakenings would eclipse anything known in the eighteenth century, revivals had never completely ceased. In addition to the remarkable revival among the Methodists in 1787, there had been general awakenings in New England in 1763 and 1764, although statistically they could not compare with the Great Awakening of the 1740s. In 1787 Hampden-Sydney, a small Presbyterian college in Virginia founded during the Revolution, became the center "of the great inter-denominational Awakening which marked the final triumph of evangelical Christianity in Virginia, and . . . left Hampden-Sydney throbbing with a new zeal for its mission."[24] Revivals had broken out in several towns, most of them in Connecticut: Norfolk in 1767; Killingly in 1776; Lebanon in 1781; New Britain in 1784; East Haddam and Lyme in 1792; Farmington and New Hartford in 1795; and Milford in 1796.

Now suddenly, revivals seemed to be everywhere in New England. Edward Dorr Griffith, a perceptive observer of these events, wrote that the period of awakening began in 1792 and that he "saw a continued succession of heavenly sprinklings at New Salem, Farmington, Middlebury, and New Hartford . . . until, in 1799, I could stand at my door in New Hartford, Litchfield County, and number fifty or sixty contiguous congregations laid down in one field of divine wonders, and as many more in different parts of New England."[25]

One of the most important of these had occurred in the small town of Lee, Massachusetts, in 1792. According to the report of its pastor, Alvan Hyde (1768–1833),

> This people had been for nine years without a pastor, and were unhappily divided in their religious opinions. Some were Calvinists, and favored the church, but the largest proportion were Arminians. . . . Contrary to my expectations, I found, on my first visits, many persons of different ages, under serious and very deep impressions. . . . Before I was aware, and without any previous appointment, I found myself, on these occasions, in the

109

midst of a solemn and anxious assembly. . . . All our religious meetings were very much thronged, and yet were never noisy or irregular, nor continued to a late hour. They were characterized with a stillness and solemnity, which, I believe, have rarely been witnessed.[26]

The awakening lasted for eighteen months, and further revivals occurred in the town in 1800 and 1806.

Dwight—Reformer at Yale

Those seeking awakening in New England found their leader and theologian in Timothy Dwight. A grandson of Jonathan Edwards through his mother, Dwight was born at Northampton in 1752. A precocious lad, he graduated from Yale College in 1769 and immediately thereafter began teaching grammar school at the age of seventeen. He received an appointment as tutor at Yale in 1771 and found that at the age of nineteen he was younger than most of those he was responsible to teach. But he faced the situation undismayed, overcoming the handicap of youthfulness by energy, tact, and firmness—qualities that served him well throughout life.

Always a prodigious worker at whatever task he undertook, Dwight threw himself into his teaching with enthusiasm, and his students loved him for it. He allowed himself a total of four hours' sleep each night, with no time for exercise, in order that he might be a good teacher. Under the heavy regimen of a meager diet, long and exacting hours, and little exercise, his eyesight and general health failed him at the same time, and he became almost blind. He was forced to abandon his position at Yale for a time, during which his health recovered, but his eyes were weak for the remainder of his life. As he returned to teaching, the stirring days of the Revolution's beginnings were upon the College, and the students felt the continual upset of threatened coastal raids and other distractions.

Timothy Dwight had by this time decided to follow the Edwardsean footsteps into the ministry, and on June 9, 1777, he was ordained. Shortly before, on March 3, 1777, Timothy married Mary Woolsey. His uncle, Jonathan Edwards, Jr., officiated. Patriotism and unavoidable confusion combined to close Yale—many of the students were joining the army— and Dwight became a chaplain that October 6. In his service with the First Connecticut Brigade, Dwight saw much of the misery of war's desolation. He exhibited his patriotism as well as his abilities as a poet in composing songs and hymns for the army, many of which attained wide popularity. An especially famous one concluded,

> Columbia, Columbia, to glory arise,
> The Queen of the world, and the child of the skies.

*Timothy Dwight, Jonathan Edwards' grandson, was both poet
and scholar, but he showed himself the master apologist
for Christianity as president of Yale College.
(Yale University Art Gallery)*

At the war's end, Dwight opened his own academy at Northampton, and this prospered. In 1777 Ezra Stiles was made president of Yale, although some favored the election of Dwight because of his excellent work as tutor before the war. Despite his success as an educator, Dwight still had ministerial intentions, and in May 1783 he was called by the congregation of Greenfield Hill, a parish in Fairfield, Connecticut. He had a successful ministry there until June 1795, when, upon the death of Dr. Stiles, the corporation of Yale College elected Dwight as president. Ministerial and public opinion throughout Connecticut immediately acknowledged Dwight as the right choice.

"A Ruined College"

Yale College at this time was not a large and thriving institution. With only 110 students, it was struggling. Ezra Stiles had not provided many answers to the problems. Dwight expressed his sentiments in a letter written just before his election: "I do not court the appointment; let those who do, take it. I am already happily settled, and in a station little exposed to envy or obloquy. To build up a ruined college is a difficult task."[27] Nevertheless, when chosen, Dwight accepted and immediately threw his characteristic energies into the task.

Among the school's problems, discipline was notoriously slack. Lyman Beecher noted that infidelity was the students' creed. Stiles, an older man of declining vigor, had clung tenaciously to the methods of the mid-eighteenth century.

Dwight, however, came to the presidency in the prime of life; he possessed, at forty-three, a great deal of experience, boundless energy, and an openness to new ideas. Although he was certainly unhappy with the licentiousness of the students, he had no intention of alienating them and making his work harder. By example he would show the rebellious student body the integrity and dignity of the Christian.

The students felt the change immediately. One reported home, "We now see the advantage of having an able director at the head of affairs, one whose commands are energetic, respected, and obeyed. . . . It is surprising to see what a difference there is in the behavior of the students since last year; at present there is no card playing, at least but little of it, no nightly revelings, breaking tutors' windows, breaking glass bottles, etc. but all is order and quietness, more so I believe than was ever known for any length of time in this college."[28] Other students testified with amazement to the studiousness of all, and to the fact that most were "much more steady at prayers than formerly." Although his instruction and administration impressed the students, above all they came to admire Dwight's character, his "sound understanding," "open, candid and free behavior," his "handsome and graceful person," and "engaging manners."[29]

Dwight introduced new methods, new textbooks, and new courses. Although by 1800 the college had achieved greater prestige than ever before, his purpose was not merely to make the academic machinery hum briskly. Concern with the honor of the Christian faith and the students' spiritual condition led Dwight to give highest priority to building faith and character. The students admired his concern for the welfare of their souls. Among his admirers was Lyman Beecher, patriarch of a distinguished family and leader of the forces of evangelism after Dwight's death. In later years Beecher exemplified the intimate association of evangelism with social reform and benevolence. Looking back on his days at Yale, Beecher recalled how Dwight handled delicate problems:

They [the students] thought the Faculty were afraid of free discussion. But when they handed Dr. Dwight a list of subjects for class disputation, to their surprise he selected this: "Is the Bible the word of God?" and told them to do their best.

He heard all they had to say, answered them, and there was an end. He preached incessantly for six months on the subject, and all infidelity skulked and hid its head.

He elaborated his theological system in a series of forenoon sermons in the chapel.... To a mind appreciative like mine, his preaching was a continual course of education and a continual feast. He was copious and polished in style, though disciplined and logical.

There was a pith and power of doctrine there that has not been since surpassed, if equaled. I took notes of all his discourses, condensing and forming skeletons. He was of noble form, with a noble head and body, and had one of the sweetest smiles that ever you saw. He always met me with a smile. Oh, how I loved him! I loved him as my own soul, and he loved me as a son. And once at Litchfield I told him that all I had I owed to him. "Then," said he, "I have done a great and soul-satisfying work. I consider myself amply rewarded."

He was universally revered and loved. I never knew but one student undertake to frustrate his wishes.[30]

Drawing the Battle Lines

After Dwight's inauguration as president of Yale, the battle lines were soon drawn. There were two alternatives, Christianity or infidelity, with no middle ground. Not only were the students generally without faith, but some of the faculty could not claim to be Christian. Tutor Benjamin Silliman was regarded as a Deist. President Dwight began a sledge-hammer attack on infidelity, and he entered with customary zeal into a battle that lasted seven years. His sermons carefully explained the dangers to church, state, and morals of all departures from revealed truth, so that no one could misunderstand. In debate he encouraged free and open discussion of religious doubts and difficulties, thereby having opportunity to refute points raised by his opponents. His great series of sermons in the college chapel lasted for the four years a student would be at Yale. Then they would be repeated. Every student heard the whole system of Dwight's divinity and his answers to the philosophy of skepticism.

At Dwight's coming, most students denounced organized religion and divine revelation as loudly as Voltaire had shouted down superstition. Christianity was literally dead at what had once been its proudest Connecticut fortress. The recovery of Yale was the highest priority for the new president and for all of Connecticut's clergy. After the students had learned to admire and appreciate Dwight's abilities, the atmosphere changed perceptibly. Early in 1796 a group of undergraduates organized to improve moral conditions, and in 1797 the Moral Society of Yale College was founded. Many students turned to the president as their favorite counselor on realizing that he was a sympathetic and concerned listener. A number left his study with a new determination and direction, often to enter the ministry.

Early in the spring of 1802, two seniors were overwhelmed with conviction for their sins. In a short period they came to faith in Christ and assurance of forgiveness. After making a public profession of their faith, they joined the college church. This made an impact on others, who in turn sought peace and consolation. In the ten days preceding vacation, fifty young men declared themselves "serious inquirers." On the day of junior exhibitions, a student reported that the "greater part of the scholars" felt more like attending "a prayer meeting than anything of a sportive kind."

Conviction multiplied; wherever the students gathered—in their rooms, at meals, and around New Haven—the great subject of conversation was eternal salvation. "The convictions of many were pungent and overwhelming; and 'the peace in believing' which succeeded, was not less strongly marked," Professor C. A. Goodrich reported after an intensive study.[31] During the awakening that followed, no regular college activities were suspended, nor was preaching more frequent than usual. Dwight disapproved of "enthusiasm" or wild displays of emotion such as had been seen during the Great Awakening; orderliness and lack of fanaticism typified all that was done.[32]

The Revival Spreads

Many feared that, when the students dispersed for spring vacation, the revival might cease. The reverse occurred. The young men carried home with them news of Yale's turnabout in sentiments, and the impulse spread. When they reassembled in New Haven, more offered their lives to God. Half of the seniors were by then rejoicing in salvation, and one-third of the class eventually entered the ministry. With great happiness Dwight witnessed the formal conversion of eighty men out of the 160 enrolled. Among the converts was tutor Silliman, who wrote to his mother, "Yale College is a little temple, prayer and praise seem to be the delight of the greater part of the students, while those who are still unfeeling are awed into respectful silence."[33]

The Brothers and Linonian debating clubs were transformed into centers of spiritual exhortation and prayer. When graduation day arrived, the departing seniors signed an agreement to pray for one another on a certain hour of each day. Since the student body changed constantly, the effects gradually faded. But under Dwight's concerned ministry for his students, a new awakening in April 1808 was almost as powerful as that of 1802. Succeeding revivals came to the students in 1813 and 1815.

114

These revivals in Yale and New Haven marked only the beginning of a movement that swept Connecticut. For many years there was little danger of a pagan Yale. Dwight's biographer, Charles Cuningham, commented:

> God having thus again blessed Yale, an ardent student carried the news from that favored institution to Dartmouth, where soon afterwards a revival was in full swing. That same year, Princeton, too, enjoyed a shower of grace. In giving thanks for these events the editors of the *Connecticut Evangelical Magazine and Religious Intelligencer* lamented that Harvard, founded with many prayers, and nurtured by the strong faith of pious progenitors, had been, for many years, passed by. At Yale, President Dwight, skilled gardener that he was, labored in a fruitful vineyard. No weeds of infidelity throve long there.[34]

Dwight was not only the central figure in the collegiate revivals that radiated from Yale. Through his writings, the devoted students who carried on his work, and his leadership of Connecticut Congregationalism, he also became a crucial innovator in American revivalism from 1800 until the beginning of the Civil War. Timothy Dwight represents a watershed in the history of awakenings in America.

Ongoing Influence

To understand Dwight's distinctive contribution, it is necessary to review theological development after the death of Jonathan Edwards. For decades, Edwards' theological descendants had from his works developed the *Edwardsean* or *New Divinity School*. Another and larger group were the *Old Calvinists*, who counted themselves completely orthodox but did not hold up Edwards as their mentor. Still a third group were the *rationalists*, represented by Charles Chauncy, who eventually turned Unitarian and repudiated Calvinism.[35]

Interestingly, Dwight agreed more with the Old Calvinists than with the Edwardseans in stressing the "means of grace": prayer, the preaching of the gospel, the searching of the Scriptures, fellowship with Christians, and attendance at divine services. Through these and any other means that allowed the efficacious grace of the Holy Spirit to descend upon the soul, one could be roused from spiritual stupor, made aware of guilt, and made open to the Spirit's work. In his multi-volume *Theology,* Dwight rejected the belief in the utter sinfulness of all "unregenerate doings," asserting that "it is the soul, which is thus taught, alarmed, and allured, upon which descends" the Holy Spirit. Therefore, "the Means of Grace ought to be used by sinners; and by Christians, for the purpose of promoting the salvation of sinners." Pastors "ought to advise, and exhort, sinners to use the Means of Grace."[36] In this Dwight ran directly counter to the tenets of most Edwardseans, especially those of the more rigid Hopkinsian school.

115

It was not that Dwight felt the prayers of a convicted sinner had any moral goodness; goodness could not come until the Holy Spirit imputed Christ's righteousness to the soul through regeneration. But according to Dwight, the sinner's agonized prayers for deliverance and the experience of being under conviction of sin had a definite purpose. Unless sinners knew their guilt and danger, unless they recognized their total dependence upon God's grace in Christ, they could not appreciate the love and goodness of God that rescued them. Indeed, it was to every person's eternal interest to use the means of grace, for they were plainly the usual methods by which God regenerates the lost soul. God would not have provided them if they were forbidden.

Thus Timothy Dwight prepared the way for free will by attempting to break the log jam of human inability that had stymied and brought ridicule upon Calvinism. He heightened the role of human choice in salvation, and reduced the prolonged period of convictions, believing conversion could come after a brief time of crisis. In reducing the time span between the first conviction of sin and final conversion, and giving a rationale for the sinner's own will to choose God, Dwight mounted a program for evangelism behind which he hoped Calvinists could unite. It was, of course, an "Arminianized Calvinism," which would erode crucial doctrines of the Reformed view and fall in behind John Wesley's ideas. But it was the wave of the future for American Protestantism and set the stage for the teachings of Nathaniel William Taylor (1786–1858) and Charles Grandison Finney (1792–1875).

The second great change brought about largely by Dwight thrust at the very heart of how awakenings were understood to operate. Sidney Mead has expressed the change well:

> As for the revivals, Edwards' connection with the First Awakening was much different from Dwight's connection with the Second. Edwards preached sincerely and vividly of what he had experienced and apparently was genuinely surprised when the revival began. Dwight deliberately set out to start a revival in the college and among the eminent men of the state, and Beecher and Taylor perfected methods of fostering them. To Edwards the revival was a by-product of his shared experience; to the latter men revivals were the calculated means to an end.[37]

All these men were utterly convinced that awakenings were the work of the Holy Spirit, but there was an increasing feeling that God *invited* men to cooperate with him in praying and preaching for revival. It is a fascinating study in American church history to note what five generations of an eminent family line—passing through Stoddard, Edwards, and Dwight—contributed to the theology of awakenings.

116

*Asahel Nettleton applied Timothy Dwight's theology of evangelism
to those in Connecticut, Massachusetts, and eastern New York.
He was the great revivalist of the Second Great Awakening until his health failed.
(Connecticut Historical Society)*

As any good strategist, Dwight organized his forces while he was at the peak of his powers, assuring that the work would be effectively continued after his demise. He was fortunate in having several very capable lieutenants, not only Lyman Beecher but also Nathaniel Taylor and Asahel Nettleton (1786–1844).

The preeminent leader in evangelism during the early phase of the Second Great Awakening was Nettleton. During his postgraduate theological studies at Yale, he was asked to take a temporary preaching assignment in eastern Connecticut. Nettleton adopted methods reminiscent of the strongly intellectual approach practiced by Jonathan Edwards and immediately achieved phenomenal success. In his meetings he always avoided emotionalism of any kind, and the atmosphere he cultivated was quiet, dignified, and solemn. Conservative in practice, he involved local pastors in his evangelistic work and emphasized the need to teach and nurture any who were converted. He found himself in great demand throughout New England and New York, and saw as many as thirty thousand conversions. A bachelor, Nettleton lived simply, accumulated no property, and charged no fees.

From 1811 to 1822, Nettleton shared the leadership of evangelism with Beecher, and in the latter year his health failed. In a few years Finney began his meteoric career, and Nettleton's place in the front rank of evangelists was taken by this man who differed from him in almost every respect. Till the end of his life Nettleton was outspoken in criticizing Finney for his innovations. He thought Finney's informal approach was not as dignified and reverential as it should be. Nor did he like Finney's method of pressing for immediate decisions. Nonetheless, Finney's modern form of mass evangelism was the wave of the future, and it succeeded in achieving many conversions and prolonging the Second Great Awakening well into the 1830s.

The Methodist Revival

As revitalization came to the Congregationalists and Presbyterians after 1800, the Methodists were coming to prominence. After John Wesley's conversion in 1738 Methodism became an Anglican renewal movement. Across England, small groups of dedicated laypeople formed for Bible study and prayer and to encourage vital religion. Inevitably the attention of Methodists shifted to the New World. As early as 1760, Robert Strawbridge, a lay preacher from Northern Ireland, settled at Sam's Creek, Maryland, and began an itinerant ministry that took him into Pennsylvania, Delaware, and Virginia. At about the same time, a party of German refugees who had been in Ireland for some years came to New York. Among them were Barbara Heck and Philip Embury. Embury was a Methodist class leader, a preacher and schoolmaster. By 1766, Heck persuaded Embury to hold services for their small group. Jesse Lee, the first historian of Methodism, gives an account of what happened:

> They then rented an empty room in their neighborhood adjoining the barracks, in which they held their meetings for a season. . . . Some time after that, Captain Thomas Webb, barrack-master at Albany, found them out, and preached among them in his regimentals. The novelty of a man preaching in a scarlet coat soon brought great numbers to hear, more than the room could contain. Some more of the inhabitants joined the society, they then united and hired a rigging loft to meet in, that could contain a large congregation.[38]

Francis Asbury built the Methodist church
in America into the first truly national
church in the United States.
(Courtesy of the Billy Graham Center Museum)

Captain Webb rendered invaluable help to the infant congregation. He had heard John Wesley preach in Bristol in 1764 and joined the Methodists. Almost immediately he was licensed to preach. "A man of fire," Wesley characterized him, "the power of God constantly accompanies his word." In 1774 John Adams, later president of the United States, described him as "one of the most eloquent men I ever heard."[39] Largely through Webb's efforts, Methodism spread through Long Island, New Jersey, Pennsylvania, and Delaware. Chapels were built and preachers were recruited from England.[40]

Each year at the annual Methodist conference in England, the matter of sending preachers to America—the new circuit and by far the largest—was presented. In 1771 the conference met in Bristol with more than one hundred preachers present. At one point Wesley arose and solemnly stated, "Our brethren in America call aloud for help. Who are willing to go over and help them?" To this appeal five responded, out of which two were appointed, Francis Asbury (1745–1816) and Richard Wright. Although several people had already contributed much to American Methodism—especially Webb—Asbury was to contribute far more to its spread and success than would any other person.

119

Asbury—Missionary to America

Francis Asbury was twenty-six years old in 1771. He had been converted at age fourteen. He was slender, with piercing blue eyes, a clear
and resonant voice, commanding presence, lofty forehead, and flowing
hair. Asbury was already a seasoned local preacher on the Bedfordshire,
Colchester, and Wiltshire circuits when he arrived in New York. He found
the situation disappointing. Church discipline was lax, some members
had a casual attitude, and the leader, Richard Boardman, insisted that
Asbury remain in that city rather than travel afield to set up new
Methodist societies along circuits.

Asbury was obsessed with the vision of an evangelized America. To
remain in one spot, he thought, betrayed the genius of Methodism. Later
events proved Asbury correct. The circuit system designed by John Wesley for England kept the preachers constantly circulating. This itineracy
system was even more practical for America than it had been for England. American congregations were separated by large distances and a
system of settled pastorates would be impossible for some years.

As tensions between American colonies and England threatened to
explode, friction continued between Asbury and other leaders. In 1775
Wesley ordered all lay preachers to return to England. All did—except
Asbury. Many thought the preachers' departure would be a disaster for
the movement, but it actually proved fortunate. Shifting the burden to
native leaders forced them to develop.[41] It was particularly fortunate for
Asbury. He was looked upon as a hero, particularly in the North, for
refusing to return to England. Largely due to his work, the membership
roughly doubled during the war years.[42]

By 1784, four-fifths of the Methodists in America (15,000) lived south
of what would one day become the Mason-Dixon Line.[43] Many factors
were pressuring American Methodism to separate from the Anglican
Church. Preferring to view Methodism as a renewal movement within
the Anglican Church, Wesley had always resisted the impulse to create
a new denomination with an independent hierarchy. In December 1784
the "Christmas Conference" convened at Baltimore. The sixty preachers
present unanimously elected Thomas Coke (1747–1814) and Asbury to
be "joint superintendents." In 1787 Coke and Asbury agreed that the title
of *bishop* was more suitable to the American situation. John Wesley was
outraged, but in this, as in other matters, his wishes did not prevail.

Like a Mighty Army

After the Revolution, the opening frontier was a major influence on the
virile spirit of the new nation. Tens of thousands moved into the open-

Harper's Weekly *(12 October 1867) caught the spirit of the circuit rider's life of determination and courage. (Courtesy of the Billy Graham Center Museum)*

ing lands. This proved an awesome challenge to the churches, but one that Asbury and his dedicated circuit riders accepted. Frontier life was harsh and dangerous. There were few social contacts and no luxuries. A visitor was an event of importance, for he brought news of the outside world. The arrival of a clergyman was an epochal event that would draw settlers from miles around. He performed marriages, baptized children, served communion, and told people that God had not deserted them.

The first reason for the rapid growth of Methodism was the circuit system. Under Asbury the system became the answer to the demands of the advancing frontier. After the war he began to consolidate his forces for the great campaign he had anticipated for years. Asbury deployed circuit riders as a military leader moves troops. Selecting a definite objective for a new circuit, perhaps an area one hundred miles or more wide, riders would make the initial contacts. After the area had been awakened by their exhortations, Asbury moved these men on and brought in others with administrative abilities to organize churches and establish regular preaching circuits. Under his command was a highly mobile cadre who covered a large territory. His small army often had little education, but education was of little use on the frontier. A powerful voice, hearty constitution, dedication, and concern were the essential qualities of the circuit riders. Their courage and disregard for danger became proverbial.

The second reason for the rapid spread of Methodism was its theology. The Christian message was simplified: God loves all people and provided Jesus Christ as the Savior. Humans are sinful, yet have the power to accept or reject this divine offer. When they accept, they must, with the aid of the Holy Spirit, seek the Methodist goal of "perfection" or freedom from deliberate sin. Their legalistic approach to moral issues included prohibitions against the use of alcohol and slaveholding. These demands gave Methodism a moral earnestness and zeal. While many writers have described this as a "democratic gospel" and "frontier faith," it was simply the way Wesleyanism stressed God's sovereignty and human depravity.[44]

The third major factor in the spread of Methodism was the camp meeting, which Asbury promoted. More than twenty thousand people could be reached at once. They were a welcome break from the bleakness of frontier life. In addition, camp meetings required few preparations. The preachers simply sent out notices of where and when one would be held. Asbury wrote of them, "I pray to God that there may be a score of camp-meetings a week, and wonderful seasons of the Lord in all directions. . . . I rejoice to think there will be perhaps four or five hundred camp meetings this year."[45]

"Fainting under My Burden"

Asbury imposed stern demands upon his preachers and greater demands upon himself. His constant travels on horseback over trackless wilderness are staggering to contemplate, especially in view of his chronic illnesses. He encountered hostile Indians and dangerous animals. Roads were primitive or nonexistent, and he and his horse had to cross rivers as best they could. Beginning in 1798, he made a complete circuit of as much territory as he could cover, calling conferences of his itinerants, teaching, and overseeing the work. These journeys reached from Maine to Georgia, and west as far as the frontier had advanced. He summarized his responsibilities in his journal entry for October 26, 1799: "I tremble and faint under my burden; having to ride about six thousand miles annually; to preach from three to five hundred sermons a year; to write and read so many letters, and read many more: all this and more, besides the stationing of three hundred preachers; reading many hundred pages; and spending many hours in conversation by day and by night, with people and preachers of various characters, among whom are many distressing cases."[46]

Constant privations, hardship, and illness plagued Asbury. Frequently he went without food except for wild vegetables he picked along the trail and boiled over an open fire. Sometimes he stopped at crude inns where the ribald occupants with their violence, swearing, gambling, thievery, and disregard for religion oppressed him more than the miseries of the road. His annual salary for the greater part of his life was under twenty British pounds. Because of year-round travel in all types of weather, rheumatism crippled his arms and legs, consumption ravaged his chest, ulcers burned his stomach and throat, his feet were usually swollen, and he itched terribly from skin diseases and insects. He never married and never owned a home. He carried all his belongings—always pathetically few—in his saddlebags, along with the Bibles and books he gave out.

Asbury gladly endured the hardships in view of the spectacular results. In 1780 there were 42 preachers and 8,504 members. In 1790 there were 227 preachers, and 45,949 white and 11,862 black members. By 1803 there were 383 preachers, and 104,070 white and 22,453 black members. By 1820, after Asbury's death, there were 904 preachers and 256,881 members.[47] Revivals came frequently, especially in the South.

Altogether Bishop Asbury preached an estimated 16,500 sermons, spoke informally many times more, ordained more than four thousand preachers, traveled on horseback 275,000 miles, and wore out six faithful horses. He was the best-known man in America. When he arrived in a seat of government, mayors and governors immediately invited him to dine. He was regarded with awe and veneration.[48] Sydney Ahlstrom has written:

With Francis Asbury positively at its head, American Methodism would begin its great forward surge [in 1784]. . . . Throughout the next century it would be the chief engine of evangelical Arminianism in this country. Expanding almost exclusively by domestic evangelism, it would exceed in its rate of growth all other large Protestant churches. By direct impact and negative reaction it would work large effects on nearly every other denomination, until by degrees it imparted its energy and spirit to American Protestantism as a whole.[49]

*T*he Second Great
Awakening in the West

The awakening that fell upon Virginia from 1787 through 1789 wore off in the turbulent 1790s. During that decade thousands poured westward in search of cheap land and a new life. Kentucky was opened after the French and Indian War, with the first permanent settlement established at Harrodsburg in 1774. In 1775 Daniel Boone, as agent for the Transylvania Company, blazed the Wilderness Road and founded Boonesboro. Meanwhile, fur traders and "long hunters" from Virginia and the Carolinas penetrated Tennessee, establishing the first settlement in the Watauga River Valley in 1769. Jonesboro, today the oldest town in Tennessee, was founded in 1779. Settlers floated into Ohio on flatboats and barges and bounced overland by wagon. The first truly American city of the Northwest Territory, Marietta, was founded in 1788 in what later became Ohio. By 1800, the census recorded 220,955 people in Kentucky; 105,602 in Tennessee; and 51,006 in the Northwest. Tens

The preaching of a small number of ministers,
among them Barton W. Stone, ignited the camp-meeting
"Pentecost" in the western wilderness.
(Courtesy of the Billy Graham Center Museum)

of thousands more lived in western Virginia, North Carolina, and other parts of the expanding frontier territory. Then came the crowning achievement of Thomas Jefferson's presidency—the Louisiana Purchase in 1803—which doubled the area of the United States. This added even more impetus for western migration.

These auspicious years for national expansion, however, darkened the horizon for church leaders. How could the resources of religion possibly keep abreast of the vast movement of farmers, land speculators, hunters, lawyers, miners, merchants, millers, blacksmiths, artisans, rogues and saints—"all rubbing elbows on the trails that led to the Mecca beyond the mountains."[1] The churches of the seaboard states were greatly weakened as members followed the siren song. The circular letter of the Charleston Baptist Association in 1799 pointed to one of the causes of the decline in churches being "that prevailing spirit of moving from place to place, just as fancy, whim, or supposed interest may dictate, without a due regard to the call of providence, or the interests of religion; by which churches are often greatly weakened, or, as it were, wantonly, and sacrilegiously, broken up."[2]

The Harsh Frontier

Not only was this profound social disruption causing unrest in the East, but also the lawlessness of the opening lands was a concern to Christians. Hopes that faith would take quick hold in the new settlements, as the Southern revivals of the 1780s promised, were soon dashed. The tours of Bishop Francis Asbury in behalf of Methodist expansion convinced him of the great danger of the unchurched wilderness to the souls of these people. "When I reflect," he wrote in his journal, "that not one in a hundred came here to get religion, but rather to get plenty of good land, I think it will be well if some or many do not eventually lose their souls."[3] In every Southern state, leaders of the denominations voiced their concerns.

In addition to deistic propaganda, postwar materialism, and westward migration—all of which impeded the growth of Christian faith in the South and West—the denominations themselves did not always help the situation. Intradenominational squabbling and rivalries were frequent, although eventually the various groups cooperated to some extent in the common task. Little wonder that one commentator in 1794 pointed to Kentucky "with concern . . . that religion appears to be at a very low ebb with every denomination in this state."[4] The same was true in Tennessee, where one respected citizen said that, "especially among the upper classes, deism and irreligion ruled beyond all bounds."[5]

Christians in the East confronted an appalling problem. The evils that prevailed throughout the country took on worse forms along the frontier. Lawlessness seemed to be the order of the day. Christianity was mocked and disregarded, Deism and infidelity were rife, and morals low. The early settlers of Kentucky named some of their towns after eminent French infidels: Altamont, Bourbon, La Rue, Rousseau, and others. In 1793 the Kentucky legislature voted to dispense with the services of a chaplain, considering them no longer necessary. In many towns of considerable size, no place of worship could be found, and religious services had never been held. Therefore, several hundred thousand people were beyond the reaches of the gospel and were "hair-hung and breeze-shaken over the pit of hell."

What was the purpose of the Almighty in all of this? In 1797 Silas Mercer surveyed the lamentable situation in Georgia, comparable to the rest of the South and West, and in one of the more profound interpretations of the time endeavored to trace the finger of God:

126

But why are these things so? To which we answer. The great Governor of the Universe does not always work by miracles, neither offers violence to the human will. It cannot be thought, but that he could have made his people perfect in soul, body, and spirit, at the same time when he converted their souls. But it appears to us, that Jehovah, in his wise providence, saw proper to continue them in connection with an old corrupt nature, in order to properly discipline them, that by the various combats between flesh and spirit, they may be weaned from sensual delight, and learn to trust their all in him. But again: in a lively time of religion, hypocrites and formalists are apt to creep into the Church, therefore, a time of trial is necessary to purge these, as dross from the pure gold or real Christians. And further: the Lord intends, it may be, by this way to prove that salvation is by grace alone; for in a time of declension no man or set of men, no, not all the people in the world, can make a stir of religion. So this proves that religion is of the Lord.[6]

God undoubtedly has his seasons—the East had seen both lean years and fat in spiritual harvests. But the vast areas of the West had not known any season of faith at all. The pressing question was, would the West *ever* be evangelized? Wild and dangerous, could it also be impervious to the gospel?

A City Set upon a Hill

Increasingly, another dimension of thinking entered the picture as the enormity of the West became apparent: *the divine mission of America as a light to the other nations of the world.* In one sense there was nothing new about this conviction, for the Puritans of New England were confident that in setting up a theocracy in the New World God had fulfilled his long-concealed purpose. Edward Johnson declared in 1650, "When England began to decline in religion," Christ raised "an army out of our English nation, for freeing his people out of their long servitude under usurping prelacy," and created "a New England to muster up the first of his forces in." The New World, Johnson continued, "is the place where the Lord will create a new heaven, and a new earth in, new churches, and a new commonwealth together."[7] The role of God's people in America, John Winthrop instructed, was to be "a city set on a hill" to exemplify before "the eyes of the world" God's new purpose and the power of his gospel.

But at the dawn of the nineteenth century came new meaning and urgency to the conviction that America was to be God's light to the world. In Puritan days, the concept of missions was still embryonic, and missionaries were sent only occasionally. By 1800, however, a new dynamic had arrived, and ambassadors of the cross were going to distant lands.

This was undoubtedly an extension of God's original purpose in colonizing the New World, that as it matured America might send missionaries back to Europe and throughout the world to spread the good news of Christ. Therefore, as Charles Hodge (1797–1878) proclaimed later, the character of America was of "unutterable importance to the world." If God intended to use America as a major base for the evangelization of all people, had "a generation ever lived on whose fidelity so much depended?"[8] The corollary of this was the imperative that the West be won for Christ. If it was not evangelized, Hodge argued, it would threaten to paganize the rest of the country.

McGready—Fire on the Frontier

Such earnestness, such zeal, such powerful persuasion, enforced by the joys of heaven and miseries of hell, I had never witnessed before. My mind was chained by him, and followed him closely in his rounds of heaven, earth, and hell with feeling indescribable. His concluding remarks were addressed to the sinner to flee the wrath to come without delay. Never before had I comparatively felt the force of truth. Such was my excitement that, had I been standing, I should have probably sunk to the floor under the impression.[9]

Thus young Barton W. Stone (1772–1844) recalled his first exposure to a central figure of the Awakening in the West, James McGready. Scotch-Irish McGready (1762?–1817) was a fiery Presbyterian preacher whose evangelical theology was ignited at John McMillan's academy in Western Pennsylvania. He observed the interdenominational revival of 1788 in Virginia and was influenced by the dignified evangelistic preaching of John Blair Smith, president of Hampden-Sydney College. The awakening at this Virginia college convinced McGready that revivals could be conducted without emotionalism and with lasting results, since in this instance more than thirty men had gone into the ministry.

Rogues' Harbor

Frontier people lived, worked, and died hard. They were impatient with the fine theological points that interested Eastern congregations. So McGready discarded Smith's model of dignified evangelism. Although he began his sermons in a calm and orderly way, as he went on he warmed to the topic and, with his thunderous voice, achieved an intensity that thrilled his backwoods congregations. In 1796 McGready became pastor of three small churches at Muddy River, Red River, and Gasper River in Logan County, Kentucky. This was in the southwestern part of the state and, as Peter Cartwright (1785–1872) described it, "was called Rogues' Harbor. Here many refugees from almost all parts of the Union fled to escape justice or punishment. . . . Murderers, horse-thieves, highway robbers and counterfeiters fled here, until they combined and actually formed a majority."[10]

McGready preached in this dangerous area with telling effect. He went directly to the heart of the spiritual problem. He described heaven so magnificently that his rustic hearers would "almost see its glories and long to be there." When he came to speak of hell, he preached no subtleties; he would "so array hell and its horrors before the wicked, that they would tremble and quake, imagining a lake of fire and brimstone yawning to overwhelm them, and the wrath of God thrusting them down the horrible abyss."[11] The response was not long delayed, and by the summer of 1798 many were "struck with an awful sense of their lost estate." But not until June 1800 did the first extraordinary manifestation of divine power occur.

On that occasion, four or five hundred members of McGready's three congregations gathered for a communion service at Red River. For many this was the third year that they had prayed for a display of God's power. Three Presbyterian ministers (McGready, William Hodge, and John Rankin) were joined by two brothers, the Presbyterian William McGee and the Methodist John McGee. The first three days of the meetings were solemn and reverent. On the final day, John McGee exhorted the people that "there was a greater than I preaching," and that they should "submit to him." At this insistence that God was at work, the congregation joyously and frantically began to shout and cry.

What was happening amazed the preachers; though they were New Side, pro-revival Presbyterians, they agreed it was beyond anything they had experienced. When one woman "shouted" for mercy, John McGee moved toward her. He then recounts what ensued.

> Several spoke to me: "You know these people. Presbyterians are much for order. They will not bear this confusion. Go back and be quiet." I turned to go back and was near falling; the power of God was strong upon me. I turned again, and losing sight of the fear of man, I went through the house shouting, and exhorting with all possible ecstasy and energy, and the floor was soon covered with the slain; their screams for mercy pierced the heavens.[12]

Although McGready was a forceful preacher who was accustomed to emotional response, he was astounded. Eventually, as Rankin wrote, "On seeing and feeling [John McGee's] confidence, that it was the work of God, and a mighty effusion of his Spirit, and having heard that he was acquainted with such scenes in another country, we acquiesced and stood in astonishment, admiring the wonderful works of God."[13]

Above and right: *These renderings of camp meetings from different areas of America show that they differed little with respect to the forest setting, preaching stand, or intensity of the participants. (Courtesy of the Billy Graham Center Museum)*

The Camp Meeting

Convinced that the Lord was moving, McGready and the other ministers planned another sacramental service for late July 1800 at Gasper River. Unprecedented crowds assembled at the appointed time, many from distances as great as one hundred miles. This was the first true camp meeting—where continuous outdoor services were combined with camping out—although the term *camp meeting* was first used in late 1802,[14] and large outdoor services have had a long history. Tents were set up everywhere, wagons with provisions brought in, and the underbrush near the church cleared. The preaching went well, with anticipation and hopes building that God would perform a mighty work.

The continuous preaching evoked much response, and the clergy were kept active counseling the convicted penitents. On Sunday—after three long, tense days—the pent-up emotions of the huge throng were ready to burst. That evening, with the rude pulpit lighted by flaming torches, William McGee preached a powerful message on the doubting Peter sinking beneath the waves. McGready recalled that

130

Above: Harper's Weekly *(10 September 1859) shows a typical camp meeting of the mid-nineteenth century with large and substantial tents capable of housing entire families. (From the author's collection).*
Below: *Camp meetings became extremely popular from Maine to Georgia, and by the 1840s they were attended by calmer preaching and a more refined clientele. (Courtesy of the Billy Graham Center Museum)*

the power of God seemed to shake the whole assembly. Towards the close of the sermon, the cries of the distressed arose almost as loud as his voice. After the congregation was dismissed the solemnity increased, till the greater part of the multitude seemed engaged in the most solemn manner. No person seemed to wish to go home—hunger and sleep seemed to affect nobody—eternal things were the vast concern. Here awakening and converting work was to be found in every part of the multitude; and even some things strangely and wonderfully new to me.[15]

Later it would become apparent that the Gasper River camp meeting was the turning point in the Awakening in the West. In the next months, similar revivals broke out and spread into Tennessee. But the full force was yet to be felt.

Barton W. Stone, a Presbyterian minister in Bourbon County, Kentucky, had been influenced by McGready some years before. Stone was pastor of the Cane Ridge and Concord churches, northeast of Lexington, and this area was still sunk in spiritual lethargy. Having heard of the work of grace in Logan County, in the spring of 1801 Stone traveled across the state to view for himself what God was doing. He reported that in the camp meetings "the scene was new to me and passing strange. It baffled description." Convinced that this was indeed a good work, Stone returned home to plan a similar protracted meeting at Cane Ridge in August 1801.

Cane Ridge

The Cane Ridge camp meeting was memorable because, being better publicized than its predecessors, amazing numbers responded and spread its fame throughout the country. The crowd was estimated to be between ten and twenty-five thousand. People came from as far away as Ohio and Tennessee. Ten thousand was an immense number, since Lexington, the largest town in Kentucky, had less than eighteen hundred inhabitants.

Stone, dumfounded at the numbers pouring in, reported that "the roads were crowded with wagons, carriages, horses, and footmen moving to the solemn camp." Arrangements had been carefully made so that the crowds could be dispersed into several congregations of somewhat manageable size, but were strained to the breaking-point by the unanticipated throngs. Invitations had been sent by the Presbyterians to Baptist and Methodist preachers from distant points, and Stone rejoiced that "all appeared cordially united in it. They were of one mind and soul: the salvation of sinners was the one object. We all engaged in singing the same songs, all united in prayer, all preached the same things."[16]

132

Numerous descriptions of the Cane Ridge meetings remain. One of the best is from John Finley to his uncle, dated September 20, 1801:

> I attended [Cane Ridge] with eighteen Presbyterian ministers, and Baptists and Methodists, I do not know how many, all either preaching or exhorting the distressed with more harmony than could be expected. The Governor of our state was with us and encouraging the work.
>
> The number of the people computed from 10 to 21,000 and the communicants 828. The whole people serious, all the conversation was of a religious nature, or calling in question the divinity of the work. Great numbers were on the ground from Friday until the Thursday following, night and day without intermission engaged in some religious act of worship. They are commonly collected in small circles of ten or twelve, close adjoining another circle, and all engaged in singing Watts' and Harts' hymns; and then a minister steps upon a stump or log and begins an exhortation or sermon, when as many as can hear, collect around him. On Sabbath night, I saw above one hundred candles burning at once— and I saw I suppose one hundred persons at once on the ground crying for mercy of all ages from eight to sixty years. When a person is struck down he is carried by others out of the congregation, when some minister converses with and prays for him; afterwards a few gather around and sing a hymn suitable to his case. . . . The sensible, the weak, learned and unlearned, the rich and the poor are the subjects of it. At Cynthiana, Paris, Flat Creek, Point Pleasant, Walnut Hill and Georgetown, great congregations are in all these places, and exercised in the manner as above described.
>
> . . . I see several things I do disapprove; but can say, if only the tenth person convicted is truly converted, 'tis a great work. In Cumberland the work is also great; they often meet in congregations of twenty-five thousand, and spend sometimes two weeks together.[17]

Revival Excesses

Cane Ridge also became identified with the same excesses that had earlier been condemned by Congregationalists and Presbyterians when James Davenport and others brought discredit on the Great Awakening of New England in the 1740s. "Enthusiasm" was viewed with great distaste and suspicion by most pro-revival evangelists. The years following Davenport had brought awakenings admirable for the absence of excesses, with some minor exceptions in the rural South. Beginning with the Kentucky revivals of 1800 and 1801, however, two factors combined to break down the resistance to uncontrolled emotionalism: first was the bleak roughness of pioneer life, with its absence of restraint and sparsity of social contact; second was the fact that the traditional prolonged process of conviction of sin, despair, faith, and assurance of salvation was compressed into a few days at the camp meeting. Pent-up emotion produced dramatic effects when finally released. Recognizing these elements, McGready and the others accepted the inevitable.

At first, shouting, crying, and falling down were the only physical reactions to rousing preaching. But with the release of tidal waves of feeling from these early camp meetings, however, convulsive physical "exercises" became somewhat common. Hysterical laughter, occasional trances, the "barking" exercise, and the "jerks" were frequent in Kentucky but did not produce the disastrous results they would have engendered in more settled communities. John Boles states, "These grossly exaggerated revival exercises, which have been cited widely to discredit the revival, were probably restricted to a comparative few. Only among some of the splinter groups that developed in Kentucky did they become ultimately respectable. . . . Except at the very start, they were never a significant factor in the camp meetings."[18] Professor Bernard Weisberger agrees: "Many stories of unusual transports of holy joy and anguish were undoubtedly stretched. Some came from supporters. . . . Others were planted by opponents, who were trying to underscore the element of caricature in the meetings."[19]

Frontier evangelist Peter Cartwright became something of an authority on the excesses in the Western Revival. He declared that "the old starched Presbyterian preachers" and "the Methodist preachers generally preached against this extravagant wildness."[20] But there was no denying that some illiterate preachers and ranters, with their ignorant blusterings, brought discredit on the awakening by allowing or encouraging excesses. The jerks were the most notorious of these physical manifestations, and Cartwright witnessed them occasionally.

No matter whether they were saints or sinners, they would be taken under a warm song or sermon, and seized with a convulsive jerking all over, which they could not by any possibility avoid, and the more they resisted the more they jerked. If they would not strive against it and pray in good earnest, the jerking would usually abate. . . . To see these proud young gentlemen and young ladies, dressed in their silks, jewellery, and prunella, from top to toe, take the jerks, would often excite my laughter. The first jerk or so, you would see their fine bonnets, caps, and combs fly; and so sudden would be the jerking of the head that their long loose hair would crack almost as loud as a waggoner's whip. . . .

I will relate a very serious circumstance . . . at a camp meeting. . . . The jerks were very prevalent. There was a company of drunken rowdies who came to interrupt the meeting. These rowdies were headed by a very large drinking man. They came with their bottles of whisky in their pockets. This large man cursed the jerks, and all religion. Shortly afterward he took the jerks, and he started to run, but he jerked so powerfully he could not get away. He halted among some saplings, and although he was violently agitated, he took out his bottle of whisky, and swore he would drink the d——d jerks to death; but he jerked at such a rate he could not get the bottle to this mouth, though he tried hard. At length he fetched a sudden jerk, and the bottle struck a sapling and was broken to pieces, and spilled the whisky on the ground. There was a great crowd gathered around him, and when he lost his whisky he became very much enraged, and cursed and swore very profanely, his jerks still increasing. At length he fetched a very violent jerk, snapped his neck, fell, and soon expired, with his mouth full of cursing and bitterness.[21]

The awakening spirit, with many conversions, spread over the entire South and West with amazing speed. Portions of the Ohio Territory, western Pennsylvania, Maryland, Tennessee, Georgia, and the Carolinas received showers of divine grace within a short time—although seldom with the vast congregations of Cane Ridge and Gasper River. The moral tone of the frontier improved. The sins McGready, Stone, the McGees, and others scourged—drunkenness, profanity, gambling, horse racing, cockfighting, dueling, fornication, and adultery—dramatically declined. In the East, church people rejoiced, particularly upon hearing reports from such eminent eyewitnesses as George A. Baxter, president of Washington College, Virginia, who toured Kentucky in 1801. He relates:

> On my way I was informed by settlers on the road that the character of Kentucky travelers was entirely changed, and that they are as remarkable for sobriety as they had formerly been for dissoluteness and immorality. And indeed I found Kentucky . . . the most moral place I have ever seen. A profane expression was hardly ever heard. A religious awe seemed to pervade the country. Upon the whole, I think the revival in Kentucky the most extraordinary that has ever visited the church of Christ; and all things considered, it was peculiarly adapted to the circumstances of the country into which it came. Infidelity was triumphant and religion was on the point of expiring. Something extraordinary seemed necessary to arrest the attention of a giddy people who were ready to conclude that Christianity was a fable and futurity a delusion. This revival has done it. It has confounded infidelity, awed vice into silence, and brought numbers beyond calculation under serious impressions.[22]

Cartwright—Frontier Evangelist

One of the most eminent of the frontier evangelists, following the first years of the Awakening in the West, was Peter Cartwright. Because Cartwright was already a frontiersman, he did not have to adapt methods derived from more cultured areas as his predecessors had done. He understood the people as no outsider could, exhibiting a rough and rugged style of evangelism.

*Peter Cartwright used his first-hand knowledge
of the early American frontier to become one of the most
successful Methodist evangelists and church planters.*

Peter Cartwright was born September 1, 1785, in Virginia. His relatively poor parents joined the migrants moving west in a few years, settling in Kentucky, a few miles from the Tennessee border. This was Logan County, the infamous Rogues' Harbor. To control the multitude of desperadoes out of the reach of law, a vigilante group formed, called the "Regulators." One of the most exciting episodes of Cartwright's boyhood was on a court day at Russellville, Kentucky, when the two groups met head-on. "A general battle ensued between the rogues and Regulators, and they fought with guns, pistols, dirks, knives, and clubs. Some were actually killed, many wounded, the rogues proved victors, kept the ground, and drove the Regulators out of town."[23] Such was frontier life.

Young Peter assisted his father in the farm, which was surrounded by wilderness. People were seldom seen except on occasional journeys to

136

towns. The few towns that existed were sparsely settled. In 1800 Nashville, Tennessee, boasted only 350 citizens, and most of the towns were much smaller than that. "When my father settled in Logan County," Cartwright recalled, "there was not a newspaper printed south of Green River, no mill short of forty miles, and no schools worth the name."[24] Sunday was for hunting, fishing, horse racing, dances, and anything else. Meat for the family table was killed in the woods, and much of the remainder of their diet came from their native state, as well. The farm raised cotton and flax, and from these Peter's mother and sisters made all the family's clothing.

On the whole, frontiersmen were a hardworking group. They were rough and ready in speech, impatient with hypocrisy and ceremony, and accustomed to harsh conditions. Their entire lives were simple and direct. No churches existed. And though this was not true of the Cartwrights, Peter knew of men forty-five years of age who had never seen a wagon.

The men spent at least part of their time trapping and hunting; some did little else. Hunters might be seen with their long rifles over their shoulders, perhaps some small game hung from their belts, and a pack of bear-dogs yelping after them. After a day of hunting or work on the farm, the evenings were spent in story-telling interspersed with gulps of hard liquor.

Among the literate, Tom Paine's Deism had a great impact. But most did not read books; for them unbelief was not a reasoned system. A large number of the Kentucky and Tennessee migrants had come from Virginia, where churches had some strength, and many coming to Ohio hailed from Pennsylvania and New England, where the Christian faith was widely followed. Most frontiersmen were not opposed to Christianity, but simply lived in a moral and spiritual vacuum since moving to the frontier. Many pioneers knew something of Christian teachings, however inadequate. But on the frontier, spiritual life was not cultivated, Bibles and other literature were few, and worship services were fewer.[25] Not till 1783 did the first itinerant preacher enter Kentucky. Later, when they came in greater numbers, the supply was still inadequate for the great distances and meager congregations.

Peter's mother was one of those who longed for the ministry of the church of Christ, and any missionary who came by was invited to hold services in their cabin. To her great joy, a Methodist congregation was organized about four miles from the Cartwright farm, and young Peter and his mother attended regularly. Yet Peter recounts that he was "a wild, wicked boy, and delighted in horse-racing, card-playing, and dancing. My father restrained me but little, though my mother often talked to me, wept over me, and prayed for me."[26] His father presented Peter with a race-horse, which was a great delight for several years. When he was six-teen, Peter became convicted of sin. "It seemed to me, all of a sudden, my blood rushed to my head, my heart palpitated, in a few minutes I turned blind; an awful impression rested on my mind that death had come, and I was unprepared to die."[27] After several days of agonizing over his lost condition, during which his friends came "to try to divert my mind from those gloomy thoughts of my wretchedness," he heard a voice from heaven saying, "Peter, look at me." He took this as encour-agement from the Lord to hope for his mercy.

It was widely taught, from Puritan days onwards, that although con-version could be almost instantaneous—as with the apostle Paul—the period of preparation should last awhile. Even for young people, who might have less sin to repent of than adults, conversion was not a thing to be taken lightly. Once sins were recognized and repented of for the guilt and misery they brought, renouncing them included the determi-nation to commit them no more. Following this pattern, Cartwright underwent a three months' search for the pardon of his sin. After this time, notices of a camp meeting to be held in the vicinity were circu-lated, and Peter went, feeling like "a guilty, wretched sinner." There, with many other "mourners," he found release. "Divine light flashed all round me, unspeakable joy sprung up in my soul. My mother raised the shout, my Christian friends crowded around me, and joined me in prais-ing God."[28] Peter Cartwright was a redeemed soul.

Thereafter, although he was only sixteen, Cartwright seemed destined for the ministry. Sooner than he expected, he was given a license "to exercise his gifts as an exhorter in the Methodist Episcopal Church." According to the common practice, exhorting could be done by anyone, not necessarily an ordained person. Often these exhorters showed more zeal than knowledge. Cartwright had almost no formal education. He had attended two small schools intermittently, but left each after a short time. He felt his lack, and following the pattern set by Francis Asbury for traveling preachers, Cartwright attempted to supplement his meager schooling by continual reading throughout his life. His library was typ-ical of all the circuit riders: a pocket Bible, a hymnbook, and the *Book of Discipline*. These were carried in the saddlebags, along with Bibles and books they sold or gave away as they traveled.

One New Suit a Year

Cartwright was so successful as an exhorter that in October 1803 he was urged to become a preacher, the next rank higher, and placed on a wide circuit. It was a hard life, full of danger, but for a young man of eigh-teen it was a great challenge to serve the living God in this way. It meant constant travel through barely-cut trails and across unbridged rivers, in the heat and storms of summer and the cold and snow of winter. Preachers often did not know where their next meal might come from. Nearing the end of his long life, Cartwright remembered, "We walked on dirt floors for carpets . . . had forked sticks and pocket or butcher knives for knives and forks; slept on bear, deer, or buffalo skins before the fire, or sometimes on the ground in open air . . . and one new suit of clothes of homespun was ample clothing for one year. . . ."[29]

Although circuit riders were supposed to receive eighty dollars a year, Cartwright declared, "I think I received about forty dollars this year; but many of our preachers did not receive half that amount. These were hard times in those Western wilds; many, very many pious and useful preachers were literally starved into a location. I do not mean that they were starved for food; for, although it was rough, yet the preachers generally got enough to eat. . . . Money was very scarce in the country at this early day."[30] In spite of this trifling salary, Cartwright thought it his duty to marry. So on August 18, 1808, he was wed to Frances Gaines. Nine children were born to that marriage, and all but one lived to maturity.

"Behold the Lamb of God!"

As he became a seasoned circuit rider and preacher, Cartwright became one of the most famous evangelists and planters of new churches that the West knew. He found himself constantly in difficult situations. Conducting worship several times each day, the substance of his message was "a text that never wore out nor grew stale: 'Behold the Lamb of God, that taketh away the sin of the world.' " Contemporaries recorded that he had a booming voice that made women weep and strong men quail. His evangelistic method was the same as other successful preachers of the West: Portray in the most vivid terms the terrors of hell; and then proclaim the gospel of God's love, grace, and forgiveness, and the beauties of the Lord Jesus Christ in his resurrected power and glory. Congregations demanded exactly this, and if the preacher was weak or derelict, woe betide him! Usually, under powerful preaching those in the congregation who were converted "got happy and shouted aloud for joy" and prayed for those who were still outside the kingdom.

One reason Cartwright became so well known was his dexterity in handling difficult situations. Disturbances caused by rowdies sometimes called for bare fists. In 1814 a gang threatened one camp meeting in Tennessee:

> The ringleaders of the rowdies went by the names of J.P. and William P., two brothers. . . . I found it would be hard to keep order, and I went to J.P., and told him I wanted him to help me keep order. Said I, "These rowdies

139

are all afraid of you; and if you will help me, you shall be captain, and choose your own men." He said he did not want to engage in that way; but if I would not bind him up too close, but let him have a little fun, away off, he would then promise me that we should have good order in the encampment through the meeting. I said "Very well. . . ."

There came into the congregation a young, awkward fellow, that would trespass on our rules by seating himself all the time among the ladies. It was very fashionable at that time for the gentlemen to roach their hair; and this young man had a mighty bushy roached head of hair. I took him out several times from among the women, but he would soon be back again.

I told J.P. I wished he would attend to this young man. "Very well," said he, and immediately sent off and got a pair of scissors, and planted his company about a half-mile off; then sent for this young fellow under the pretense of giving him something to drink. When they got him out there, two of them, one on each side, stepped up to him with drawn dirks, and told him they did not mean to hurt him if he would be quiet; but if he resisted or hallooed, he was a dead man. They said they only wanted to roach his hair, and put him in the newest Nashville fashion. The fellow was scared almost to death, but made no resistance whatever. Then one with the scissors commenced cutting his hair, and it was haggled all over at a masterly rate. When they were done shearing him, they let him go; and he came straight to the camp ground. Just as he entered it, I met him; he was pale as a cloth. He took off his hat, and said, "See here, Mr. Cartwright, what those rowdies have done!" I had very hard work to keep down my risibilities [laughter]; but I told him he had better say nothing about it, for if he did, they might serve him worse. He soon disappeared, and interrupted us no more during the meeting.[31]

For decades, Peter Cartwright was a leading organizer of camp meetings throughout his circuits in Ohio, Kentucky, Tennessee, Indiana, and Illinois. He fervently believed that they were the best way to bring sinners to Christ and into the membership of the church. He could quote statistics proving that tens of thousands had been converted through them.

Pioneer, Evangelist, and Politician

Cartwright completed one of the longest and most useful ministries in the West, living to see much that was once untamed wilderness grow to become settled and civilized. Vexed by his circuits in Kentucky and Tennessee because of his distaste for slavery, he requested a transfer to Illinois in 1824 where he served as presiding elder for forty-five years. Twice he was elected representative to the Illinois legislature, and in 1846 he ran against Abraham Lincoln for an Illinois seat in Congress, losing that election.

He calculated that in his lifetime he had preached at least 14,600 sermons, had received at least 10,000 members into the church, and had baptized almost as many children. Up to the close of the Civil War he served his people well, and contributed greatly to saving the West for Christianity. Hundreds of churches were organized under his direction, and his friends were everywhere. His amazing stamina carried him to the age of eighty-seven, and he laid down his labors for the Master confident that they would be revealed at the last day.

$\mathcal{F}$inney: Developer of Planned Mass Evangelism

O ne writer has described Charles Grandison Finney before his conversion as a "splendid pagan—a young man rejoicing in his
strength, proudly conscious of his physical and intellectual supe-
riority to all around him."[1] He was six feet, two inches tall and weighed
185 pounds. Strikingly handsome, he was regarded by the opposite sex
in the area of Jefferson County, New York, as a most eligible bachelor.
Young Finney was well-known for his dancing, cello playing, and athletic prowess. As a man studying for a career as a lawyer and the leader
of the church choir, his influence was especially large among admiring
young people. There was, however, one problem: Finney was not a Christian. That thought increasingly gnawed at him.

Finney related in his *Memoirs* that in the autumn of 1821 he resolved
to settle the issue of his soul's salvation. Since no one else was in the law
office one Monday and Tuesday, he had opportunity to study his Bible
and pray. He stopped up the key hole so he could not be heard; "but still

Alone in the woods near Adams, New York,
Finney wrestles in prayer during his conversion.

it seemed as if my heart grew harder. I could not shed a tear; I could not pray. . . . Tuesday night I had become very nervous; and in the night a strange feeling came over me as if I was about to die. I knew that if I did I should sink down to hell."[2]

The questions still weighed on his mind Wednesday morning as he started for the office. Convinced that he could evade the issue no longer, he turned into the woods north of town, resolving to "give my heart to God, or I never will come down from there." Finney found a spot near a tangle of fallen trees where he might evade prying eyes. As he dropped to his knees, a reassuring passage of Scripture, Jeremiah 29:12, came: "Then shall ye go and pray unto me, and I will harken unto you." He had believed the Bible intellectually, but the truth had not come to him that faith was a voluntary trust and not merely an intellectual state. Now, by faith he became a Christian.

After hours of prayer, Finney left the woods to go to the office. He attempted to play his bass viol and to sing some sacred pieces, "but as soon as I began to sing those sacred words, I began to weep. It seemed as if my heart was all liquid."[3] He was interrupted when his law partner, Benjamin Wright, came in. After Wright left for the day, the emotional impact of Finney's decision struck him again. One of the choir members dropped by and was amazed to see Finney weeping loudly. Finney said that he was not crying because in pain, "but so happy that I cannot live."

The next morning, as he described it,

There I was having the renewal of these mighty waves of love and salvation flowing over me, when Squire Wright came into the office. I said a few words to him on the subject of his salvation. He looked at me with astonishment, but made no reply whatever, that I recollect. He dropped his head, and after standing a few minutes left the office. I thought no more of it then, but afterward found that the remark I made pierced him like a sword; and he did not recover from it till he was converted.

Soon after Mr. Wright had left the office, Deacon B—— came into the office and said to me, "Mr. Finney, do you recollect that my cause is to be tried at ten o'clock this morning? I suppose you are ready?" I had been retained to attend this suit as his attorney. I replied to him, "Deacon B——, I have a retainer from the Lord Jesus Christ to plead his cause, and I cannot plead yours."[4]

Thus Finney soon moved in the direction of Christian ministry.

Leadership of the Second Awakening

At the time of Finney's conversion it had been four years since the death of the leader of New England's awakenings, Timothy Dwight. The Yale president's carefully organized campaign to promote dignified, orderly revivals in the settled East had met with unexpected success after 1800. Dwight, the uncontested leader of Connecticut Congregationalism, was also a sagacious planner who understood that the blessings of the revivals must not be terminated by his death. Accordingly, he chose and carefully groomed promising Yale men to succeed him. The most outstanding of these were Lyman Beecher, who became an energetic pastor in Litchfield, Connecticut, and later in Boston; Asahel Nettleton, who became the leading itinerant evangelist throughout New England; and Nathaniel W. Taylor, whose career led him to become a pastor in New Haven and later the first professor of theology at Yale Divinity School. Dozens of Yale graduates provided excellent leadership under Dwight's paternal encouragement, in an effort to bring about a general awakening along the eastern seaboard. Things seemed even more hopeful after 1801, when the Congregational churches of New England and the leading Presbyterian denomination in the remainder of the states agreed upon a *Plan of Union* "to promote harmony and to establish as far as possible a uniform system of Church government." Thus, by 1821 these Yale graduates and the Presbyterians of New York, where Finney lived, had officially been members of the same ecclesiastical body for twenty years. Ministers easily intermixed, and there was general agreement on matters of church government and on the urgent question of awakenings.

Great numbers had been converted and were energizing the churches of the East. Between 1800 and 1835, while the national population tripled, church membership increased fivefold. In 1800, 7 percent of Americans belonged to a Protestant church, but by 1835 the proportion had jumped to 12.5 percent. While membership in Protestant churches stood at only 365,000 in 1800, by 1850 it had soared to 3.5 million.[5] Evangelism flamed in the healthiest churches of America, and an expectant spirit of awakening made the clergy and the laity alike vitally concerned for the salvation of the lost. The future of the churches appeared bright indeed.

With this dynamic spirit surging onward, a successor to Dwight was sought after his death. Lyman Beecher had been Dwight's lieutenant in the leadership of the campaign for awakenings, and he appeared to be the likely commander of aggressive evangelism for the future. Beecher enlarged the existing structure of institutional revivalism in New England and New York through the Plan of Union network. In 1826, by which time he was one of the well-known preachers in America, he was called to the Hanover Street Church of Boston. From there he carried his campaign for revivals into the heartland of unitarianism. In Boston he found distressing conditions. Many congregations were split between trinitarians and unitarians, and court battles over church property were in progress. Joining forces with the Baptists, Beecher began "inquiry meetings" in various parts of town and was rewarded at the next communion with seventy converts in his church alone.

But Dwight's mantle was not to fall upon the shoulders of Lyman Beecher, Asahel Nettleton, Nathaniel W. Taylor, or any other of Dwight's protégés. Rather, it was an unknown young lawyer, Charles Finney, who was to become the chief evangelist in America, and the head of the "Benevolent Empire" of reform movements in the nation. "No religious leader in America since [Jonathan] Edwards commanded such attention," the historian Perry Miller has declared, "and no one was to do it again until Dwight Moody."[6]

Finney's Early Development

Finney was born in Warren, Litchfield County, Connecticut, on August 29, 1792, in the very path of the migration of thousands of New Englanders into the beckoning New York frontier. "When I was about two years

145

old," Finney recalled, "my father removed to Oneida County, New York, which was at that time, to a great extent, a wilderness. No religious privileges were enjoyed by the people. . . . My parents were neither of them professors of religion. . . . I seldom heard a sermon, unless it was an occasional one from some traveling minister."[7] Charles was the seventh child, and when he was sixteen the family settled in Henderson, on the Lake Ontario shore. After receiving the training available from the backwoods schools of his boyhood, Charles attended the Hamilton Oneida Academy at Clinton, New York, for two years, from 1806 to 1808. Although regular church attendance was not his custom, he must have been inspired by the academy's headmaster, Samuel Kirkland, the famous missionary to the Oneida Indians.

Increasingly, Charles was convinced he wanted to be a teacher and not a farmer and that he needed more education to attain his goal. Leaving the academy, he taught school from his sixteenth to his twentieth years, and in the fall of 1812 he enrolled in a school at Warren, Connecticut, where he lived with an uncle. He contemplated attending Yale College, but a teacher advised him against it, saying he could master the entire curriculum by himself in two years. Finney then set himself to acquiring some knowledge of Latin, Greek, and Hebrew, and was offered a position teaching school in New Jersey, which he accepted. Again, as before, he was a successful teacher, but much of his formula for success came from his ability to win the students' unbounded admiration. One former student asserted,

> There was nothing which anyone else knew, which Mr. Finney didn't know, and there was nothing which anyone else could do, that Mr. Finney could not do—and do a great deal better. He was the idol of his pupils. . . . He was very dignified, and kept perfect order. Should any boy attempt to create a disturbance, one flash of Mr. Finney's eye would quell the sinner at once. Oh, I tell you, they all loved and worshipped him, and all felt that some day he would be a great man.[8]

This admirer went on to say that in the school yard, Finney kept the students' loyalty by out-wrestling and out-fighting the best of them, even several of the boys at once. But after a time his interest in teaching waned; Finney was in his mid-twenties, and turned instead to a career in law. The custom at that time was to study under the tutelage of a local lawyer, and he entered the law office of Wright in Adams, New York, not far from his parents' farm. This, then, was to be his life's work—or so he thought. But the Christian faith had a strange allure.

> Thus when I went to Adams to study law, I was almost as ignorant of religion as a heathen. I had been brought up mostly in the woods. I had very little regard for the Sabbath, and had no definite knowledge of religious truth.

> At Adams, for the first time, I sat statedly, for a length of time, under an educated ministry. Rev. George W. Gale, from Princeton, New Jersey, became, soon after I went there, pastor of the Presbyterian Church in that place. His preaching was of the old school type; that is, it was thoroughly Calvinistic. . . .
>
> In studying elementary law, I found the old authors frequently quoting the Scriptures. . . . This excited my curiosity so much that I went and purchased a Bible, the first I had ever owned. . . . This soon led to my taking a new interest in the Bible, and I read and meditated on it much more than I had ever done before in my life. However, much of it I did not understand.[9]

Charles Finney's musical talents enabled him to take the position of choir director in the Adams Presbyterian Church, even though he was all too aware he was not yet converted. Gale in time became a good friend, probably feeling that Finney needed special attention for conversion. An additional motive, no doubt, was that Finney's influence was keeping some of the choir out of the Kingdom! In their many discussions over theology, the basis of disagreement was Gale's Calvinism, which stressed the sovereignty of God, the absolute depravity of man, and his utter inability to bring about his own salvation. Whatever his own views, through these discussions Finney was "brought face to face with the question whether I would accept Christ as presented in the Gospel, or pursue a worldly course of life."[10]

An Offer to be Accepted

Finney's own intense study of the Bible and his debates with Pastor Gale led him to different conclusions about human ability than those of high Calvinism. He agreed that he and the remainder of mankind were at enmity with God. But Finney became convinced from his own study that this broken relationship with God could be healed if he would turn in repentance to Christ. His innate self-assurance asserted itself, but his understanding of the gospel showed him that he must admit that he was a sinner. His acceptance of what Christ had done on the cross of Calvary would bring salvation to him. What held him back was not that he was not one of the elect, but his own obstinacy and lack of determination. "Gospel salvation seemed to me to be an offer of something to be accepted; and that it was full and complete." All that was necessary to receive it "was to get my own consent to give up my sins, and accept Christ."[11]

These thoughts overwhelmed him on that October Wednesday in 1821. His conversion experience epitomized the influences of his formative years, his confidence in himself and in his free will, and the theology he had been hammering out in discussions with Gale. Regeneration seemed

George W. Gale, Finney's mentor, initially resisted Finney's means-centered evangelistic approach. Later, however, he became one of his student's supporters. (Courtesy of Knox College)

simpler than the version Gale presented; it involved only the admission of one's lostness and sin and the willing acceptance of the Savior's redeeming grace and forgiveness. With that—in all its beautiful simplicity—the believer immediately was regenerated, through God's grace.

Finney now turned completely from his irreligion. Wherever he went he told people of his conversion and urged them to think seriously of Christ and salvation. When he found the son of a church elder advocating universalism—that all would go to heaven—he demolished the young man's arguments in short order. Finney seemed from his conversion to be destined for the ministry, and one witness remembered him saying that if he ever served God, he would be in earnest and "pull men out of the fire."[12]

The news spread quickly that Finney professed conversion. While some friends counseled him not to leave a most promising career in law, others, such as Gale, recognized that, if Finney could bring to the Christian faith all the intensity he focused on other areas, he would have much to offer. As it was, his legal training gave him valuable experience in dealing with people and in speaking. Indeed, his style in preaching for the rest of his life showed his law training; few who heard him failed to see that he owed much of his success to the conversational, direct, and persuasive style of argument he had cultivated as a lawyer. The electrifying way he spoke to congregations previously accustomed to duller preaching styles showed far greater affinities to the law-court than to the written sermons then in vogue.

At Gale's urging Finney placed himself under the care of the local presbytery as a candidate for the ministry in the spring of 1823. The assembled clergy put the usual queries to him and then urged him to enroll at Princeton to study theology. They were dumfounded when he informed the august body "that I would not put myself under such an influence as they had been under; that I was confident they had been wrongly educated, and they were not ministers that met my idea of what a minister of Christ should be. I told them this reluctantly, but I could not honestly withhold it."[13] As they struggled to regain composure and dignity, the presbytery saw they were not dealing with the average young man and reluctantly allowed Finney to pursue studies under Gale's direction. Delighted with this arrangement, the two friends continued the discussions that had begun before Finney's conversion, but the large gulf that separated their views was not easily bridged.

The Presbytery of St. Lawrence was again called together at Adams in December 1823. On their agenda was Finney's licensure to preach, and they were to check his progress. When asked if he received the Westminster Confession of Faith, Finney answered that he did as far as he understood it but that he had never actually read it. Nevertheless, in March 1824 the Female Missionary Society of the Western District of New York retained Finney as a missionary to Jefferson County, a rural northern district bordering Lake Ontario. And on July 1, 1824, he was ordained a Presbyterian minister, and began pastoral work in the towns of Antwerp and Evans Mills.

The Wave of the Future

Already Finney was honing the techniques he would use as an evangelist. He disagreed with the form of Calvinism expressed in the Westminster Confession and disliked the ornate, elevated preaching style practiced by Gale and most Congregational and Presbyterian clergymen. His preaching style, Finney determined, would reach people where they were. But the complaints went in both directions. Many clergymen were displeased at his pulpit performances, for in their view Finney destroyed the dignity of the pulpit by his colloquial and familiar speech and his vivid, energized homiletics. He was hurt that "Mr. Gale, when I preached for him immediately after I was licensed, told me that he should be ashamed to have any one know that I was a pupil of his. . . . They would reprove me for illustrating my ideas by reference to the common affairs of men. . . . I sought to express all my ideas in few words, and in words that were in common use."[14]

Whether preachers of the time liked his ways or not, he was the voice of the future, and their methods were destined to become obsolete. Soon, under Finney's direct and challenging preaching, the communities of Antwerp and Evans Mills were ablaze with an awakening. He avoided the excesses of the western "Cane Ridge" revivals. His methods were based on civilized decorum—directness, relevance to life, and animation, yes, but without sensationalism. He once was asked to preach at a schoolhouse three miles from Antwerp. He decided to preach on the story of Abraham and Lot, of Lot's poor choices, and of God's destruction of the city of Sodom after Lot had been warned to flee. As he preached, the congregation showed a strange restlessness. Later, after a revival had broken out, he learned that the community was named Sodom, and the old man who had invited him to preach there was named Lot.

In October 1824 Finney married Lydia Andrews of Whitestown in Oneida County. A year later, leaving the revivals in Jefferson County, Finney and his wife planned to return home from a synod meeting in Utica in time to celebrate their first year of marriage. They were unaware of the events that would soon catapult Charles Finney into national prominence.

Seven Years of Intense Revivals

In the small town of Western, near Lake Oneida, they happened to meet George Gale. He had retired to a farm near the village and was concerned about the low moral condition of the area. Finney, already well known in the region, was implored by Gale and the church leaders to stay a short time to preach. He began conducting services almost every evening and three times on Sundays. His preaching series touched off seven years of the most intense revivals in American history, setting a revival fire that brought in thousands of converts and began the Oneida County revivals of 1825–27.

Immediately after he finished his brief stay in Western, Moses Gillet invited Finney to preach at his Congregational church in Rome, New York. Soon Gillet was able to declare that "religion was the principal subject of conversation in our streets, stores, and even taverns."

Finney's personal and extemporaneous pulpit style had a rapid-fire impact on the packed congregation, but also his uncannily penetrating and hypnotic eyes riveted his audience. Set under firm brows in a handsome face, those eyes were "large and blue, at times mild as an April sky, and at others, cold and penetrating as polished steel."[15] In addition to those unforgettable eyes, observers were always impressed with Finney's grace in the pulpit, his fitting illustrations, his appropriate but not exaggerated gestures that dramatized his delivery. A fitting companion to the eyes was his majestic voice.

Finney once preached a sermon against those who believed that hell was not perpetual punishment but that people might serve some time there for their sins and be released. (Finney, of course, held that Scripture taught *eternal* punishment for unbelievers.) One theological student recounted:

> The tones of the preacher . . . became sweet and musical, as he repeated "Worthy is the Lamb that was slain, to receive power, and riches, and wisdom, and might, and honor, and glory, and blessing." No sooner had he uttered the word "blessing" than he started back, turned his face . . . fixed his glaring eyes upon the gallery at his right hand, and gave all the signs of a man who was frightened by a sudden interruption of the divine worship. With a stentorian voice he cried out: "*What* is this I see? What means that *rabble-rout* of men coming up here? Hark! Hear them shout! . . . 'Thanks to hell-fire! We have served out our time. Thanks! Thanks!' . . . Then, after a lengthened pause, during which a fearful stillness pervaded the house, he said in gentle tones: "Is this the spirit of the saints? Is this the music of the upper world?"[16]

Finney was able to modulate his rich voice persuasively, and he could thunder out verbal pyrotechnics. Many warned him at first that being dramatic in the pulpit might woo the lower classes, but it would turn away the educated. As Finney suspected, just the opposite proved to be the case. "They found that, under my preaching, judges, and lawyers, and educated men were converted by scores; whereas, under their methods, such a thing seldom occurred."[17]

The Burned-over District

A socioeconomic factor also worked in Finney's favor in promoting awakenings. Beginning with the revivals at Western and Rome, he came into an area that was being turned upside down by rapid industrial development, spearheaded by the completion of the Erie Canal in 1825. This, plus the opening of multitudes of small factories, mills, distilleries, and packing houses, attracted tens of thousands of migrants. Some were bound for the Midwest, others settled along the canal. Bernard Weisberger has stated, "Steadily, upstate New Yorkers watched the crumbling of certain eternal verities—fixed land tenure, a stable populace, small class distinctions, isolation from the outside world."[18]

People searched for certainties they could cling to, and enthusiastic religion filled the void admirably—although not necessarily orthodox Christianity. New York west of the Hudson River Valley was called the "burned-over district" before Finney's time, because of the number of scorchings it had received from various excitements. Just as in Kentucky and Tennessee, the winter of 1799–1800 was the time of the "great revival," although the New York awakening was far more decorous and well-behaved—to suit the Yankee taste—than in the West. From then on, one enthusiasm after another agitated the area. During the quarter century 1825–1850, New York State produced a remarkable variety of groups: Mormonism, perfectionism, spiritualism, millennialism, and the anti-Masonic, Liberty, and Free Soil parties!

Finney left five hundred new converts behind at Rome. Samuel C. Aikin, pastor of the First Presbyterian Church in Utica, begged Finney to preach there, and soon that city was ablaze with spiritual concern. Aikin reported that the services were made "solemn and sometimes terribly so by the presence of God which made sinners afraid and Christians humble and still."[19] By May 1826 five hundred had been added to Aikin's church, and more than a thousand converts were added to other churches. Demands for Finney increased; in the summer of 1826 he led meetings in Auburn, and in the fall he preached in Troy. Again, spiritual concern flooded these cities, and multitudes were converted.

As Finney's fame grew, his practices came under increasing criticism. Asahel Nettleton, particularly, charged that Finney had introduced "new measures"—that he had changed the previous practice of keeping awakenings firmly in the hands of settled pastors and was using more than the ordinary "means of grace." The "new measures" included praying for persons by name, allowing women to pray and testify, encouraging persons to come forward to the "anxious seat" (a front pew for those under conviction), mobilizing groups of workers to visit all the homes of the community, and displacing the regular services with "protracted meetings" (lengthy services held each night for several weeks).[20]

Yet, for every critic who found fault, more supporters lauded his aggressive evangelism and especially his insistence on order and dignity. "Beyond some unaffected, yet striking peculiarities of voice and manner," wrote one observer of Finney's preaching, "there is nothing to attract curiosity, or offend even the most fastidious or carping sense of propriety."[21] The "new measures" were successful and logical extensions of evangelistic techniques, his supporters urged, and the real difference between Finney's efforts and those of others was in the "power and passion" of his meetings.

In another significant change from the ways of older evangelists, Finney gathered around himself like-minded associates to promote the work. In 1826, Finney formed the Oneida Evangelical Association with Daniel Nash (a retired pastor), Herman Norton (a recently ordained evangelist), Nathaniel Smith (another Presbyterian preacher), and, ironically, Gale (whose views now were in line with Finney's). The purpose of this society was "to send forth . . . evangelists" to "establish and benefit the Redeemer's Kingdom."[22] As Garth Rosell says, "For the first time in the nation's history, professional evangelists banded together for the 'salvation of the world.' "[23]

In addition to these members of the Association, a circle of supporting friends also was gathering. Nicknamed the "Holy Band," it consisted mainly of pastors in whose churches Finney had ministered, such as Nathan Beman of Troy, Dirck Lansing of Auburn, Aikin of Utica, and Gillet of Rome. Others became convinced that God's hand was upon Finney and joined, among them John Frost, pastor at Whitesboro; Charles Stuart, principal of the Utica Academy; Noah Coe, pastor in New Hartford; Edward N. Kirk, pastor at Albany (who later aroused the spiritual concern of a young D. L. Moody); Horatio Foote, evangelist in New York; and Theodore Dwight Weld, who would later become a famous abolitionist. Many leaders of the Presbyterians and Congregationalists in New York were rallying around Finney and moving their denominations closer to the new type of evangelism.

The New Lebanon Convention

The methods and increasing impact of the Oneida Association were bound to stir controversy. Beecher called a meeting of concerned evangelical leaders on July 18, 1827, at New Lebanon, New York (just west of the Massachusetts line). Rumors of Finney's deviation from accepted evangelistic practices had been filtering into New England, fueled by the complaints of Nettleton, co-leader with Beecher of New England orthodoxy. Sensibly, Beecher did not want to be stampeded into anything rash, and wrote to Nathan Beman, "Satan, as usual, is plotting to dishonor a work which he cannot withstand." He had no doubts as to Finney's orthodox theology: "I have confidence in the piety and talents of brother Finney, and have no doubt that he brings the truth of God to bear upon the conscience with uncommon power."[24]

*Lyman Beecher promoted both benevolent societies
and revivals. He called the New Lebanon Convention
to end internecine fighting in the evangelical
community over Finney's "new measures."
(Courtesy of the Billy Graham Center Museum)*

After some discussion of Finney's methods, the first formal resolutions at the convention were passed by unanimous vote. One stated in part:

> That revivals of true religion are the work of God's Spirit, by which, in a comparatively short period of time, many persons are convinced of sin, and brought to the exercise of repentance towards God, and faith in our Lord Jesus Christ.
>
> That the preservation and extension of true religion in our land has been much promoted by these revivals.
>
> That . . . greater and more glorious revivals are to be expected, than has ever yet existed.[25]

In the subsequent discussion of possible extravagances and enthusiasm, Finney and the other New Yorkers made clear to the New Englanders that they were as firmly opposed to the ignorant bombast and physical excesses of the "Cane Ridge" tradition as was Beecher. It was again unanimously agreed that it was wrong to condemn settled pastors; to deprecate education; to justify any measure simply because it might be successful; to hold inquiry meetings till late at night; to exaggerate accounts of revivals; to encourage "audible groaning, violent gestures and boisterous tones" among the congregation; or to name particular individuals in public prayer.

The convention reviewed allegations about Finney's past revivals, but it soon became apparent that these problems were exaggerated. None of the New Yorkers wanted to condemn Finney in any way, whatever their sentiments may have been when they arrived. Discussion turned to the question of whether it was proper for women to speak and pray in public. Here the New Englanders were adamant; the Apostle Paul had forbidden women to speak in church (1 Tim. 2:12; 1 Cor. 14:34) and that ended the matter. Then it was shown that the First Presbyterian Church of Utica had been encouraging women to pray in public before Finney arrived to begin his meetings, and Finney simply went along with the practice. Three days were spent debating this, but the two groups could not agree. Howard Morrison has said, "Still, the female issue was not in any way a question of an excess which could discredit Finney. Indeed, although Beecher and Nettleton had planned to use the convention to put Finney in his place, none of the resolutions passed by the delegates were in any way a censure of Finney . . . but actually supported and reinforced him."[26] After a great deal of prayer the group adjourned, and Charles Finney emerged the victor, his views exonerated.

Beecher left New York, realizing that younger men with newer ways were supplanting those represented by Nettleton and himself. He said he had "crossed the mountains expecting to meet a company of boys, but . . . found them to be full-grown men."[27] He then took action to silence the dissension, and to align himself with Finney. At the General Assembly of the Presbyterian Church in the U.S.A. in May 1828, an agreement was drawn up between the two sides that stated, "The subscribers . . . are of the opinion that the general interests of religion would not be promoted by any further publications on these subjects, or personal discussions."

Finney thus emerged, at age thirty-six, as the leader of the Congregational-Presbyterian campaign for awakening in America, the recognized head of this part of the Second Great Awakening, and the inheritor of Dwight's mantle. Demands for his preaching in the major cities of the eastern seaboard drew him first to Wilmington, Delaware, in the fall of 1827. Here in the Philadelphia-Princeton area was the heart of the Old School views of Calvinism—that Christ had made atonement only for the elect, and that only the Holy Spirit could initiate faith. The individual was seen as completely passive, for he or she had no means or will to pursue faith. Finney, agreeing with the "New Divinity" of Taylor, held that sin was a voluntary act and theoretically avoidable. He taught, at the very outset of his *Lectures on Revivals,* "[A revival] is not a miracle, nor dependent on a miracle, in any sense. It is a purely philosophical result of the right use of the constituted means—as much so as any other effect produced by the application of means."[28] As Christians could use scriptural means to bring about revivals, so could the unregenerate person exercise his will—actively—to choose or reject Christ and his claims. Old School adherents were horrified.

During the Wilmington meetings Finney received an invitation to preach in the pulpit of James Patterson in Philadelphia. He had some misgivings about entering the fortress of the Old School,

> but I was preaching to please the Lord, and not man. I thought that it might be the last time I should ever preach there; but purposed, at all events, to tell them the truth, and the whole truth, on that subject, whatever the result might be.
>
> I endeavored to show that if man were as helpless as their views represented him to be, he was not to blame for his sins. If he had lost in Adam all power of obedience, so that obedience had become impossible to him, and that not by his own act or consent, but by the act of Adam, it was mere nonsense to say that he could be blamed for what he could not help. . . . Indeed, the Lord helped me to show up, I think, with irresistible clearness the peculiar dogmas of old-schoolism and their inevitable results.[29]

Surprisingly, Finney soon received invitations to speak in several of the leading pulpits of Philadelphia, including the First Church of James P. Wilson. As a friend wrote to Finney in February 1828, "Dr. Wilson having taken you into his pulpit it has almost petrified opposition here. He has more weight here than perhaps any Minister in the Presbyterian Church."[30] Opposition continued, but Finney moved on to preach to great crowds in the largest German Reformed church in the city.

Meanwhile, a group of new measures laymen in New York City were appealing for his aid. Zephaniah Platt wrote in March 1828, "Our New York churches are generally in a cold stupid state but I am happy to tell you there is a very general change of sentiment here in regard to yourself and the Western Revivals."[31] Finney responded in the fall of 1829 and preached for a year in New York under the patronage of Anson G. Phelps and Arthur Tappan.

156

Finney at the height of his career, in 1834
(Courtesy of Allen Memorial Art Museum, Oberlin College, Oberlin, Ohio)

The Rochester Revival

Finney received an invitation to conduct a city-wide campaign in Rochester, New York, in the fall of 1830. He welcomed the opportunity to return to the scene of his first successes. The Rochester revival of 1830–31 was the most successful in Finney's entire ministry. The entire city and area for miles in every direction seemed to band together in spiritual concern. Here all of the theories and techniques Finney had developed were put into practice, and they worked remarkably well. For six months, from September 10 to March 6, Finney and a number of co-operating evangelists held forth in pulpits in Rochester and surrounding

157

towns, so that few people were left untouched. This was the first city-wide evangelistic endeavor in American history that deserves to be compared with the urban campaigns of the post-Civil War era. As William McLoughlin has written, "In conducting it Finney made full use of the theories and practices of modern revivalism which he bequeathed to all professional evangelists. . . . In Rochester he proved himself a master of the respectable, efficient, carefully organized revivalism of the future."[32] And Whitney Cross has declared,

> No more impressive revival has occurred in American history. Sectarianism was forgotten and all churches gathered in their multitudes. . . . But the exceptional feature was the phenomenal dignity of this awakening. No agonizing souls fell in the aisles, no raptured ones shouted hallelujahs. Rather, despite his doses of hell-fire, the great evangelist, "in an unclerical suit of gray," acted "like a lawyer arguing . . . before a court and jury," talking precisely, logically, but with wit, verve, and informality. Lawyers, real-estate magnates, millers, manufacturers, and commercial tycoons led the parade of the regenerated. The theatre became a livery stable. Taverns closed. . . .
>
> More remarkable yet was the way the fire threw off sparks. . . . Finney later quoted Lyman Beecher's testimony that a hundred thousand in the nation made religious affiliations within a year, an event "unparalleled in the history of the church."[33]

Hundreds were won to Christ at the meetings that winter, including most of Rochester's leading citizens, and the life of the entire area was profoundly influenced. The awakening spread far beyond Rochester as other evangelists and pastors who came to see the Lord's working carried its message and fervency back to their own areas.[34] Finney then accepted invitations to conduct meetings in New England, first in Providence and then in Boston. Convinced that Finney would not give the Unitarians anything to condemn, Beecher and the Congregational ministers' association of Boston requested that he come "as a general labourer among the Evangelical churches in this city." He stayed in Boston for nine months, from August 1831 to April 1832, but he was quite critical of the spiritual climate there. When Lewis Tappan, a wealthy businessman, rented the Chatham Street Theater for another series of meetings in New York City, Finney gladly accepted the call and named the place the Second Free Presbyterian Church, since it had issued from his previous work there.

Since the late 1820s Finney had been moving in the direction of including social reform in his program for awakening. Converts would immediately be put to urgent work in the battle against sin; as he preached, "Every member must work or quit. No honorary members."

Arthur Tappan and his brother Lewis were wealthy entrepreneurs who helped finance Finney's endeavors and many Benevolent Empire undertakings. They lost most of their wealth in the Panic of 1837.

The Benevolent Empire

During the first three decades of the nineteenth century, intensely zealous Christians organized thousands of societies, intending to create an empire of benevolence that would alleviate every vice and problem. By 1834 the total annual income of the benevolence societies reached the then incredible amount of $9 million.[35] Finney entered zealously into the leadership of the movement, aided by reformers such as Weld and Tappan. Almost no phase of life in America was untouched. Temperance, vice, world peace, slavery, education, Sabbath observance, profanity, women's rights, the conditions in penal institutions—all those and more issues had societies devoted to them. In the Rochester awakening of 1830–31, Finney introduced his growing social concern by focusing attention on the temperance crusade. From then on he lent his influence to the entire spectrum of causes. In his first sermon in the Chatham Street Chapel of New York City during the May "anniversary meetings" of 1832, Finney assumed the role of spokesman for the benevolence empire by outlining the framework within which American benevolence might function.

Finney first borrowed the concept of "universal benevolence" from Jonathan Edwards, picturing America as the center of a theocratic world, a nation ruled by the moral government of God. "Laws of benevolence" are deeply graven into human society, he declared, and Christ commanded specifically that people love both God and neighbor. The obligation of each Christian is therefore inescapable, he thundered; every child of God is to "aim at being useful in the highest degree possible," preferring the interest of God's kingdom above all other interests. In that way, God's millennium will be hastened by each faithful Christian.[36]

It was a great vision. To a remarkable degree the reform movements achieved their goals in the middle third of the nineteenth century—making genuine and lasting contributions to national life, eliminating much evil, and bringing important Christian values into the mainstream of society. By coupling awakenings with the reform impulse, Finney deserves much of the credit, sharing it with a host of lesser-known but equally devoted figures.

Finney also created problems. His statement, "A revival . . . is a purely philosophical result of the right use of the constituted means," with its emphasis on the *human* production of revivals and conversions, was consistent with his self-confident conviction that all that was needed for God to save a sinner was the person's own consent. In time this led to his stress on perfectionism—the idea that sin was a voluntary act, and sinlessness was a human possibility.[37] This was a startling and dangerous idea in those parts of the United States where the influence of Calvinism was strong, and it led many to object to Finney's theology. Also, for all his contributions to the rise of urban evangelism and the benefits that flowed from the benevolence empire, Finney was a rather divisive person. Throughout much of his life, first as a Presbyterian and later as a Congregationalist, he polarized opinion on many issues. Heated disputes arose over his new measures, his concept of revivals, his constant attacks on Old School Calvinism and its adherents, and especially his doctrine of perfectionism (which he developed at Oberlin College after 1836).

An Academic Career

Charles Finney began another phase of his long career when he left New York City to become professor of theology at Oberlin Collegiate Institute in Ohio. This new school was founded (with much financial help from Arthur and Lewis Tappan, and others) in order to attract young converts from Finney's revivals as well as supporters of his new measures and New School views. Another, more demanding issue was then hanging over the United States—slavery. Finney had become an ardent supporter of abolitionism, and, with the admission of a large number of fervent antislavery students, soon the preoccupation of Oberlin College was to train and send out young men to denounce slavery in the harshest terms. With the ominous prospect of civil war looming on the horizon, Oberlin became a major stop along the Underground Railroad, which helped slaves fleeing to freedom in Canada.

Although Finney strongly supported the abolitionist cause, his greatest interest remained evangelism. His work at Oberlin did not satisfy his desire to practice mass evangelism. In December 1834 he had begun a long series of lectures at the Chatham Street Chapel that later became a book entitled *Lectures on Revivals of Religion.* Of this powerful book Perry Miller has written,

> Not only could [Finney] slay his thousands in the frenzy of a revival, but in 1835 could articulate his *Lectures on Revivals of Religion,* indisputably the most powerful theoretical statement of the significance of the titanic enterprise. Overnight it sold 12,000 copies in America, soon was translated into Welsh, French, German. No religious leader in America since Edwards had commanded such attention. . . . Hence Finney's book stands . . . as the key exposition of the movement, and so a major work in the history of the mind in America. Its study is imperative if one wishes to pursue the mental adventure of the country.[38]

Lectures on Revivals covered many topics related to the bringing of awakening to a region and the proper treatment of converts. Rejecting the doctrine of predestination, Finney held that revivals—with mass conversions— *could* and *should* happen. And if people used sanctified common sense, by God's grace they *would* happen. The book has had a great impact on an enormous number of people since its first publication. Among those it influenced were the founders of the Salvation Army— Catherine and William Booth— and George Williams, the founder of the Young Men's Christian Association.

Finney left the Presbyterian denomination in March 1836 and took the position of pastor of New York's Broadway Tabernacle, a superb new building designed according to Finney's specifications. He held that post for a year, but resigned it to give more of his time to Oberlin. Each year, however, he would take some time from his teaching duties to hold revivals in Boston, Rochester, and other cities. On November 6, 1849, he arrived in England to hold meetings in a number of cities, finally preaching in Whitefield's Tabernacle in London until March 1851. He was elected president

The Broadway Tabernacle in New York City was Finney's third settled pastorate, though not for long. Its sanctuary measured 10,000 square feet and seated 2500. (From the author's collection)

of Oberlin College in August 1851, and held this post until 1865. He died in 1875, a titan in the field of evangelism. It has been estimated that he was responsible for half a million conversions during his long lifetime.

Aftermath of the Second Awakening

The sheer number of converted people flooding into the churches in the Second Awakening made it an immense movement. Add to this the great number of interests promoted after 1800 by American evangelicals whose consciences were sensitized by revival, and its impact becomes truly astounding. The results of the Second Awakening and its vast social concerns were, by any standard, far more widespread than those of the First Great Awakening. This was to be expected given the rather brief duration of the first revival, and the very extended nature—roughly 1795 to 1835—of the second. However, it can also be argued that some impulses to benefit society at large were generated in embryonic form during the First Awakening and took time to mature. Whitefield's concern for orphans and slaves, and his promotion of these causes, is a prominent example of this.

Movement Toward Abolition

The fight against slavery was one of the positive effects of the Wesleyan Revival in England and the worldwide Evangelical Awakening of the nineteenth century. Among the prominent English converts of this time was William Wilberforce (1759–1833), whose influence against slavery was also strong in America. Wilberforce was elected to Parliament in 1780 and became associated with the Clapham Sect, a group of evangelicals who were active in public life. He was involved with many good causes, including an attempt to evangelize England's upper classes as Wesley had the lower classes. Through the influence of his friends Thomas Clarkson and John Newton, and William Pitt in Parliament, he was persuaded to put his energies into the abolition of the British Empire's slave trade. By a brilliant use of all available weapons, he and his friends gradually won over Parliament to their view. In 1807 the slave trade was abolished. The complete abolition of slavery throughout the Empire was achieved just before his death in 1833. The end of slavery in the British Empire added moral pressure upon the United States to do the same, although many strongly resisted. Few people have achieved more for the benefit of humankind than did Wilberforce.[39]

Of all the side-effects of the awakening, none is more striking than its influence on the abolition of slavery movement in America. Most dedicated opponents of slavery, especially in the 1820s and 1830s, were concerned Christians who had been active in the Second Great Awakening: the Tappans, Weld, Charles Stuart, James G. Birney, Beecher, Finney, Henry B. Stanton, and others. Yet some secular historians, just as they have misrepresented the character of evangelism and awakenings in general, are distorting the history of the antislavery movement. To them, the fact that most abolitionists were dedicated Christians is almost entirely incidental; they see no correlation between their faith and their convictions regarding slavery. Wilberforce's committed faith is also thought to have had little bearing on the campaign against slavery in Britain.

To support this argument, some have established William Lloyd Garrison (1805–1879) as the primary force behind American abolition. Garrison, the emotionally high-strung editor of the Boston *Liberator* (one of the most extreme abolitionist papers in the nation), was not at first anti-Christian. However, when all the ministers did not at once accept him as their leader, he began to vilify the "black-hearted clergy" in his paper, calling the Methodists "a cage of unclean birds and a synagogue of Satan" and the Presbyterians "anathema." Thomas Bailey has written, "The error persists that Garrison was the 'voice' of the abolitionists. The truth is that he and his colleagues were only a small minority—the 'lunatic fringe'—of the whole abolitionist movement. But his voice was so piercing, and his antics were so spectacular, that he overshadowed and obstructed the efforts of the more levelheaded anti-slave majority."[40]

Gilbert H. Barnes, in his book *The Antislavery Impulse, 1830–1844,* has accurately shown that great numbers of Christians were in the forefront of the effort to end slavery in America. He writes:

> The conjunction of so many elements of the Great Revival [the Second Great Awakening] in the antislavery agitation was more than coincidence. . . . In leadership, in method, and in objective, the Great Revival and the American Anti-Slavery Society now were one. It is not too much to say that for the moment the anti-slavery agitation as a whole was what it had long been in larger part, an aspect of the Great Revival in benevolent reform.[41]

A Vast Social Movement

While the abolition of slavery may be the most important, it was only one of many reform efforts born of the Second Great Awakening. There were many things wrong in the United States and Britain in the first half of the nineteenth century, and the British were the first to address them. The first steps in England were in reaction to the outrages of the French Revolution, particularly after the French king Louis XVI was beheaded in January 1793. At the heart of the French Revolution was atheism, and Britons were horrified at the possibility that such an evil might invade their nation.

Even in 1790, before Louis's death, the British statesman Edmund Burke had published his *Reflections on the Revolution in France . . . ,* in which he declared, "We are resolved to keep an established church, an established monarchy, an established aristocracy and an established democracy." Burke saw these as part of a divine order—"that religion is the basis of civil society, and the source of all good and all comfort."[42] With this reassurance from a leading statesman, the English turned to strengthen, not dilute, their religious loyalties. "In the face of a dangerous foe, denominational tensions eased," C. I. Foster writes. "There was a loyalty transcending sectarian differences . . . [that] laid the foundation for a new British institution, nonsectarian Christianity. All of these impulses the United States would accept, adopt, and adapt in its own way, in its own good time."[43]

As happened frequently in America, it was that evangelical man-for-all-seasons, Lyman Beecher, who headed up many of the American causes and contributed perhaps more than anyone else to what was to become the Benevolent Empire. In 1815 Beecher sought to bring the government of the Almighty down to the nation in a practical way by launching what was to become the American Education Society. The United States needed a more homogenous character in order to bind it together, he declared. This was best achieved through intelligent pastors who "would establish schools, and academies, and colleges, and habits, and institutions of homogeneous influence. These would produce a sameness of views, and feelings, and interests, which would lay the foundation of our empire upon a rock. Religion is the central attraction which must supply the deficiency of political affinity and interest."[44]

The visions of Beecher and hundreds of others caught on in a remarkable way, and cooperation to improve society became a flaming watchword among Americans. "No period has existed since the creation of the world," exclaimed one observer, "when it was so easy to do good."[45] Commenting on the Second Great Awakening from a sociological perspective, Donald G. Mathews notes that it brought forth "a general social movement that organized thousands of people into small groups. . . . Its expansion was in large part the work of a dedicated corps of charismatic leaders who proposed to change the moral character of America. . . . Mobilizing Americans in unprecedented numbers, it had the power to shape part of our history."[46]

Largely unknown now even to Christians, the united social and spiritual crusade of almost forty years was indeed a Benevolent Empire, awe-inspiring in its scope.[47] Laypeople were recruited for a smorgasbord of causes, and thousands enthusiastically contributed their energies and funds. "Ours is an age of societies," British commentator Sir James Stephens observed of American religious life. "For the redress of every oppression . . . there is a public meeting," for the "diffusion of every blessing, there is a committee."[48] In the words of the *First Annual Report of the American Bible Society* in 1816, most agreed that there was nothing remotely to be compared "to the importance of spreading the knowledge of the one Living and True God."[49]

There was yet another reason for Christians to dedicate their energies to reform: the eschatological expectation of the millennium, in which the kingdom of God would come swiftly to earth, ending sin and death. Most Protestants at this time were postmillennialists and believed that their efforts for the kingdom of God would help to bring in the thousand-year golden age foretold in Scripture. They based this belief on passages like Isaiah 2, 4, and 65 and Revelation. Their optimistic hope was that as evil *decreased*, goodness and the gospel would *increase* to the point of bringing in the millennium. Gradually their view was replaced by the now-dominant premillennialism, a more pessimistic view holding that evil will increase globally until Christ returns to set up his full earthly kingdom and begin the millennium. (Premillennialists set the return of Christ *before* the millennium, whereas postmillennialists place it *after* it.) The thought that one's own efforts could help to bring in the kingdom contributed an obvious urgency to the Benevolent Empire's activities.

A great number of reform organizations spread good works through America, but much of the enthusiasm revolved around the "Great Eight" societies, which came to New York City each May in the 1820s and 1830s for their "anniversary meetings." It was always a time of jubilation, for the eight had expanded "beyond the most sanguine expectations of their founders." Great contributions of money were rolling in, and they had become, in the view of one observer, "immense institutions spreading over the country, combining hosts . . . a gigantic religious power, systematized, compact in its organization, with a polity and a government entirely its own, and independent of all control."[50] The Great Eight were:[51]

1. The American Board of Commissioners for Foreign Missions (founded 1810; headquarters Boston)
2. The American Education Society (founded 1815; headquarters Boston)
3. The American Bible Society (founded 1816; headquarters New York City)
4. The American Colonization Society (founded 1816; headquarters New York City)
5. The American Sunday School Union (founded 1817; headquarters Philadelphia)
6. The American Tract Society (founded 1826; headquarters New York City)
7. The American Temperance Society (founded 1826; headquarters New York City)
8. The American Home Missionary Society (founded 1826; headquarters New York City)

Missions around the Globe

Under such exemplary leaders, the Evangelical Awakening inspired the sending of missionaries to every part of the globe. One United States missions leader, Samuel J. Mills, Jr. (1783–1818), had been converted in 1801 in a revival in Connecticut. Mills entered Williams College in western Massachusetts and there developed a great interest in foreign missions. On a hot day in August 1806, he and four other students were praying in a field by the college campus. A sudden thunderstorm forced them to take shelter under a nearby haystack where they continued their prayer meeting. The "Haystack Prayer Meeting" is considered the birth of the foreign missions movement in America, resulting in the formation of the American Board of Commissioners for Foreign Missions in 1810 and the sending of the first five missionaries in 1812. Mills remained in the United States, making journeys throughout the West to determine

The ordination of the first missionaries sent by the American Board of Commissioners for Foreign Missions. Kneeling, not necessarily in order, are Luther Rice, Gordon Hall, Henry Nott, Samuel Newell, and Adoniram Judson.

the need for Bibles and missionaries. Then he sailed for Africa in 1818 to purchase what would become Liberia, a colony for freed blacks. He died of fever on the voyage home, but his valiant efforts to spread Christianity and help people inspired multitudes to take up the challenge.[52]

The approximate number of converts during the forty years of the Second Great Awakening in America can be determined by examining the membership records of many Protestant churches. In 1855 Robert Baird reported the number of evangelical Protestants as 4,176,431.[53] While some of this increase was through other means, a gain of almost 3 million within fifty years must be due in part to intensive evangelism. The one hundred thousand new converts reported for the revival year 1831 alone indicates how intensive the evangelism was.[54] Based on available statistics, it would seem that the Second Great Awakening converted, by conservative estimate, at least 1 million people from 1795 to 1835.

Beecher, the Tappan brothers, Finney, and a host of other Christians envisioned a truly Christian America and promoted this ideal. In 1835 it seemed attainable.

*T*he Third Great
Awakening and the Civil War

Prior to Charles Finney, few itinerant evangelists were welcomed. George Whitefield was widely recognized in his time as a divinely-anointed messenger, and Asahel Nettleton was in constant demand throughout New England and New York. Other itinerants, however, tended to be looked upon as intruders. Although Nettleton did much to change this attitude, Finney's "Holy Band" of itinerant coworkers would hardly have been welcome in Boston or Philadelphia in 1826. Rural New York State, however, was relatively open to them.[1]

The situation had improved significantly by the time Finney went to Oberlin in 1835. Evangelists had become quite respectable in most ecclesiastical circles, although some feared introduction of a class of "professional" evangelists. One writer in the *Quarterly Christian Spectator* attacked Connecticut laity who called for "a corps of Evangelists

*Phoebe Palmer and her husband Walter stimulated
the holiness movement through their lectures in the United
States and Canada. Mrs. Palmer did most of the speaking
and writing, and was also a leader in the early feminist
movement. (Courtesy of the Billy Graham Center Museum)*

to be employed for life exclusively amidst revivals of religion."[2] Laypeople would think settled pastors incapable of conducting revivals, that only experts could do it, the writer feared. Finney did not intend to create a special branch of clergy. He taught that every settled pastor should be an evangelist. If they did not win souls the fault could be found in the system of ministerial education. "The end of the ministry," Finney declared, "is the salvation of the soul. . . . He must understand how to wake up the church, and get them out of the way of the conversion of sinners. This is often the most difficult part of a minister's work."[3] When he went to teach at Oberlin, Finney intended to remedy what he saw as deficiencies in the typical seminary education, which trained future ministers in all the wrong ways. Oberlin would raise up "revival ministers."

Whatever Finney's intentions, the result was an increase in the number of itinerant evangelists. One of the first to become almost as famous as Finney by the 1840s, was Elder Jacob Knapp (1799–1874), the first professional Baptist evangelist. He graduated from Hamilton College and became an evangelist in 1833 after a pastorate in Watertown, New York. He accepted the New Divinity and new measures of Finney, and conducted more than 150 revivals. Although he claimed to have been instrumental in the conversion of one hundred thousand people, Knapp was criticized frequently. Preferring to conduct evangelistic campaigns in cities rather than towns, between 1835 and 1842 he held campaigns in New York, Washington, Baltimore, New Haven, Hartford, Providence, Boston, Rochester, Albany, and Brooklyn. He described his methods as follows:

> My reliance has been upon the power of God's truth, made effectual by His own Spirit and the hearty cooperation of the church, as "workers together with Him." If the work drags, I preach on some subjects which are applicable to both saints and sinners: appoint a fast requiring all who join in it to abstain from all business and all food during the twenty-four hours. Sometimes we have held three or four such seasons in one meeting. Thus by prayer and fasting, by preaching and exhortation, by humiliation and confessions, we have sought the Lord, until He has "come and rained righteousness upon us." When the church is aroused and consecrated, and the presence of the Spirit realized, then pour on God's truth, hand over hand. . . . Preach Christ crucified; knock out every prop on which sinners lean. Sometimes the prop is one thing, sometimes it is another. It may be Universalism, or Unitarianism, or morality.[4]

Other evangelists active in the 1830s also deserve mention. The Baptist Jabez S. Swan was a tall, slender man who brought a sense of humor into his preaching. He began his career with a four-day campaign in 1832. Like Finney, temperance was one of his chief concerns, and no one was considered converted at his meetings who did not also sign the temperance pledge.

Edward Norris Kirk (1802–1874), initially a Presbyterian, was a graduate of Princeton and exponent of the new measures. As pastor of Fourth Presbyterian Church in Albany he welcomed Finney to preach there. In 1837 he became an evangelist and was very successful until 1842, when he was called to the Mt. Vernon Congregational Church in Boston. This church was organized after the revivals he conducted there that year, and soon became the chief evangelistic institution in Boston. Its work with young men in 1852 produced the first YMCA in the United States. In 1854 a young man of seventeen named Dwight L. Moody came to Boston and began attending Kirk's church. Moody was converted and discipled through the church's ministry.

170

By 1840, more evangelists were on the field. Religious journals constantly referred to such respectable itinerants as the Methodists James Caughey, John Newland Maffitt, and Dr. and Mrs. Walter Palmer; Baptist Francis Wayland; and such men as Orson G. Parker, Daniel Baker, Arthur Granger, A. C. Kingsley, James Gallagher, Emerson Andrews, Thomas Sheardown, Samuel G. Orton, and Lewis Raymond. A great number of ordained men became evangelists between pastorates but did not engage in it permanently.[5]

National Agitation

By the mid-1830s the nation's attention was diverted by intense agitation over the slavery question. Then, as the year 1837 dawned, entrepreneurs and financiers recognized that economic trouble was coming. The primary problem was the scarcity of credit, at any rate of interest. Businessmen canceled orders or begged extensions on their arrears. Firms went bankrupt across the country. As money became scarce, the banks themselves were hard-pressed and collapsed by the hundreds as the Panic of 1837 began. The Tappan brothers—who had generously supported Charles Finney, Oberlin College, and a host of other causes—were among the best-known businessmen in the nation. Nevertheless, after unsuccessful attempts to raise cash, on May 1, 1837, the Tappan brothers announced their bankruptcy as well. Their indebtedness (due in part to a December 1835 fire that leveled their dry-goods store in New York City) was $1.1 million, an unpayable amount. The effects of the panic cast a pall over all the affairs of the nation for years.

From 1837 to 1857 the spiritual life of America declined for many causes—political, social, economic, and religious. Churches were vexed over the extremes of the Millerites. William Miller (1782–1849) and his followers had proclaimed that Christ would return to earth between March 21, 1843, and March 21, 1844. Many sold their belongings and waited with mounting anticipation. Whitney R. Cross has written, "Probably well over fifty thousand people in the United States became convinced that time would run out in 1844, while a million or more of their fellows were skeptically expectant."[6] The editor of the Millerite paper advised his readers to "dispose of *all* you have which you do not actually need for the present wants of yourself and family . . . to aid in sending out the truth to the perishing."[7] When the dates passed with nothing out of the ordinary occurring, Miller reset the date for the Second Coming to October 22, 1844, and again many trusted. All churches were mocked, though most had nothing to do with the Millerite delusion. "At Ithaca, Dansville, Scottsville, and Rochester, mobs stormed the Adventist meeting places, wrecking or burning as they could. . . . Tar and feathers abounded in Toronto, Canada."[8] This was a major setback for all the denominations, since they were lumped together by the skeptics and ridiculed indiscriminately. Between 1845 and 1855 the number of new members in the churches scarcely kept pace with losses due to death and discipline.

Eventually the effects of the Panic of 1837 and the 1843–44 Millerite delusion wore off, but the agitation over the slavery issue grew with each year. Allegiances among Christians became strained, and whole denominations separated into Southern and Northern divisions. The influences radiating from Oberlin and the Underground Railroad, the extremism of abolitionist William Lloyd Garrison, the passage of the Fugitive Slave Law, the work of Wendell Phillips, the incredible popularity of Mrs. Stowe's *Uncle Tom's Cabin,* the bloody fighting in Missouri and Kansas, the Dred Scott decision of the Supreme Court, and a score of other factors fueled the upheaval.

The financial crisis that hit late in 1857 was not as bad economically as the Panic of 1837, but psychologically it was probably the worst of the nineteenth century. Over five thousand businesses went bankrupt within a year. Unemployment was widespread, especially in major cities. As for the West, one historian has declared, "Premature railroads in the West had fostered premature cities teeming with premature traffic for a premature population."[9] Each state regulated its own banking system, resulting in unsteady bank credit and unwise mortgages covering land speculation. The Ohio Life Insurance and Trust Company failed in August 1857; other businesses toppled like ten-pins.[10] As in the Panic of 1837, interest rates soared and money was soon almost impossible to obtain. Factories ground to a halt, and the ranks of the unemployed grew.

Stopping to Hear the Spirit

Said Methodist Church Bishop Warren A. Candler, "And now that the wheels of industry stood still and the noisy cries of greed were hushed, men stopped to hear the voice of the Spirit calling them to repentance. And they heeded the heavenly call. Another revival of national extent began."[11] The origins of the Third Great Awakening can be traced most directly to the Methodists. Far outstripping all other Protestant groups by 1855, the various branches of Methodism could claim 1,593,794 members, while the closest competitor, the Baptists, had 1,322,469 adherents.[12] With the extremely rapid growth of the Methodists since Bishop Asbury's day, a vital tradition of soul-winning and revivals was deeply imbued into the life of the church. Timothy L. Smith states: "The fact that only four noteworthy full-time evangelists appeared in the church before 1857—John Newland Maffitt, James Caughey, and Dr. and Mrs. Walter Palmer, who were laymen—only emphasizes the point that every bishop, college president, presiding elder, and circuit rider was expected to be a constant winner of souls."[13]

A Stress on Holiness

The initial thrust for the Third Great Awakening came from Hamilton, Ontario. There Dr. Walter Palmer, a physician and layman, and his wife Phoebe were preaching in church services and camp meetings. Mrs. Palmer usually did most of the speaking. For years this pair was a potent force in Methodism, urging the doctrine of perfectionism upon their hearers with striking effect. Mrs. Palmer's career in speaking began in the mid-1830s with the Tuesday Meeting for women in her home in New York City. These meetings drew increasing crowds, requiring two moves to find a house that would accommodate those who wished to attend. In addition, Mrs. Palmer wrote a number of influential books—*The Way to Holiness, The Promise of the Father, Faith and Its Effects, Entire Devotion, Incidental Illustrations of the Economy of Salvation*, and others—all of which went through a number of editions. One of her most important contributions was the founding of the Five Points Mission in New York City in 1850. The area was one of the worst slums of the city, and from this issued the beginning of Christian institutional work among America's poor.[14]

The Palmers devoted about half of each year after 1850 to revivals and camp meetings in Canada and the eastern United States. From June through October 1857 they were in Quebec and Ontario, conducting camp meetings with attendance of five thousand or more. While waiting for a train connection to New York City at Hamilton, Ontario, they were approached by Samuel Rice, a Wesleyan pastor, who invited them to speak at the McNab Street Wesleyan Methodist Church. The meeting was so well received that they were invited to speak again the next evening, and twenty-one people were converted. The Palmers remained for several weeks, during which six hundred people professed faith in Christ. This was the first instance of an unusual power of conviction in the movement that was to sweep the world.[15] The revival in Hamilton was declared by Canadian and American newspapers to be a model of orderliness. That winter the Palmers traveled to Binghamton, Owego, and Union Center, New York, for meetings that drew interdenominational support. The Third Awakening had begun.

The Fulton Street Prayer Meeting

While the Palmers' work gave the impetus for the awakening, others contributed to the widespread nature of this unusual revival. In September 1856 the New York Sunday School Union asked each of its participating churches to send visitors to homes, and two thousand people covered the city, imploring people to attend the churches. Everywhere, it seemed, people were gathering for prayer. Perhaps the ominous state of the nation drove them to pray; certainly the perilous economy and impending Civil War gave reason. In cities, large and small, interdenominational prayer sessions were conducted, usually by laypeople. One in Bethel, Connecticut, met daily at 4 P.M. and reported four hundred converts.

In downtown New York City, a quiet businessman named Jeremiah Lanphier, forty-eight years of age, began work as an urban missionary for the North Dutch Reformed Church in July 1857. He was born in Coxsackie, New York in 1809 and had been converted in 1842 in Finney's Broadway Tabernacle. A journalist described Lanphier as "tall, with a pleasant face, an affectionate manner, and indomitable energy and perseverance; a good singer, gifted in prayer and exhortation, a welcome guest to any house, shrewd and endowed with much tact and common sense."[16]

The North Dutch Church employed Lanphier because it was losing members, and its leaders recognized that something had to be done. People were moving from the older downtown neighborhood to newer areas to the north. Lanphier decided that part of his strategy to attract people to the church would be to institute a noonday prayer meeting on Wednesdays. He printed handbills with this message:

"How Often Shall I Pray?"
As often as the language of power is in my heart; as often as I see my need of help; as often as I feel the power of temptation; as often as I am made sensible of any spiritual declension, or feel the aggression of a worldly, earthly spirit. . . .

A day Prayer-Meeting is held every Wednesday, from 12 to 1 o'clock, in the Consistory building, in the rear of the North Dutch Church, corner of Fulton and William Streets (entrance from Fulton and Ann streets).

This meeting is intended to give merchants, mechanics, clerks, strangers, and business-men generally, an opportunity to stop and call upon God amid the perplexities incident to their respective avocations. It will continue for one hour; but it is also designed for those who may find it inconvenient to remain more than 5 or 10 minutes, as well as for those who can spare the whole hour. The necessary interruption will be slight, because anticipated; and those who are in haste can often expedite their business engagements by halting to lift up their voices to the Throne of Grace in humble, grateful prayer.

All are cordially invited to attend.[17]

At noon on September 23, 1857, Lanphier opened the door to the room, and awaited those who might respond. Finally, at 12:30, someone ascended the stairs, and then another, until six people were in attendance and the meeting began. On the following Wednesday twenty came, and the next week that number doubled. Two days after this Fulton Street prayer meeting began, the Bank of Pennsylvania failed in Philadelphia, sending shock waves through the nation's financial community. As economic and social conditions grew worse the meeting was scheduled for every day. When that happened Lanphier found that the room would not hold all those attending, so the prayer meeting moved to the nearby John Street Methodist Church. Astonishingly, the Fulton Street prayer meeting continued daily far into the twentieth century.

A Growing Interest in Prayer

The city of New York was a center for the Third Great Awakening of 1858. It was then a well-churched city of predominantly evangelical Protestants, still quite inclined toward religious values. There were fifty Episcopal churches, forty-one Presbyterian, thirty-four Methodist, twenty-nine Baptist, twenty-three Dutch Reformed, seven Congregationalist, seven Lutheran, five Reformed Presbyterian, four Associate Presbyterian, and more than seventy others.[18] Finney had declared that New York "seemed to be on such a wave of prosperity as to be the death of revival effort." But this attitude changed overnight. The financial crisis triggered by the crash of the New York stock market shook people out of their complacency and served as the catalyst for the awakening. A frequent statement was, "We have had instruction until we are hardened; it is time for us to pray."

Gradually, the first effects of the awakening became public. One Brooklyn church reported seventy-five conversions during January, and in the same month in the Hudson River town of Yonkers nearly ninety were brought to faith.[19] By February the secular press began to notice that something unusual was occurring. At that time there was great rivalry among the New York papers, and each editor was looking for any newsworthy item. Horace Greeley, a pioneer in sensational newspaper editing, gave extensive coverage to the awakening in his *New York Daily Tribune*. On February 10, 1858, the following appeared:

> The Hour of Prayer.
> Some two or three years ago, a daily prayer-meeting was started in the lower portion of the city. . . . A few months ago, after a long silence, this meeting was revived at the Consistory of the North Dutch Church at the corner of Fulton and William Streets, and has been crowded every day since the commencement of the financial panic.

Another meeting has been established up town in the Ninth Street Dutch Reformed Church and was opened yesterday at noon. Upwards of two hundred persons were present. . . . These meetings are anti-denominational. The advancement of sectarian views is not tolerated in any form.[20]

The newspapers also noted that there was no fanaticism, no hysteria, nor even any preaching at these meetings; instead, everyone felt an irresistible urge to pray. *The National Intelligencer* of Washington, D.C., reported that in New York "a religious interest has been growing in the midst of the rowdyism everywhere so long prevalent."[21] A week later, on March 11, 1858, the same paper stated that "religious revivals were never more numerous or effective than at present."[22] And in New York City the arch-rival paper of Horace Greeley's *Tribune,* James Gordon Bennett's *New York Herald,* stated, "Satan is busy all morning in Wall Street among the brokers, and all the afternoon and evening the churches are crowded with saints who gambled in the morning."[23]

Where churches were not available or too small, theaters sometimes were used for the prayer services. Burton's Theater on Chambers Street was engaged for noonday prayer meetings by merchants in the vicinity. Mr. Burton, the owner, asked to be prayed for. Each day, half an hour before the time set for the service, the theater was packed to capacity, with others waiting outside. The street in front was crowded with vehicles, and the excitement was overwhelming. The *New York Times* reported that on March 19 Henry Ward Beecher (1813–1887), pastor of the large Plymouth Church of Brooklyn, led three thousand people in devotions at the theater. While he was reading Scripture, Beecher was interrupted by singing from an overflowing crowd at a prayer meeting in an adjoining barroom. He then led the people in thanksgiving that such a thing could happen in a bar.[24]

The most sensational conversion in March was that of Orville Gardner, a well-known boxer notable for his brutality in the ring. Gardner's public testimony had a widespread effect, especially on those of the lower classes. Meanwhile, all of the New York papers gave extensive coverage to the awakening, sending reporters to the meetings who wrote descriptions of what was happening. Bennett and Greeley continued to vie for revival coverage. In April, Greeley's *Tribune* devoted an entire issue of the weekly edition to the revival. With all of this coverage, some prayer meetings that had attracted only small numbers began getting huge crowds.[25]

By April more than twenty prayer meetings were being conducted throughout New York City. Still the Fulton Street meeting continued to be one of the best attended. It achieved a far-flung reputation as a place where prayers obtained answers. People began to mail in prayer requests daily, some from as far away as Canada, the British Isles, Switzerland, and Germany. At one point the following letter was received:

To the Officiating Minister
at the Union Prayer Meeting, Fulton Street.

Dear Sir:

The Mayor has directed me to enclose to you the within requests received at his office, with the wish expressed to forward them as above directed.

I am, Respectfully,
J. B. Auld
Mayor's Clerk.[26]

The conduct of the meetings was similar throughout the nation. A leader, often a layperson competent to speak before a crowd, was appointed. His purpose was twofold: to guard against disorder and to maintain the freedom of the meeting. A hymn would be sung, and then the leader would pray. Someone would read a portion of Scripture, and then the meeting was opened for prayers and exhortations, with strict observance of the rules. The leader would read several requests, and then prayers would be directed toward those objects or persons. If anyone injected a sectarian note or inappropriate idea, the leader would state that this was simply a prayer meeting and that the person was out of order. At five minutes before the stated time for dismissal the leader would announce the closing hymn, and if there was one present, request a clergyman to give the benediction. Posted signs guided the conduct.

Ignoring Sectarian Differences

The humble and reverent spirit was disarming, even to those who initially opposed the prayer meetings. As Smith writes, "Distinctions between the sects and between ministers and laymen were ignored. The joyous liberty of the camp meeting 'love feast' was thus transferred to an urban setting."[27] Sectarian differences were set aside and Christians cooperated so wholeheartedly that Methodists, Baptists, Lutherans, Congregationalists, and New School Presbyterians worked together, alongside Episcopalians, Old School Presbyterians, and even Universalists and Unitarians. The pastor of the largest Old School Presbyterian church in New York, James W. Alexander, was at first antagonistic to the revival. Gradually, however, his opinion changed, admitting to a friend that "The openness of thousands to doctrine, reproof, etc., is undeniable. Our lecture is crowded unendurably, many going away. The publisher of Spurgeon's sermons says he has sold a hundred thousand. . . . You may rest assured there is a great awakening among us."[28] Converts poured into the New York churches. Early in the awakening, on March 14, 1858, the Thirteenth Presbyterian Church received 127 new members.[29] By May, one journal calculated that there were fifty thousand new converts in New York City alone.[30]

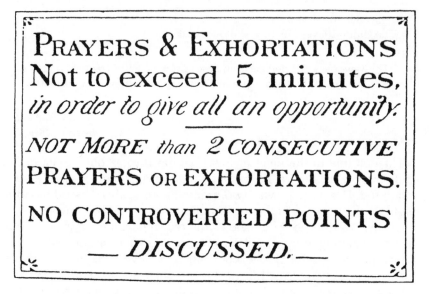

PRAYERS & EXHORTATIONS
Not to exceed 5 minutes,
in order to give all an opportunity.

NOT MORE than 2 *CONSECUTIVE*
PRAYERS OR EXHORTATIONS.

NO CONTROVERTED POINTS
— DISCUSSED.—

A sign governing conduct at a New York City prayer meeting during the 1857 awakening

A National Movement

While Manhattan and Brooklyn provided much of the momentum at the beginning, it would be a mistake to portray the awakening as exclusively urban and regional in nature. Finney recorded in his *Memoirs,* "I recollect in one of our prayer meetings in Boston that winter a gentleman arose and said: 'I am from Omaha the capital of Nebraska. On my journey east I have found a continuous prayer meeting all the way. We call it,' said he, 'about two thousand miles from Omaha to Boston; and here was a prayer meeting about two thousand miles in extent.' "[31] Smaller cities and towns made the Third Great Awakening truly national in scope. Timothy Smith has written, "In the record of the climactic five months from February to June, two facts stand out. Small towns and rural communities were as powerfully affected as the great cities; and support and participation came from major portions of every Protestant sect."[32]

Ohio provides a good example, out of many, of the breadth of this movement. *The Cincinnati Daily Commercial* of April 2, 1858, stated that "Religious excitement in the city is unabated, and the churches are becoming more popular every day with citizens unaccustomed to modes of grace."[33] Cleveland was especially involved; out of its population of forty thousand, the united attendance at the daily prayer meetings throughout the city was about two thousand.[34] The most startling of awak-

178

enings in public high schools was in Cleveland, where all but two students converted.[35] Ohio's dedication to revival and prayer was encouraged by church authorities. The bishop of the Episcopal Church, Charles Pettit McIlvaine, gave over most of his annual diocesan report to a review of revival blessings, adding, "Pray for our whole church, that no part of it may be unvisited in these 'times of refreshing from the presence of the Lord.' "[36] Throughout Ohio, two hundred towns reported a total of about twelve thousand conversions within a three month period.[37]

Everywhere in the nation, similar stories were published. From Salem, New York, near Saratoga Springs, came the following report:

> Without any alarming event, without any extraordinary preaching, or any special effort or other means that might be supposed peculiarly adapted to interest the minds of the people, there has within a short time past been, in several towns and villages in Washington and Warren Counties, and towns and villages along the western parts of the State of Vermont, a revival so extraordinary as to attract the attention of all classes of the community. In one town, over a hundred have been brought to conviction and conversion, and the glorious work is still going on; they expect the whole town will be converted—for this they pray. This work does not appear to be confined to the churches; hundreds are converted at prayer meetings, in private homes, in the workshops, and at their work in the fields. Men of fortune and fashion, lawyers, physicians, and tradesmen and indeed all classes, ages, and sexes, are the subject of it.[38]

New England was especially moved. The Congregationalists added 11,744 members during 1858. Two hundred sixty towns and small cities declared a total of more than ten thousand conversions in several months.[39] The towns of Winchester and Holliston each reported about 250 conversions. In New Bedford, one in twenty of the population claimed to be converted in the revival, and similar awakening struck Haverhill and Lynn. In Springfield, nearly every minister held inquiry meetings. Maine and Rhode Island were similarly moved. In Rutland, Vermont, two hundred people were brought to salvation, seventy in a single meeting. Yale claimed that forty-five seniors, sixty-two juniors, sixty sophomores, and thirty-seven freshmen had experienced conversion, and that the college had experienced an awakening where, overall, it was "impossible to estimate the conversions." The president of Amherst College stated that nearly every student there claimed to have received God's grace and regeneration.[40]

New Jersey experienced a moving as early as October 1857. Near Trenton and Princeton several towns claimed that more than one hundred people had been converted before the New Year.[41] By March 1858 the revival in New Jersey was as powerful as anywhere. Newark, with a population of about seventy thousand, recorded almost three thousand conversions in a few months. In New Brunswick, 177 joined the Methodist Church, and in Trenton, the Methodists gained more than seventeen hundred.

The movement swept across Pennsylvania and was equally powerful west of the Allegheny and Appalachian Mountains. Within a few months, five hundred towns reported a total of fifteen thousand conversions.[42] *The Presbyterian* announced that the entire West was involved, with powerful revivals in Indianapolis, Chicago, Louisville, Detroit, St. Louis, Dubuque, Cincinnati, and Cleveland. Kentucky, Ohio, Missouri, Iowa, Wisconsin, Indiana, Michigan, and Illinois felt the effects.[43] *The Western Christian Advocate* stated ecstatically that the West truly was being won for Christ. It said that forty-two Methodist pastors had claimed 4,384 conversions in three months, more than seven hundred in one town.[44]

The city of Chicago, with almost one hundred thousand citizens in 1858, underwent an unusually long period of spiritual interest. Since 1850, it had grown from only thirty thousand into a noisy, sprawling center of trade and industry, with eleven railroad lines radiating from it. A Chicago correspondent of the *New York Daily Tribune,* on February 17, 1858, gave an unvarnished description of the city that was fast becoming a giant: "Within a dozen years, men have come together on a low swamp of the lake, where there was no foundation for houses, and from the midst of a mammoth mudpuddle have raised a large, wealthy, and wicked city. . . . The city looks as though a horde of wandering Tartars with movable houses had come along and set them down for the night."[45]

The churches of Chicago united for solemn prayer services. By March the excitement caused the press to notice, and on March 13 the *Chicago Daily Press* carried a full column of religious news entitled "The Religious Awakening: Its Manifestations in Chicago." In addition to the local meetings, the huge Metropolitan Theater was leased, and on March 24 the *Daily Press* stated that twelve hundred were gathering daily. The next day, the same paper declared that it was so "unusual and almost unprecedented that the secular press should be called upon to refer beyond a brief notice to religious affairs in the community," and said that the number coming daily to the Metropolitan Theater had jumped to almost two thousand. A few days later, the *Daily Press* said that "nothing like the present general interest has ever occurred in the history of Chicago," and it commented positively on the cordial cooperation of all the different Christian groups.[46]

In Philadelphia and New York City, low-church Episcopalians were led in the awakening by Stephen Higginson Tyng and his sons, pastors of enormous congregations in those cities. In Philadelphia great prayer services were held not only in churches but also in the American Mechanics Auditorium, Handel and Haydn Hall, and Jayne's Hall. The first prayer meeting was conducted in the Union Methodist Episcopal Church on November 23, 1857. On February 3, 1858, space was acquired in the larger Jayne's Hall. At first only a small room was used, but on March 10 the meeting moved to the twenty-five-hundred-seat main hall. The place was soon filled, and the galleries and other areas were opened; eventually over six thousand filled every part of the place each noon.[47] When Dudley A. Tyng gave an evangelistic invitation at one meeting, the response was so great that one observer said no sermon of modern times had produced so many inquirers.[48] With warmer weather on the way, it was thought wise to buy a great canvas tent and transfer some of the services there. The tent was erected in a central location and opened on May 1. During the next four months a total of 150,000 people crowded into the tent night after night.[49] The churches of Philadelphia—Episcopalian, Baptist, Presbyterian, Lutheran, Methodist, and many of the Quakers—were all involved and received a large harvest of new members during the next year.

In Boston, unusual characteristics manifested themselves because of the constant theological controversies that agitated the city. Frequent disputes between the Unitarians and the orthodox had produced the most volatile radicals and the most rigid conservatives to be found anywhere in America. For this reason, the awakening was not expected to take solid root there. But that assumption proved to be incorrect. By March, the awakening in Boston had spread generally. The Boston correspondent of the *National Intelligencer* reported "that there are several New England towns in which not a single adult person can be found unconverted."[50] The Boston *Daily Transcript* on March 26 noted: "On account of the crowd that daily throngs Father Mason's chapel, in North Street, unable to gain admittance, Father Taylor has thrown open the Bethel in North Square, and a Prayer Meeting will be held daily in that place from 12 to 1 o'clock."[51]

The meetings were staggered during the day to fit work schedules. South Baptist Church held a daily service from 8 to 9 A.M.; Old South Chapel had two services, 8:30 to 9:30 and noon to 1 P.M.; a number of churches held services at noon, and others convened after work, including one at the YMCA from 5:30 till 6:30 P.M. Another held explicitly evangelistic night meetings where inquirers could be counseled in a more leisurely fashion than was possible during working hours. Perhaps the most amazing aspect was the interest of Unitarians, some of whose clergy organized daily prayer meetings in their churches.

The Rural South

Several writers on the Third Great Awakening have suggested that the South was not affected as greatly as the East, New England, and the West. But other authorities argue that the effect was real—only different. Warren A. Candler has written, "In the South there were no large cities, but a widely scattered rural population, remote from both the perils and privileges of urban life. The results in that part of the country, therefore, were not heralded in the press nor flashed over the telegraph wires. But they were not less abundant and blessed. And they were achieved in the main by the churches and in the churches."[52] Candler cites the growth record of his own denomination, the Methodist Church South. In 1858, 43,388 new members were admitted; in 1859, 21,852; and in 1860, 36,182—a total for those three years of 101,422. "Its sister churches in the same section were proportionately prosperous, especially the great Baptist denomination, which divides so nearly with the Methodists the rural communities of the South."[53]

Effects Abroad

While the Third Great Awakening was at its peak in America for only nine months (October 1857 to June 1858), its influence continued unabated for years in Ulster, Scotland, Wales, and England. Reports of the happenings in the United States were read eagerly in the British Isles, especially in the large cities. Awakenings began in Glasgow, Belfast, London, and elsewhere in the summer and fall of 1858, and continued for several years. This happened despite frequent opposition from the British press, which was generally unfavorable toward the revival. *The Times* of London took an especially sneering attitude, intentionally distorting the facts about the awakening.

Aftermath of the Third Great Awakening

In America the most apparent result of the awakening was the great wave of converts that injected new vitality and enthusiasm into churches. Frank G. Beardsley, in his *History of American Revivals*, estimates that between three hundred thousand and 1 million people were converted as a result of the revival.[54] Finney, in his *Memoirs*, estimated five hundred thousand in the North alone.[55] J. Edwin Orr, who has thoroughly researched this awakening, believes 1 million is probably closer. This agrees with the calculations of Candler.[56]

Of the 5 million evangelical Christians in America in 1858, about 411,000 (better than 8 percent) joined the churches in that year alone. And a large ingathering was going on even before the awakening came to full force. The following figures show some of the growth:[57]

182

Baptists:

> 1857: American, 63,506 (double the annual average of the previous ten years)

> 1858: American, 92,243; Free-Will Baptists, 5,714 (the equivalent of over 10 percent of denominational membership); all major groups, 111,647; all small groups, 130,000

> 1859: American, 72,080

Methodists:

> 1858: All groups, almost 200,000; Methodist Episcopal (North), 135,517; Methodist Episcopal (South), 43,388

Presbyterians:

> 1858: New School and Old School combined, 34,650; Dutch Reformed and other Presbyterian groups, 10,065

Congregationalists:

> 1858: 21,582

Protestant Episcopal:

> 1858: 14,822

Another beneficial result was that with the many student conversions at colleges, large numbers of enthusiastic students entered the ministry and foreign missions.

The Young Men's Christian Association became vitally involved in the awakening. In such cities as Chicago and Philadelphia, YMCA-sponsored prayer meetings drew large crowds. For years this specifically evangelical Christian organization had provided religious training and a wholesome atmosphere for underprivileged young men who lived and worked in the cities. The mid-century YMCA was closely tied to the churches, with clergymen active at all levels. Typical of YMCAs across the nation, in 1858 the Philadelphia YMCA prayer meeting drew more than three hundred daily. It began at noon, but people would start gathering at 11 A.M. to be assured of a seat. An evangelistic campaign using a tent could hold twelve hundred people. The Chicago YMCA was a training school for laypersons. Moody found it to be a home away from home while he worked in Chicago. He received his first opportunities for Christian service there and rose through its ranks until he was president.

Coming on the eve of the Civil War, the Awakening of 1858 was unique. It was led by laymen, with an emphasis on prayer rather than preaching, and it brought about a vast number of conversions. God seemed to be strengthening his people for the great trial that would begin in 1861. But the Awakening did not end with the opening shots of the Civil War.

During the conflict, both the Northern and Southern armies experienced awakenings in the camps.

Onset of the Civil War

By April 11, 1861, eight states had seceded to form the Confederate States of America. Fort Sumter, a Union garrison on an island in the harbor of Charleston, South Carolina, was deep in Confederate territory. Sumter's commander, Major Robert Anderson, knew his situation was hopeless. On April 11, General Pierre G. T. Beauregard sent to Major Anderson a demand of surrender. At 3:30 A.M. the following morning the note arrived: "[Beauregard] will open fire . . . in one hour from this time." Anderson, like many other officers on both sides, was a Christian. He shook hands with the Confederate messengers, saying, "If we never meet in the world again, God grant that we may meet in the next." Promptly at 4:30 A.M., Confederate Captain George S. James pulled the lanyard of a ten-inch mortar, sending a huge shell arcing into the air toward the fort. Some forty thousand shells later, at 2:30 P.M. on April 13, Anderson surrendered the fort. No lives had been lost and the wounded were few on either side, but the Civil War had begun.

In the early stages of the war, there was little evidence of religion in the soldiers' lives. When the troops left their homes, they seemed to leave their Christianity behind as well. In the camps, day-to-day life was so repetitious and dull that the soldiers were frequently tempted to do wild things. Drunkenness, profanity, sexual licentiousness, gambling, and thievery became common. The hearts of the soldiers grew bitter as the war and its miseries dragged on, especially when a battle was lost or one army was forced to flee to escape the enemy.

The agonies of conflict were everywhere. One officer described the battlefield after the fight at Murfreesboro (or Stone's River), Tennessee, on December 31, 1862:

> Here are sights to sicken the bravest hearts . . . One [soldier] lies upon his face literally biting the ground, his rigid fingers fastened firmly into the gory sod; and another with upturned face, open eyes, knit brow, compressed lips, and clenched fists, displays all the desperation of vengeance imprinted on his clay. Dissevered heads, arms, legs, are scattered everywhere; and the coagulated pools of blood gleam ghastly in the morning sun.[58]

After the hideous battles, troops often spent weeks doing nothing, waiting for another engagement. Besides homesickness and boredom, cold rainy weather depressed privates and generals alike. Christians complained that Sundays were like any other day, especially in the Union

A sketch from Harper's Weekly *of a Sunday worship service
at General McClellan's headquarters (Courtesy of the Billy Graham Center Museum)*

Army. Several Union generals, such as Oliver O. Howard and George McClellan, tried to make a difference, but for the most part military duties were carried out as if Sunday meant little. When the Union suffered its great defeat at the first Battle of Bull Run on July 21, 1861, General Howard blamed it on the decision to attack on a Sunday. McClelland agreed and ordered that the Sabbath henceforth be observed throughout the Union Army, with services held whenever military demands did not absolutely prevent worship and rest.

Christians in the armies and at home sensed the lack of spiritual influences in the military. The entire nation had just received a soul-stirring baptism of the Holy Spirit's power in the Revival of 1858. Was all of the power and grace of Almighty God now to be forgotten, as if it had never been experienced? Christians prayed as never before. Multitudes of soldiers—hardly more than boys—were searching for confidence and hope. Some had come from homes, now far away, where Christian faith was strong. But the temptations of army life and the huge number of war casualties brought bitterness and hopelessness.

Prior to the Civil War, it was rare to find chaplains in America's armies. A number of men, such as Timothy Dwight and James Caldwell, had served as chaplains under Washington. But after the Revolutionary War, the service of chaplains dwindled. During the first years of the Civil War, however, leaders such as Generals Robert E. Lee and McClellan recognized the need and sought clergymen who could provide spiritual direction for the two armies. Hundreds of pastors temporarily left their churches to meet this need.

Spiritual Work among the Soldiers

The first evidence of awakening among the soldiers seems to have come in 1862. Although later there were powerful revivals in the Northern armies, it was in the Confederate armies that the earliest movings of the Holy Spirit were felt over a wide area. Chaplain E. J. Meynardie—who was working at the camp on Sullivan's Island near Charleston, South Carolina—reported that "on Thursday evening, 25th [of September], the religious interest, which for some time had been quite apparent, became so deep and manifest that I determined to hold a series of meetings, during which, up to last night, ninety-three applied for membership in the various branches of the Church, nearly all of whom profess conversion. Every night the church at which we worship was densely crowded, and obvious seriousness pervaded the congregation."[59]

Similar things were happening to one Union regiment, the 63rd Pennsylvania. After the Northern defeat at First Bull Run in July 1861—when the war began in earnest—a spirit of discouragement came over the troops. Recognizing that the best antidote to that was spiritual revitalization, Chaplain James Marks bought a tent and began services, continuing this for months. Hundreds of soldiers soon professed conversion.

After a number of costly and desperate battles such as Shiloh and Second Bull Run, any levity or irreligion among the troops on both sides was swept away. The war was becoming more serious and prolonged. But after the major campaigns at Gettysburg, Chattanooga, and Vicksburg in 1863, evangelistic services for the troops became almost commonplace. Many letters sent home to waiting loved ones tell of spiritual changes among the troops. One lieutenant testified: "I am glad to state that I am a better man than when you saw me last. There are about two thousand officers here, and I have never seen so great a change in the morals of any set of men as has been here in the last four months."[60] The Rev. Neil Gillis gave this report from an army camp on the Chattahoochee River,

I never heard or read of anything like the revival at this place. The conversions were powerful, and some of them very remarkable. One man told me that he was converted at the very hour in which his sister was writing him a letter on her knees praying that he might be saved at that moment. Another, who was a backslider, said to me at the altar that his case was hopeless. I tried to encourage him; discovered hope spring up in his countenance . . . he bounded to his feet and began to point others to the Cross with most remarkable success.[61]

The deep faith evident in the lives of many high-ranking officers, and the Christian dedication common among the enlisted men, made possible the broad evangelistic efforts and great revivals that relieved these dark days. J. William Jones, a chaplain in the Army of Northern Virginia, later recalled a scene he had witnessed:

> Let us go some bright Sabbath morning to that cluster of tents in the grove across the Massaponax, not far from Hamilton's Crossing. Seated on the rude logs, or on the ground, may be seen fifteen hundred or two thousand men, with upturned faces, eagerly drinking in the truths of the Gospel. That reverent worshipper that kneels in the dust during prayer, or listens with sharpened attention and moist eyes as the preacher delivers his message, is our loved Commander-in-Chief, General Robert E. Lee; that devout worshipper who sits at his side, gives his personal attention to the seating of the multitude, looks so supremely happy as he sees the soldiers thronging to hear the Gospel, and listens so attentively to the preaching, is 'Stonewall' Jackson; those "wreaths and stars" which cluster around are worn by some of the most illustrious generals of that army; and all through the congregation the 'stars' and 'bars' mingle with the rough garb of the 'unknown heroes' of the rank and file who never quail amid the leaden and iron hail of battle, but are not ashamed to 'tremble' under the power of God's truth. I need not say that this is Jackson's headquarters, and the scene I have pictured one of frequent occurrence.[62]

Lee was a man of sterling character. He served gallantly in the Mexican War and later became superintendent of West Point. In 1861 he refused chief command of the Union forces and became a general for the Confederacy. Consistently throughout the war, he worshipped with his men and vigorously supported the work of the chaplains. The following was General Lee's order to his army for the observance of a fast-day on Friday, April 8, 1864:

> The commanding general invites the army to join in the observance of the day. . . . All military duties, except such as are absolutely necessary, will be suspended. The chaplains are desired to hold services in their regiments and brigades. The officers and men are requested to attend. Soldiers! let us humble ourselves before the Lord our God, asking through Christ the forgiveness of our sins, beseeching the aid of the God of our forefathers in the defense of our homes and our liberties, thanking Him for His past blessings, and imploring their continuance upon our cause and our people.
>
> R. E. Lee, General.[63]

With dedicated Christian officers such as Lee, "Stonewall" Jackson, J. E. B. Stuart, William Pendleton, Leonidas Polk, John B. Gordon, and A. H. Colquitt, it is little wonder that there was a great deal of evangelism in the Confederate Army, and many revivals.

As soon as the war began, the YMCA prepared to send representatives to army camps to distribute tracts and Bibles. An offshoot of the YMCA, the United States Christian Commission, became its evangelistic arm in 1861. George H. Stuart, a resolute YMCA leader, served as president of the Christian Commission and recruited a team of several thousand dependable men to minister to the troops as the armies moved. Among these, and typical of their dedication, was the young Moody. Their main tasks were: to undergo hardships with the soldiers, to distribute Bibles and other reading materials, to witness in every available way, to write letters to the parents of wounded men, and, particularly, to go into the hospitals of both armies and comfort the wounded and dying. Stuart chose William E. Boardman, a Presbyterian pastor, as executive secretary to organize the overall work. Almost fourteen hundred clergymen were recruited to work alongside the lay ministers. The clergy were also to assist the regular chaplains, conducting services in the camps whenever they were called upon.

In addition to the work of the YMCA and the Christian Commission, Protestant denominations and other agencies carried forward the work of evangelism. Among them were the Bible Society of the Confederate States and the Evangelical Tract Society. Eleven million Bibles and tracts were distributed in the first year, and by 1863 the report of one agency—the Southern Methodist Episcopal Soldiers' Tract Association—showed receipts of $95,456, and distribution of 7 million pages of tracts, 45,000 hymn books, 15,000 soldiers' almanacs, 15,000 Bibles, 15,000 Bible readings for soldiers, 50,000 copies of *The Soldier's Paper,* and 20,000 copies of *The Army and Navy Herald.* And this was only one agency.[64]

As the revivals in the Northern and Southern armies gathered in intensity, one Confederate worker wrote,

I was assured by the post chaplain (Rev. G. B. Taylor) that a great and blessed reformation had been effected in the hospitals. He said that in the early stages of the war it was very difficult to secure the attention of the men to the preached word. Many would sit with hats on during religious services, engage in conversation, smoke, walk about, etc. But now the room is filled with earnest, solemn, and often weeping listeners, while multitudes eagerly embrace any and every opportunity for securing the prayers of God's people. What is stated by this chaplain of his hospitals is substantially true of almost every hospital (and of many camps) throughout the Confederacy.[65]

General Lee is depicted attending a soldiers' prayer meeting.
(From J. W. Jones, Christ in the Camp)

Further Military Revivals

In the Union Army of the Potomac, awakenings began during the winter of 1863–64. A number of regiments erected chapel tents and churches
for prayer meetings and services. In a religious journal one writer con-
jectured that the spirituality of the Union army might win the entire
nation for Christ! General McAllister stated that he had never seen a better interest in spiritual things among his troops.

At approximately the same time, the fall of 1863, what was later called
the "Great Revival" spread through the Army of Northern Virginia.
Approximately seven thousand men, roughly 10 percent of Lee's troops,
were converted. Evangelism continued in a determined way until Ulysses
Grant's forces attacked in May 1864.

William W. Bennett, president of the Southern Methodist Episcopal
Soldiers' Tract Association, believed that the revivals in the Confederate armies were stronger than those in the Union forces. In his extensive
travels following the movement of the troops, Bennett thought the Con-

federate camps truly "a school of Christ," where men facing danger would actually become better men. In his book *A Narrative of the Great Revival Which Prevailed in the Southern Armies,* Bennett wrote, "In the army of General Lee, while it lay on the upper Rappahannock, the revival flame swept through every corps, division, brigade, and regiment. One of our chaplains said, 'The whole army is a vast field, ready and ripe to the harvest. . . . The susceptibility of the soldiery to the gospel is wonderful, and, doubtful as the remark may appear, the military camp is most favorable to the work of revival.' "[66]

S. M. Cherry, central distributing agent for the Soldiers' Tract Association for the army camped in Georgia, reported in May 1864,

> The army was in the midst of a most extensive revival at the beginning of the month. Protracted meetings were being held in almost every brigade; thousands of our soldiers were thronging our rude camp altars, hundreds were giving their hearts to God, and scores were nightly asking for certificates of Church membership. About 300 were baptized on the first day of May, and the great work seemed to be growing in depth and interest all the while. . . . Not less than five hundred professed to find peace in believing the first week of the month, and two thousand were publicly seeking salvation. But these interesting meetings have been interrupted by the advance of the enemy, who has despoiled our country and desecrated our arbors and altars consecrated to the worship of God.[67]

By 1864, powerful revivals were reported throughout the Confederate armies. In Tennessee, Atticus G. Haygood, missionary to Bryan's Brigade, wrote to the Knoxville *Register:*

> I write you this hasty note to let your readers know that we are in the midst of a glorious revival. . . . In every brigade of this grand old division there is a deep and wide-spread religious interest. I have seen more excitement; but profounder feeling, as manifested in the great crowds that flock to every service, the reverent attention given to the preaching of the Word, the large number of earnest penitents that crowd our rude altars, I have not seen, at home or in the army. . . . I have attended meetings in three brigades in this division of Longstreet's Corps . . . and in all I have found the most remarkable religious awakening.[68]

Workers at first wondered if all this religious concern was simply because of the extreme danger the soldiers were facing. Was it genuine? Would this religious interest have a practical effect on the lives of the soldiers? But again and again they became convinced that the soldiers' faith was bearing fruit in concern for others. J. William Jones related one remarkable instance illustrating this:

In the winter of 1863–64 the Young Men's Christian Association of Posey's Mississippi Brigade led off in a movement which was followed by a number of other brigades, and deserves to be written in letters of gold on one of the brightest pages of our country's history. They solemnly resolved *to fast one day in every week in order that they might send that day's rations to the suffering poor of the city of Richmond.* Think of it, church members, who, in these days of plenty, plead poverty as an excuse for giving nothing to the cause of Christ; here were these poor soldiers (away from home, and many of them cut off from all communication from home), receiving only eleven dollars per month *in Confederate currency,* never getting more than half rations, and very frequently not that, voluntarily *fasting one day in the week* (poor fellows, they were often compelled to fast) in order to send that day's rations to God's poor in the city, for whose defence they were so freely and so heroically offering and sacrificing their lives.[69]

Jones wrote that he had seen soldiers, after a battle, "despite their almost complete exhaustion, going over the ground to hunt up and care for the wounded of the enemy," and taking enemy soldiers to their own hospitals where they might receive medical care, "sharing with them their scant rations."[70]

Examples of selfless courage and dedication to Christ in both armies continued throughout the war. The best estimates of conversions in the Union forces ranged between one hundred and two hundred thousand, between 5 percent and 10 percent of the Northern army. As for the Confederate armies, Bennett wrote:

Up to January, 1865, it was estimated that nearly *one hundred and fifty thousand* soldiers had been converted during the progress of the war, and it was believed that fully one-third of all the soldiers in the field were praying men, and members of some branch of the Christian Church. A large proportion of the higher offices were men of faith and prayer, and many others, though not professedly religious, were moral and respectful to all the religious services, and confessed the value of the revival in promoting the efficiency of the army.[71]

A conservative total of the converts for both armies would be three hundred thousand men. "But figures cannot, of course, give a tithe of the results of a great revival," Jones wrote. "The bringing back of backsliders, the quickening of the zeal, and faith, and general consecration of God's people, the comfort, the joy, the peace, the strength for hardships, privations, sufferings, trials, temptations—*these* cannot be *counted,* but are really of far more value than mere numbers of professed converts."[72] In both the North and South, a large number of ex-soldiers entered the ministry.

191

*M*oody: *Perfecter of Urban Evangelism*

G eorge Whitefield, for all his widespread ministry, remained an itinerant evangelist. Charles Finney succeeded in making evangelism a profession. But for a nation that was rapidly industrializing, Dwight Lyman Moody gave evangelism a different cast, organizing and unifying campaigns with the methods of the business world. One friend said of Moody's 1876 New York campaign, "The Hippodrome work is a vast business enterprise, organized and conducted by business men, who put their money into it on business principles, for the purpose of saving souls."[1]

Much had changed since Finney's heyday in the 1820s and 1830s. Just as Whitefield had taken his enormous crowds outside because no building could hold them, Finney had to contend with cramped facilities. But by 1880 the spiritual climate and larger facilities made possible evangelistic enterprises on a scale Finney could not have imagined, though he pioneered many of the techniques. The desire of church members to

The Moody Family in Massachusetts, around 1860.
Dwight stands in the center of the back row.
(Moody Bible Institute Archives)

reach the lower classes, general acceptance of mass evangelism, increased cooperation between denominations, rapid urbanization, growth in lay involvement, widespread use of print media, and vastly improved transportation and communication all allowed mass evangelism to reach far greater numbers than ever before.

Immediately after his conversion, Moody began preparing for a life of Christian service. As his first major endeavor he chose one of the toughest parts of Chicago, "the Sands," to establish a Sunday school. Moody concluded that no one else cared for the souls in this notorious slum section. It was the red-light district of the booming young city, filled with tumble-down shanties, saloons, and gambling halls. In the spring of 1859, when Moody was twenty-two, he secured use of the North Market Hall, a city-owned market with a large, dingy hall on the second floor. Although hardly conducive to worship or study, it was large enough for Moody's vision.

Moody persevered in filling the huge place with hundreds of children. Not knowing the conventional methods used to attract children, he simply applied common sense. On one occasion he offered a squirrel in a cage as a prize to the child who could bring in the largest number of friends. Recruiting pupils was only the beginning. "I would have to be up by six o'clock to get the hall ready for Sunday school," he related. "Every Saturday night a German society held a dance there, and I had to roll out beer kegs, sweep up sawdust, clean up generally, and arrange the chairs."[2] The urchins' initial scorn was soon replaced by curiosity, and then by eager attendance. By degrees, the school increased to five hundred children, and in time to fifteen hundred, the largest attendance at a Sunday school in Chicago. Abraham Lincoln's visit to the school, on his way to Washington to begin his first term as president, gave it favorable publicity and won for it public acceptance. One teacher described a typical Sunday:

> The scholars were bubbling over with mischief and exuberance of vitality and sorely tried the patience of the teachers; but the singing was a vent for their spirits, and such singing I had never heard before. The boys who sold papers in the street had an indescribable lung power, and the rest seemed not far behind. . . . It was no easy task to govern such a boisterous crowd, but the teachers seemed to interest their classes, and the exercises passed off with great enthusiasm.
>
> At the close of the school Mr. Moody took his place at the door and seemed to know personally every boy and girl; he shook hands and had a smile and a cheery word for each. They crowded about him tumultuously, and his arm must have ached many a time after those meetings. It was easy to see the hold he had on those young lives, and why they were drawn to that place week after week. The institution was a veritable hive of activity—meetings almost every evening, with occasional picnics and sociables, and services on the Sabbath that occupied most of the day.[3]

Moody always kept his pockets full of candy when he toured the Sands looking for prospective pupils. But even a presidential visit was not enough to secure for his school the consent of all parents. Many fathers were indolent loafers, with a great suspicion of visiting missionaries.

On one occasion Moody was greatly irritated by some Irish Catholics sent to cause disturbances. He went to the top to rectify the situation—to Bishop Duggan, the prelate of the diocese. The maid who answered the door doubted Moody would be granted an audience. But stepping over the threshold, he said cheerfully that he would wait until the bishop was at leisure. Eventually the bishop appeared in the hall, and Moody briefly stated his mission, asking if the bishop would use his influence to stop the interference. The bishop replied that it would be easier for Moody to work among these people if he were a Catholic. Moody countered that then he could no longer work among Protestants. Not at all, came the episcopal reply. Did the bishop mean that Moody could pray with a Protestant if he became a Catholic? asked the missionary innocently. Oh yes, that was indeed possible, the bishop responded. Well, said Moody, that was very good, but would the *bishop* pray with a Protestant? Again the answer was affirmative. Then, the missionary added once more, would the bishop kneel and join him in prayer that Moody might be led aright in this matter? Bishop Duggan, no doubt startled at this turn of events, did as Moody asked, and there were no further disturbances at the Sunday school. Moody did not join the bishop's fold, however, but the bishop must also have breathed a sigh of relief that he had not been recruited to teach a class in Mr. Moody's Sunday school![4]

Moody knew his limits in education and left the teaching to those better qualified. He recruited, administrated, and disciplined. Before the lessons, he would take control of the large roomful of toughs with names like Red Eye, Madden the Butcher, Darby the Cobbler, Black Stove Pipe, and Rag-Breeches Cadet.[5] One young troublemaker repeatedly created disturbances. Moody had decided never to throw anyone out, but he recognized that—grace having failed—recourse to law might at times be necessary. On this occasion he turned to John V. Farwell, the wealthy businessman who superintended the school, and said, "If you see me go for him and take him to the anteroom, ask the school to rise and sing a *very loud hymn* until we return." Soon sacred strains muffled the noise of a loud battle. After a few minutes, master and pupil reappeared, red-faced and perspiring. The boy subsequently became a model student.

Moody's concern extended also to the illiterate and indigent parents of these waifs. He developed evening classes three nights a week "for instruction in the common English branches." By 1863 the school had outgrown its depressed surroundings. With substantial gifts from Farwell and other concerned Christians, a lot was purchased at the corner of Wells and Illinois Streets. By the spring of 1864 a large brick building stood on this spot, with a fifteen hundred-seat auditorium, numerous classrooms, and a chapel. Initially, Congregationalists helped with this Illinois Street Church, but it later grew into a nondenominational evangelical ministry.

Budding Businessman

By any estimate, Moody was an unusual fellow. When he began the Sunday school in 1859, he was a shoe salesman who earned five thousand dollars in commissions above his salary, a huge sum. But during his earlier years no one could have foreseen his future success as a wealthy business entrepreneur—or as the greatest evangelist of his time.

The booming, bustling Chicago of 1860, so congenial to Moody's aggressive personality, was not his first home. Moody was born February 5, 1837, in Northfield, Massachusetts, where both his parents' families had lived for generations. His father Edwin had followed the family trade as a stonemason, but his sudden death when Dwight was four left the family in desperate straits. Betsy Moody had seven children to care for, and twins were born shortly after her husband's death. Creditors removed everything movable from the home, including the firewood. But Mrs. Moody courageously provided for her large family, with help from numerous relatives. Each child contributed what he or she could to the home, and Dwight and his brothers worked as farmhands. This allowed little time for schooling, but Dwight attended the local academy for the equivalent of about six grades. For the rest of his life the grammatical errors in his speech reflected this deficiency.

At seventeen, Dwight left for the city to earn more money for his family. He sought employment in Boston, trudging the streets for days before getting a job. An uncle owned a shoe business there, but Dwight hesitated to ask to be hired. After looking elsewhere without success, Moody swallowed his pride and requested employment. His uncle, wary of the temptations the inexperienced youth would face in the big city, made him promise to attend church and Sunday school.

Frequent church attendance brought young Dwight under strong Christian influences for the first time. Baptized in the local Unitarian church, he had been taught nothing of consequence regarding faith.[6] So when he chose Boston's Mount Vernon Congregational Church at his uncle's direction, Moody came as one utterly untaught in the Scriptures and the basics of Christianity. Edward N. Kirk, a former associate of Finney and later an evangelist himself, led the dynamic evangelical fellowship as Mount Vernon's pastor.

In addition to benefiting from the preaching of Kirk, Moody attended the young men's Bible class taught by Edward Kimball. On Moody's first day, Kimball asked the students to turn to the Gospel of John for the lesson. Dwight began thumbing through Genesis as his snickering classmates looked on. The embarrassed youth was rescued by the alert teacher, who gave the lad his own Bible, already opened to the text. Kimball took an increasing interest in Dwight, and later wrote:

> I determined to speak to him about Christ and about his soul, and started down to Holton's shoe store. When I was nearly there I began to wonder whether I ought to go in just then during business hours. I thought that possibly my call might embarrass the boy, and that when I went away the other clerks would ask who I was, and taunt him with my efforts in trying to make him a good boy. In the meantime I had passed the store, and, discovering this, I determined to make a dash for it and have it over at once.

I found Moody in the back part of the building wrapping up shoes. I went up to him at once, and putting my hand on his shoulder, I made what afterwards I felt was a very weak plea for Christ. I don't know just what words I used, nor could Mr. Moody tell. I simply told him of Christ's love for him and the love Christ wanted in return. That was all there was. It seemed the young man was just ready for the light that then broke upon him, and there, in the back of that store in Boston, he gave himself and his life to Christ.[7]

Moody's Turnabout

From the minute Moody received Christ, his life changed. His conversion was not a highly emotional experience, and in his later evangelistic campaigns he did not try to produce overwhelming emotions in his hearers. He looked more for whether his hearers understood the essentials of the Christian faith and what a commitment to Christ entailed than for temporarily heightened emotions. With little previous religious instruction, the young Moody learned slowly. On May 16, 1855, hardly three weeks after his conversion, he presented himself before the church deacons seeking membership. The examination was a disaster. In answer to the question, "What has Christ done for you, and for us all, that especially entitles Him to our love and obedience?" Dwight replied, "I think He has done a great deal for us all, but I don't know of anything He has done in particular." Moody tried for membership again on March 3, 1856, and this time he was accepted.

But Moody was not happy in Boston; he saw no future there. So like many others from the rural areas of America, he went west to Chicago, the most rapidly growing city in the nation.[8] Chicago hustled, he once wrote. Though it had made only a beginning when he arrived, Chicago already showed tremendous potential as a mecca for immigrants. Over half the city's population was foreign-born, and the mushrooming factories and businesses needed all the help they could get. By 1856, eleven major railroad lines had laid their rails far into the grain fields of the West, transporting vast amounts of livestock, corn, and wheat. Money was easy to make, and Moody—not yet twenty—decided that here he would make his fortune.

Despite all the opportunities it afforded for business, the "wicked city" jolted him. In a letter home he remarked that "many of the folks keep the stores open on the holy Sabbath," which was "enough to sicken anyone."[9] Yet Moody had no intention of leaving behind his new-found faith. On September 25, 1856, he wrote to his mother, "God is the same here as He is in Boston, and in Him I can find peace." Great things were happening at this time; the Third Great Awakening of 1857–58 had begun. Moody was growing in grace, and becoming alert to the movements of the Holy Spirit, as he wrote to his mother on January 6, 1857: "There is a great revival of religion in this city. I go to meeting every night. Oh, how I do enjoy it! It seems as if God was here Himself. Oh, mother, pray for us. Pray that this work may go on until every knee is bowed. I wish there could be a revival in Northfield."[10]

Moody began as a clerk for E. E. Wiswall Co., a retail shoe and boot outlet. The shoe and leather business in Chicago held huge potential for ambitious young men. "I can make more money here in a week than I could in Boston in a month," he wrote to his brother George. He began to lend money to friends at high interest, and confided to some that his ambition was to be worth one hundred thousand dollars. But secular interests never overcame the spiritual; he transferred his membership to the Plymouth Congregational Church in May 1857 and shortly after became involved in YMCA work.

Moody never contented himself with mere membership; surely Christ required more. This was the era of rented pews, and out of his own pocket he rented four long ones. Early on Sunday mornings he would go into local boardinghouses to invite strangers to come to the services. He particularly singled out commercial travelers—salesmen—as his guests. At this he became quite successful, and the four pews were usually filled. But this didn't seem like enough to do for his Lord, so he sought a greater outlet for service in the YMCA. The first YMCA was organized in Boston in 1852 as an evangelistic arm of the church. Moody's work with the YMCA began much as it had with the rented pews, by encouraging other men to attend its prayer meetings. Soon he served as librarian of the Chicago YMCA and head of the visitation committee.

With boundless energy and business savvy, he began asking prospective customers out on the sidewalk to come inside for shoes. Moody soon found another method for selling shoes and boots: watching new arrivals at railroad depots and hotel registers for possible customers. Wiswall's eager young salesman was so successful that a new department had to be added to handle the increased business. In 1857 Moody transferred to the shoe firm of C. N. Henderson, where he became a close personal friend of the owner. When Henderson died late in 1858, his widow asked Moody to settle up her husband's estate worth $150,000 (the equivalent of $2 million dollars in the 1990s). He was overwhelmed by this show of trust, but declined and went to work for the prominent shoe business of Buel, Hill, and Granger. Already he had saved seven thousand dollars toward his goal of becoming wealthy. But the allure of the business world, and the great wealth it promised, had paled in his eyes by the time he began the Sunday school in North Market Hall in 1859. Perhaps he felt that he had proven himself in the intense competition of business, and working for the salvation of souls was more rewarding and challenging.

Devoting Energies to God

Soon even Moody could no longer do justice to both interests. He abruptly turned his back on commerce and offered his energies to God in June 1860. Years later, Moody often told of the time one of his teachers from the Sunday school came to his shoe store. Pale and ill, the young man was hemorrhaging from the lungs. He told Moody that his doctor had ordered him to return to New York, but he hated to leave while his class of frivolous girls was still unsaved. He asked Moody to accompany him on one last visit to their homes. "It was one of the best journeys I ever had on earth," Moody declared. Moody watched as the dying teacher implored each of his students to accept Christ, winning every one of them to the Savior. Moody later recalled:

> He had to leave the next night, so I called his class together that night for a prayer meeting, and there God kindled a fire in my soul that has never gone out. The height of my ambition had been to be a successful merchant, and if I had known that meeting was going to take that ambition out of me, I might not have gone. But how many times I have thanked God since for that meeting![11]

For the next seven years, until 1867, Moody proved his sincerity in serving Christ. Freed from the restraints of secular employment, he devoted himself entirely to the Sunday school, YMCA, and other enterprises. With the outbreak of the Civil War in 1861, a new opportunity appeared. The YMCA became a link between the evangelical churches and both the Northern soldiers and captured Confederate troops. Out of this emerged the United States Christian Commission, in which Moody played a leading role. The army established Camp Douglas south of Chicago, and Moody spent much time with the nine thousand Southern troops imprisoned there. He also saw much pain and death, accompanying the Union armies as a Christian Commission worker at the battles of Shiloh, Murfreesboro, Pittsburg Landing, Chattanooga, and in the campaign for Richmond.

During this time Moody also met Emma C. Revell—a lovely girl of nineteen—and married her on August 28, 1862. Moody always marveled that he had won the love of a young lady whose background seemed so superior to his. His brusque, impulsive, outspoken, and uneducated manner was offset by Emma's educated, conservative, and retiring nature. He relied heavily upon her excellent judgment and help. Their three children—Emma, born in 1863; William, born in 1869; and Paul, born in 1879—completed a very happy family.[12]

Even the enormous demands of the war years did not exhaust his boundless energies. In addition to his work with the troops, Moody continued with the Illinois Street Church as its unordained leader. He did much of the preaching, and occasionally invited clergymen in to preach and administer the sacraments. Few pastors could have matched his torrid pace. One deacon of the church recounted an unforgettable New Year's Day on which Moody led several men on *two hundred visitation calls*. He would burst into a home and greet the astonished family with, "I am Moody; this is Deacon DeGolyer; this is Deacon Thane; this is Brother Hitchcock. Are you well? Do you all come to church and Sunday-school? Have you all the coal you need for the winter? Let us pray." He would fall to his knees, offer thirty words of prayer, and be out the door to the next call before the bewildered family knew what had hit them.[13]

Expanding Ministry

In 1866 the Chicago YMCA elected Moody as its president, a position he held for four years. As head of one of the most important local YMCAs, he traveled widely. Meetings and conventions in Portland, Maine; Baltimore, Maryland; Albany, New York; and other places greatly expanded his contacts during this period. In addition to his work with the YMCA, he also became involved in two new interdenominational movements of great power: the Sunday School Union and the Christian Convention. Both drew together leaders of churches throughout the Midwest, and Moody became a familiar speaker at their conventions. In such meetings he tested techniques and ideas he later incorporated in his evangelistic campaigns. By 1870, when he delivered one of the principle messages at the national YMCA convention in Indianapolis, he was one of the best-known Protestant leaders throughout the Midwest.

It was at the Indianapolis convention that Moody met Ira D. Sankey (1840–1908), a delegate from New Castle, Pennsylvania. Sankey had a powerful, mellow voice and was an accomplished singer and song leader. After Moody heard him sing he approached Sankey, introduced himself, and spent some minutes inquiring about Sankey's family ties and occupation. Then he said, "Well, you'll have to give that up! You are the man I have been looking for, and I want you to come to Chicago and help me in my work."[14] Sankey soon gave in, left his occupation, went to Chicago, and became Moody's inseparable companion and co-laborer.

In the spring of 1867 Moody traveled to England to meet with British evangelicals and exchange ideas on Sunday schools, YMCA work, prayer meetings, and evangelism. Remaining there for four months, he became interested in the work of a lay group known as the Plymouth Brethren, which had been formed in the 1820s as a reaction to tendencies within the Church of England. Under the leadership of J. N. Darby (1800–1882), they preached the inerrancy of the Bible, premillennialism, and con-

Moody and Sankey do individual counseling with those
who come forward at one of the New York crusades.
(Courtesy of the Billy Graham Center Museum)

version as a deep personal experience. Darby visited America several times and probably spoke at the YMCA building in Chicago at Moody's invitation.[15] Another member of the Brethren, Henry Moorhouse, became Moody's close friend and influenced his ministry in several areas. By the end of his visit to England, Moody had become friends with many leaders of the evangelical cause in London. At a farewell reception, they gave him a substantial honorarium as a token of their esteem. On that first British trip he heard those words that were to affect him profoundly: "The world has yet to see what God will do with and for and through and in and by the man who is fully and wholly consecrated to Him." To this Moody responded, "I will try my utmost to be that man."

Arriving in Chicago in the fall of 1867, Moody completed his beloved YMCA building, Farwell Hall, containing an auditorium seating three thousand. To secure the necessary funds for building, Moody had organized a stock company with twelve trustees chosen from among Chicago's wealthy businessmen. These included Cyrus McCormick, George Armour, John Farwell, and B. F. Jacobs. But despite his popularity, successes, and host of friends, Moody now entered a period of spiritual crisis. His energies seemed no longer equal to his schedule of speaking engagements and ministry obligations. The low point of his life came when the Chicago fire of October 1871 consumed his home, personal belongings, the YMCA building, and the Illinois Street Church. Although others rallied to rebuild Farwell Hall, Moody alone had to shoulder the responsibility of raising money for a new church. He stated later that the fire was the most important reason for his decision to leave Chicago.[16]

Moody's spiritual crisis had been building for some time, and lasted at least four months. But one day God broke through the gloom. Moody did not wish to say much about it, for it was "almost too sacred an experience to name." He said, "God revealed Himself to me, and I had such an experience of His love that I had to ask Him to stay His hand." Later he referred to it as an anointing, a filling of the Spirit with unction and empowerment for service. He began to preach that a similar experience was necessary for anyone who desired to be truly effective in Christian service.[17] Moody emerged from this period as a preacher of great power.

Preaching the Love of God

Moody made a second short trip to England in 1870, and a third trip in June 1872. During both of these visits he renewed friendships with British Christian leaders. In July 1872 he delivered a major address at the annual Mildmay Conference in London. This exposed him to hundreds of the most important Christians in Britain. His growing friendship with Moorhouse caused him to reexamine and change the emphasis of his preaching. Once, Moorhouse preached seven nights in Moody's Chicago church on the theme of the love of God, using John 3:16 as his text. Moody was astounded; until then, he had always called upon sinners to repent and flee the wrath to come. Instead of emphasizing what sinners should *run from,* Moorhouse reversed this—without suggesting that God would not judge. Moody saw the important difference, and began to teach that sinners should be *drawn to* God by love—for God wants sons, not slaves.[18]

With his new consecration and revitalized preaching based on God's love, Moody set out with Sankey on a completely different course. He made his final break with the responsibilities in Chicago in June 1873, and set sail for England with Sankey at his side. On previous visits he had received many invitations to conduct extended preaching tours, especially from William Pennefeather (the founder of Mildmay Conference), Cuthbert Bainbridge of Newcastle, and Henry Bewley of Dublin. The latter two invitations included the promise of funds to meet the expenses of Moody and Sankey.

When the two docked at Liverpool on June 17, 1873, they were greeted with the news that the three friends on whom they depended for moral and financial support had died. Moody turned to Sankey; "God seems to have closed the doors," he said. "We will not open any ourselves. If

*A Currier and Ives lithograph
shows Moody at the height of his career.*

He opens the door we will go in; otherwise we will return to America."[19] Moody found an unopened letter from the secretary of the YMCA in York, England, inviting him to speak there. "This door is only ajar," he said, but having no other prospects he telegraphed York that he would be there as soon as possible. Quickly the YMCA secretary, having expected nothing of the sort, scrambled to arrange for Moody to preach in various pulpits of the city. The meetings began slowly, since Moody was unknown in York. But F. B. Meyer, the great preacher and writer, recalled,

> What an inspiration when this great and noble soul first broke into my life! I was a young pastor then, in the old city of York, and bound rather rigidly by the chains of conventionalism. Such had been my training, and such might have been my career. But here was a revelation of a new ideal. The first characteristic of Mr. Moody's that struck me was that he was so absolutely unconventional and natural. . . . But there was never the slightest approach to irreverence, fanaticism, or extravagance; everything was in perfect accord with a rare common sense, a directness of method, a simplicity and transparency of aim, which were as attractive as they were fruitful in result.[20]

After five weeks of meetings in York, with only modest success, the team of Moody and Sankey was invited to Sunderland to conduct a similar campaign. There Moody wisely took the step of inviting his good friend Moorhouse to share the preaching. These meetings went some-

203

what better, and evangelical groups began to hear of the dynamic American preacher and his singing companion. An invitation next came from the city of Newcastle, and meetings began there in September 1873. Here the team met with its first large response. To accommodate the crowds, the meetings were transferred from a church to the music hall. The newspapers also gave them favorable reviews.

Presbyterian Scotland

One of the pastors of Leith, the port city of Edinburgh, heard of the unusual evangelistic work of the two Americans in Newcastle, and went to see for himself. He was so impressed that he extended an invitation on behalf of both the established and free churches in Edinburgh to hold meetings there. The offer convinced Moody that he would get widespread support from the churches and clergy, so he accepted. Meetings began in the Edinburgh Music Hall—the largest in the city—on November 23, 1873.

Moody and Sankey knew that in strict Presbyterian Scotland they would have to be circumspect to overcome prejudices against their type of evangelism. Some were opposed to Sankey's "singing the gospel." Scottish Presbyterians were just then beginning to move beyond the exclusive use of the psalter in congregational singing; only since 1860 had organs been tolerated in the churches.[21] Sankey's portable harmonium and the catchy, simple words and tunes he had composed himself shocked Scottish sensibilities. Some derided Sankey's "kist o' whistles" as an instrument open to satanic use.

For the most part, though, the Scots were open-minded and enthusiastic. They packed the opening service "in every cranny, . . . and several thousand people went away, unable to obtain admission." The Americans' efforts gained approval from all levels. Moody's simple message and call for unity among Christians was irresistible. The hearts of the people of Edinburgh were open to the duo, and almost every minister voiced support for the meetings. So deep was the spiritual awakening after a few weeks that the following letter was sent to every clergyman in Scotland.

> Edinburgh is now enjoying signal manifestations of grace. Many of the Lord's people are not surprised at this. . . . They hoped that they might have a visit from Messrs. Moody and Sankey, of America, but they very earnestly besought the Lord that He would deliver them from depending upon them or any instrumentality, and that He Himself would come with them or come before them. He has graciously answered that prayer, and His own presence is now wonderfully manifested among them. God is so affecting the hearts of men that the Free Church Assembly Hall, the largest public building in Edinburgh, is crowded every evening with meetings for

prayer, and both that building and the Established Church Assembly Hall overflow whenever the gospel is preached. But the numbers that attend are not the most remarkable feature. It is the presence and power of the Holy Ghost, the solemn awe, the prayerful, believing, expectant spirit, the anxious inquiry of unsaved souls, and the longing of believers to grow more like Christ—their hungering and thirsting after holiness.[22]

So completely did Moody and Sankey capture the affections of the Scots that even opposition to the little organ evaporated. Professor Blaikie of New College, Moody's host during the campaign, reported, "It is amusing to observe how entirely the latent distrust of Mr. Sankey's 'kist o' whistles' has disappeared."[23]

The other great city of Scotland, Glasgow, invited the Americans to conduct meetings almost as soon as the Edinburgh campaign began, and after two months of preaching the gospel in Edinburgh, a three-month series began in Glasgo The attendance equaled that in Edinburgh, and the clergy united in support. From February 8 through May 24 as many as two or three huge meetings were held each day, and crowds frequently numbered twenty thousand. From Glasgow, Moody and Sankey went to the north of Scotland. Meetings were held in Aberdeen, Dundee, Inverness, and at every major town until most of Scotland had been reached. A year after the meetings in Glasgow, the famous preacher Andrew A. Bonar wrote, "We should like to testify to the permanence of the work among us, and any one who will come and see for himself will at once discover how extensive and sincere this work has been."[24]

Ireland and England

Moody and Sankey crossed over to Ireland, with meetings in Belfast from September 6 until October 8, 1874. They then moved to Dublin, where the entire Protestant population numbered only forty thousand, and received a very friendly welcome. The leading Roman Catholic paper of the city covered the meetings fully, and was extremely positive toward them. Moody then returned to England, beginning meetings in Manchester in December and moving to Sheffield and Birmingham in January 1875. Nothing like these enormous attendances had been seen since Whitefield spoke to crowds of twenty and thirty thousand in the open air over one hundred years earlier. Now Moody could speak to comparable numbers inside. By the time the two Americans reached Liverpool, a flood of favorable newspaper reports had made everyone in England aware of their ministry. In Liverpool not even the largest buildings could hold the anticipated crowds, so a huge temporary sheet-iron tabernacle called Victoria Hall was erected.

In England it was not as easy to get the united support of the clergy because of the diversity among the Protestant denominations. One pastor who was at first inclined to look with disfavor on Moody's work was the famous Congregationalist leader, R. W. Dale. As interest increased, however, Dale decided to observe Moody. Becoming more impressed, he eventually threw his wholehearted support behind the work, saying, "Of Mr. Moody's own power, I find it difficult to speak. It is so real and yet so unlike the power of ordinary preachers, that I hardly know how to analyze it. Its reality is indisputable. . . . On Tuesday I told Mr. Moody that the work was most plainly of God, for I could see no real relation between him and what he had done. He laughed cheerily, and said he should be very sorry if it were otherwise."[25]

The occasional opposition and attacks in the newspapers came mostly from jealous clergymen who made fun of Moody's Yankee pronunciations and his clipped "Dan'l" and "Sam'l." The *New York Times* could not believe that two Americans had achieved such notoriety in the British Isles, stating that it had reliable information that P. T. Barnum had sent them to England.[26] By the time Moody and Sankey reached the climax of their British tour—the four months of meetings in London from early March to early July 1875—such criticism could be laughed at or ignored.

London Crusade

Advance planning for the London crusade systematically applied Moody's evangelistic methods. All through January and February 1875, workers conducted house-to-house visits and hundreds of prayer meetings. The committee directing the preparations divided London into four huge sections, and rented or constructed large buildings in each section to serve as central meeting halls. They rented Agricultural Hall (the largest hall ever occupied by Moody) in Islington, the Royal Opera House in the fashionable West End, and raised two temporary structures on Bow Road and in Camberwell Green (the working-class areas).

When meetings began on March 9, much scurrilous material had been printed in papers such as *Vanity Fair*. Moody and Sankey were called "pernicious humbugs," "crack-brained Yankee evangelists," "abbots of unreason," and worse. But when many of Britain's most important people attended, the epithets had to be tempered. The *Times* of London was very positive, saying,

> Is any Christian church in this metropolis in a position to say that it can afford to dispense with any vigorous effort to rouse the mass of people to a more Christian life? The congregations which are to be seen in our

churches and chapels are but a fraction of the hundreds and thousands around them, of whom multitudes are living but little better than a mere animal existence. If any considerable proportion of them can be aroused to the mere desire for something higher, an immense step is gained.[27]

For four months in the sprawling, difficult city of London, the two Americans faithfully presented the gospel. Moody confided that four years would hardly be adequate to reach the teeming population. While Moody's great love for people inclined him to try to reach all of London, the attendance figures show that in reality a great multitude did hear him during the four months. Although many were probably repeat attenders, the statistics were:

Agricultural Hall, 60 meetings attended by 720,000

Royal Opera House, 60 meetings attended by 330,000

Bow Road Hall, 60 meetings attended by 600,000

Camberwell Hall, 60 meetings attended by 480,000

Victoria Hall, 45 meetings attended by 400,000

In all, 285 meetings, attended by more than 2.5 million people.

Back to America

After two years in the British Isles, Moody and Sankey returned to America in July 1875 in the wake of a tidal wave of favorable press reviews. Christian leaders in the United States, perhaps puzzled that Moody had risen to international stature and fame in a foreign land, quickly enlisted his ministry at home. After a rest from the grueling pace, Moody desired to conduct metropolitan campaigns in America: "Water runs down hill, and the highest hills in America are the great cities. If we can stir them we shall stir the whole country."[28]

Brooklyn, a city accustomed to great preaching from men such as Henry Ward Beecher, Thomas DeWitt Talmage (1832–1902), and Theodore L. Cuyler (1822–1909), began its preparations. The arrangements committee rented the Rink, which seated five thousand, and the trolley company laid extra tracks to its doors. On opening day, October 24, fifteen thousand were lined up for blocks waiting to get in, and Moody held excellent meetings for a month. He might have remained longer, but other cities demanded campaigns. Philadelphia, under the leadership of the widely known and respected merchant John Wanamaker, was especially eager to begin an evangelistic work before the spirit of the United States Centennial celebration took over. The recently vacated Pennsylvania Railroad freight depot was refurbished to hold

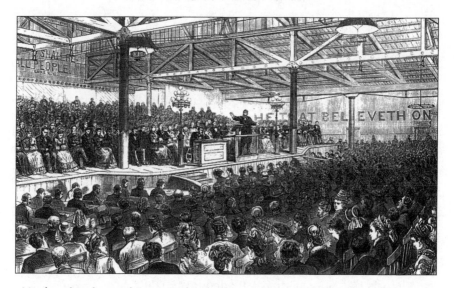

Moody and Sankey conduct a revival in the Pennsylvania Railroad freight station building in Philadelphia. (Courtesy of the Billy Graham Center Museum)

thirteen thousand seats. For two months Moody drove himself at his usual awesome pace, conducting two or three meetings a day plus innumerable prayer services and inquiry sessions. Then it was New York City's turn. The vast Hippodrome at Madison Avenue and 27th Street accommodated more than fourteen thousand each night for four months. He returned to Chicago in October 1876 for several months of meetings in a specially constructed auditorium, and then, in the spring of 1877, he preached in Boston.

The five evangelistic missions to Brooklyn, Philadelphia, New York, Chicago, and Boston—from 1875 through 1877—began an evangelistic campaign throughout the United States that spanned twenty years. Moody visited hundreds of cities before his death in 1899—in the United States, Canada, and Mexico. He returned to the British Isles in 1881. Even the *New York Times* changed its earlier negative tone in assessing Moody, saying: "Whatever the prejudiced may say against him, the honest-minded and just will remember the amazing work of this *plain man*."[29]

Plainness certainly contributed to Moody's success. He shared several characteristics with the other most successful early evangelists: (1) He was absolutely sincere, as even his worst critics admitted; (2) He had a fiery love for Christ and for people that was evident in everything he did; (3) He was unshakably sure of his own salvation, and believed that God's grace had gone to the uttermost limits to save all people who would only believe.

*During Moody's 1875 campaign, the people of Brooklyn crowd
into the 5000 seat Rink. (Courtesy of the Billy Graham Center Museum)*

World Evangelization by 1900

Although Moody transformed evangelism in America and the British Isles, his vision extended beyond these nations. In his latter years he shared with other Christian leaders the idea of converting the entire world to Christ.

In 1883 Moody hosted the first of what became the annual Northfield Conference in the Massachusetts town of his birth. On the third year of this popular gathering (1885) a Presbyterian pastor in Philadelphia, Arthur T. Pierson (1837–1911), was asked to speak about foreign missions at an evening meeting. Several years earlier he had sounded the cry that the world could be evangelized by the year 1900. He had dedicated himself to this message and was determined to make the most of this opportunity to address more than a thousand influential Christians. On the platform was Moody himself.

Pierson laid down the challenge with forceful passion: "If ten millions out of four hundred millions of nominal Christians would undertake such systematic labors that each of that number should in the course of the next fifteen years reach one hundred other souls with the gospel message, the whole present population of the globe would have heard the good tidings by the year 1900!" He continued to cite statistics to prove that the task was possible. "Believers everywhere should get busy" to complete the Great Commission by 1900.

Pierson's words so gripped Moody that he jumped up from his seat and interrupted the speaker. "How many of you believe this can be done?" Moody asked the audience. The crowd roared its approval. Not wanting to lose the momentum of the moment, Moody asked that a committee of six well-respected leaders be appointed to move on this, and he joined it himself. This small group hammered out an eloquent document within three days, entitled "An Appeal to Disciples Everywhere," which was approved at a subsequent meeting by a massive voice vote of the same influential audience. Probably for the first time in history, the idea of finishing the task of global evangelism was proposed as an attainable goal on a set schedule.

The same document called for a world-level conference at which global plans could be made. It stated:

> Even Pentecost is surpassed by the ingathering of ten thousand converts in one mission station in India within sixty days, in the year 1878. . . . and yet the church of God is slow to move in response to the providence of God. Nearly a thousand millions of the human race are yet without the gospel; vast districts are wholly unoccupied. And yet there is abundance of both men and means in the church to give the gospel to every living soul before this century closes. . . . If at some great centre like London or New York, a great council of evangelical leaders could meet, to consider the wonder-working of God's providence and grace in mission fields . . . it might greatly further the glorious object of the world's evangelization; and we earnestly commend the suggestion to the prayerful consideration of the various bodies of organizations. . . . Done in convention at Northfield, Mass., August 14, 1885, D. L. Moody presiding.[30]

In 1888 the largest missions conference ever convened up to that time opened in London to answer the summons.

Moody already had been instrumental in challenging young people to volunteer their lives for the foreign missions movement. Moody's warm, optimistic evangelicalism shone through every phase of the activity after 1880. Thousands of people committed themselves to the cause. One major event was a series of revival meetings at Yale, Harvard, Dartmouth, and Princeton that repeated his earlier successes in Britain at Oxford, Cambridge, and Edinburgh. The meetings in England had shocked all of England because of the conversion of the "Cambridge Seven"—students from some of the nation's finest families who volunteered as missionaries. Charles T. Studd (1862–1931) was one of these seven who aroused great enthusiasm in the universities. A superb athlete, he sailed for China with the China Inland Mission in 1885 and gave away his inherited fortune to Christian causes.

With the American college revival at its peak in 1886, Moody invited missions-minded students to a month-long summer session at his Northfield school. The College Student Conference brought results far beyond the aspirations of even Moody, for prior to their leaving, an even one

A photograph of Moody in his later years of involvement in promoting world missions (Courtesy of the Billy Graham Center Museum)

hundred students—"the Mount Vernon Hundred"—had volunteered to become missionaries. By the next summer the number had reached twenty-one hundred—five hundred women and sixteen hundred men. Moody began sending men such as J. E. K. Studd (C. T. Studd's brother) to canvass the college campuses in America as the Cambridge Seven had done in Britain. President Seelye of Amherst College called this movement the greatest missionary uprising in modern times. In 1888 the Student Volunteer Movement was organized, growing out of these conferences and taking as its motto, "The evangelization of the world in this generation." Soon this expanded incredibly, due largely to the leadership of John R. Mott (1865–1955), a student who had been evangelized by J. E. K. Studd. For almost half a century Mott became the leading American ambassador of missions; his impact on American Christian students during that time was phenomenal.

After Moody's partial retirement in 1892, he increasingly devoted his remaining years to mobilizing young people for Christian service and to strengthening the institutions he had founded. The Moody Bible Institute, started in 1886 as the Chicago Evangelization Society, became the pattern for similar Bible schools and colleges in cities across America. It soon became an important training ground for professional evangelists. Moody also placed great confidence in the Northfield schools and conferences, which he hoped would continue to raise up qualified young men and women for ministry to future generations.

$\mathcal{E}$vangelism at the Beginning of the Twentieth Century

S hortly after the turn of the century, a wise and scholarly Methodist bishop reflected on the work of evangelism over the past two hundred years. Contemplating what was needed for the continued expansion of the Christian faith in America, he wrote *Great Revivals and the Great Republic*. Warren A. Candler, of the Methodist Episcopal Church South, was gratified at the accomplishments of the past and both hopeful and troubled about the future. History provided abundant proof, Candler believed, that the religion of a people absolutely determined the character of the culture and political structure that was established. It was no wonder, he wrote, that the nations of Christendom enjoyed both the highest morality and the most advanced governments on the globe.

212

A 1919 Salvation Army poster
(Courtesy of the Billy Graham Center Museum)

The forms and forces of national life take their rise in the religion of the people. National life is feeble or strong according as the faith of the people is faint or vigorous. . . . The deepest and most influential thing in the life of any people is its religion, and its customs and codes must inevitably be colored and controlled by its moral convictions. Atheism breeds anarchy as like begets like, and in all the graduations of civil government, from the lowest absolutism to the highest types of free institutions, the character of the political system is exactly determined by the faith that underlies it.

The governments of all heathen lands are despotisms by the very law of their being. Civil freedom cannot live in the atmosphere of pagan superstition. . . .

The Great Republic of North America is the offspring of revivals of religion in the Old World, which aroused persecutions for righteousness' sake

213

and which led heroic souls to go forth, as did Abraham, upon migrations to preserve a spiritual religion in the earth. Its civil institutions were moulded at the outset to conform to the faith of its founders, and its subsequent progress has moved under the impulses of moral forces which have been quickened and intensified by 'the great awakenings' which have marked the subsequent course of its history. It is at once the product and propagator of evangelical Christianity. In such Christianity it had its origin, and in such faith its mission must be fulfilled.[1]

Candler was a sincere evangelical and an astute observer of the contemporary scene. His book is a penetrating analysis of the history of America and of American Christianity that gives a good view of the atmosphere in which evangelism flourished from 1880 to 1920. Candler also was formerly president of Emory College, a friend of numerous evangelists, editor of Methodism's official periodical (the *Christian Advocate*) and brother of Asa G. Candler (the Coca-Cola magnate).

In his book, the bishop traced the contributions evangelical Christianity has made to the modern world, showing that, whether directly or indirectly, all the benefits that modern people enjoy have come to them through the gospel. He also noted that wherever the gospel has been stifled totalitarianism has rushed in. "But this evangelical Christianity is not only the security of the Republic," he declared, "it is also the hope of the world. That this claim may not appear extravagant let us consider several facts that are known and read of all men."[2]

The Invincible Gospel

Candler believed that history is on the side of Christianity, and that the gospel is invincible.

> The doctrines and life of evangelical Christianity will hold the field against all comers, whether they be the forces of doubt denying all faith, or the companies of rationalism or ritualism with their pinched and paralytic faiths. ... Moreover, this is the only type of religion which they could carry throughout the earth, even if they were of a mind to try some other sort. Evangelical Christianity only has in it the elements of universality and permanence. Doubt is transient, and all forms of rationalism are the fleeting fashions with which men of an indolent and curious culture interest themselves for a season. ... But the doctrines of evangelical Christianity, incarnated in the experiences of glowing souls, are at home in all lands, potent in all times, and unembarassed in any presence. It is impervious to the assaults of infidelity and unhindered by the advance of knowledge. Its doctrines of sin, repentance, justification by faith, the new birth, the witness of the Spirit, Christian perfection and the life eternal after death, are certified by the deepest wants, the highest aspirations and the profoundest convictions of the race.[3]

And what of evangelism at the beginning of the twentieth century? Bishop Candler found that his contemporaries—especially the recently deceased Dwight L. Moody—were continuing steadfastly in the tradition of Solomon Stoddard, Theodore Frelinghuysen, Jonathan Edwards, George Whitefield, John Wesley, and Charles G. Finney. "Like all the great revivalists, from Luther to the present time, *Moody was intensely Biblical.* While preaching in an untechnical manner, he was, nevertheless, a doctrinal preacher, and his doctrines were those of the orthodox churches. He was not a liberal, nor did he boast of 'a progressive orthodoxy.' Liberalism has never produced a revival of religion, nor does it promise to do so at any early day."[4]

Evangelists of that mold, who live modestly and not for money, are to be greatly encouraged, Candler stated. Moody, Candler found, was exemplary in regard to wages.

> Not living upon an income derived from his meetings . . . he was never tempted to lower the standard of religion to win the semblance of triumph, to corrupt doctrine to conciliate popular favour, nor to berate the churches to secure the smiles and remuneration of a cynical, vindictive and godless world which stands ever ready to reward a man who will denounce the Church of God that it hates, because of the faithful rebukes of its own unrighteousness. Moody had none of the arts of the demagogue, for he was neither greedy of gain nor covetous of applause.[5]

Jones—"The Moody of the South"

At Moody's death in 1899, the man who seemed most likely to succeed him as American's preeminent evangelist was Samuel Porter Jones, who was already called "the Moody of the South." Born in Chambers County, Alabama, on October 16, 1847, the young Jones moved with his family to Cartersville, Georgia, after his mother's death. He was educated at Euharlee Academy and studied to become a lawyer. After being admitted to the Georgia bar and gaining recognition as a very capable attorney, he began to have health problems. According to one biographer, "He suffered from the worst form of nervous dyspepsia; and, in his sufferings, with his health wrecked, with sleepless nights and restless days, he became discouraged and despondent and sought relief in drink."[6] At this low point in Jones' life his father became ill. At the deathbed his father told him, "My poor, wicked, wayward, reckless boy. You have broken the heart of your sweet wife and brought me down in sorrow to my grave: promise me, my boy, to meet me in heaven." Convulsed with emotion, Jones promised his father never to drink again, and in later years he declared, "Thank God, I can say every wilful step of my life since that moment has been toward the redemption of that promise."[7]

But Jones had not yet come to Christ. Knowing that he needed a power beyond his own, he went to hear his grandfather preach at Moore's Chapel. Jones came under deep conviction, and at the close of the sermon he walked forward, gave his grandfather his hand, and said, "I give myself, my heart, and life, what is left of it, all to God and His Cause." Soon after this he felt a call to the ministry. In November 1872 he was admitted to the North Georgia Conference of the Methodist Episcopal Church South, as an itinerant preacher. Eventually he gained fame as a revival preacher throughout northern Georgia. As he was shifted from one circuit to another, he developed a style very different from that of most preachers. As Tom Watson, a young lawyer, testified:

> In the good year 1879, Sam Jones lit down in this veritable town of Thomson, and began to go for the devil and his angels in a manner which was entirely new to said devil, also new to said angels. . . . For six weeks the farms and stores were neglected, and Jones! Jones! Jones! was the whole thing. Well, the meeting wound up, the community settled back to business—but it has never been the same community since. Gambling disappeared, loud profanity on the streets was heard no more, and the barrooms were run out the county.[8]

Jones' first attempt at mass evangelism on a city-wide scale was in Memphis, Tennessee, in 1884. At the end of the campaign, one newspaper stated, "He has loomed into importance as an evangelist and revivalist, until he stands now second only to Talmage and Moody."[9] The following year Jones came to national attention in Nashville. A tent holding five thousand people was filled three times a day for four weeks, earning Jones the designation: "The Moody of the South." An associate, Walt Holcomb, said,

> In speaking of the meeting six months afterwards, the presiding elder of the Nashville district said he believed ten thousand accessions were made to the churches of Nashville, and within a radius of one hundred miles of the city. . . . Perhaps he was never so bitterly opposed in any work as that in Nashville. However, his manly and fearless way of addressing the people made a deep impression upon the audiences. They admired his courage and manliness. He completely silenced those who opposed him, and there was very little condemnation in the papers during the entire meeting.[10]

Increasingly, Jones introduced into his evangelism the element of "civic reform"—preaching against "all sorts of shams, hypocrisies, worldliness, covetousness, drunkenness, gambling and impurity"—while at the same time inviting the multitudes to accept Christ as Savior. Jones' antipathy toward liquor grew out of his own past experience. In linking evangelism and reform, Jones followed in the footsteps of Finney. While

Moody also had used this strategy to a limited degree, Jones introduced a negative emphasis that set the pattern for professional evangelism for the next forty years. Although the positive element of salvation through Christ was not neglected, a large percentage of Jones' sermons attacked societal ills. He sought in this way to build a foundation for pointing people to Jesus Christ. Jones called this determined attempt to expose hypocrisies and sins "muscular Christianity" or "practical religion." "I like a broad, useful, aggressive Christianity," he said, "a Christianity with a musket and a cartridge belt. Satan won this country by fighting and we must win it back from him in the same way."[11] Often Jones' meetings seemed largely to be Prohibition rallies, and here he differed from Moody, who distinguished between church and politics. Jones had a large effect upon his own denomination, however, for in 1886 the Southern Methodist Church officially declared the manufacture and sale of liquor to be a sin.

From 1885 until his death in 1906, Jones gradually branched out into the entire nation. As Moody had engaged the services of Ira Sankey to present music, so Sam Jones acquired E. O. Excell as his soloist. Usually his meetings included choirs of about three or four hundred, and he went beyond Moody in having assistants who arranged the details for his campaigns. In the fall of 1885 he was invited to St. Louis and St. Joseph. The following year Jones held large meetings in Chicago, Cincinnati, Indianapolis, Baltimore, Toronto, Omaha, and St. Paul. In 1887 he went to Boston and Kansas City. He conducted campaigns along the west coast—San Francisco, Los Angeles, and Sacramento—in 1889, and was in Wilmington, Little Rock, and Chattanooga in 1890. He returned to Nashville for eighteen campaigns, finding that city especially receptive to his emphases.

Losing Spontaneity

By the time of Jones, American Protestant evangelism had lost the spontaneity of Stoddard's day. In the 1700s, little was standardized about the methods of evangelists. Awakenings were viewed as unpredictable miracles sent from God, and the styles of evangelists differed greatly. Their common concern was to avoid emotionalism, although at times (as in Gilbert Tennent's preaching) "enthusiasm" broke out. Then, in the early 1800s, the revivals of the West—emanating from the Cane Ridge tradition of camp meetings in Kentucky and Tennessee—showed unbridled emotionalism. In the East, however, the dignified evangelism of Asahel Nettleton and Lyman Beecher demanded awe and solemn quiet. Finney broke all precedents with his "new measures" and logical, lawyer-like argumentation. Also new was his contention that revivals could be "prayed down" with "the right use of means" at any time. In keeping with the times, Moody introduced the organized city-wide cooperative evangelistic campaign. Each of these evangelists modified the tradition they received from their predecessors. From decade to decade evangelism changed its methods but not its timeless message of salvation through faith in Jesus.

With Moody's passing, much of American evangelism became stylized, fixed in method and content, and professionalized. Revival movements largely lost the dynamic, revolutionary spontaneity of the Puritans. Although evangelistic preaching still retained a great deal of its power, revival effects became expected and were no longer viewed as a miracle sent by a loving God. At this very time, as the effects of too much organization were being felt in America, the Welsh Revival of 1904–5 revealed the traditional type of awakening. Totally unexpected and unorganized, it was truly a layperson's revival as America's Third Great Awakening had been. G. Campbell Morgan, the renowned Bible teacher and pastor of London's Westminster Chapel, described the Welsh Revival as "Pentecost continued," in a book distributed worldwide. "I am inclined to think God is saying to us, 'Your organizations are right, providing you do not live in them and end in them. But here apart from all of them, setting them ruthlessly on one side, Pentecostal power and fire are being manifested.' "[12]

Whereas previously there had been much for Christians to praise and little to criticize, evangelists now seemed to be using the high-pressure methods of big business to get results. In 1904, out of concern for such problems, the Interdenominational Association of Evangelists (IAE) was founded at the Winona Lake Bible Conference in Indiana. The purpose was to bring some regularity and unity to the evangelistic profession, providing cohesion and oversight. For years it held annual conventions, where new methods and procedures were explored. While the intentions of the IAE were entirely good and understandable, it may have contributed to standardization and professionalizing. Certainly Edwards and Whitefield would have looked askance at such an organization. But even Finney had his "Holy Band" of itinerant evangelists.

Torrey—Institute Evangelist

Samuel P. Jones, B. Fay Mills, and to some extent Moody, set the pattern for hundreds of evangelists who ministered across the land. After Jones' work was over, the evangelist who came to greatest prominence in America was Reuben A. Torrey (1856–1928). The son of a New York banker, he was unusual in having acquired an excellent education, graduating from Yale College in 1875 and Yale Divinity School in 1878. He then studied theology at German universities. After a pastorate in a small

A postcard promotes a 1906 revival with song leader Charles M. Alexander and evangelist R. A. Torrey. (Courtesy of the Billy Graham Center Museum)

church in Ohio, he went in 1883 to the Open Door Church in Minneapolis and from 1886–89 he was superintendent of the Minneapolis City Mission Society. It was at this time that he passed through the spiritual crisis that prepared him for his future work. Torrey wrote,

> Perhaps the most decisive turning point in my life since I have been in the ministry came through reading *The Life of Trust* by George Muller. I have been a different man ever since reading that book; it led to a radical change in my whole conception of the Christian ministry, and of what Christian living really was. It led to my turning my back upon everything that I had hoped for in this world, and to just step out and obey and trust in God for everything; and since I have done it He has given me everything I have or am. I shall thank God throughout all eternity for what the words of this sainted servant of God were to me, and for what they have been to me ever since.[13]

In 1889, Moody planned the Bible institute in Chicago that bears his name. Shortly thereafter he said to E. M. Williams, "I wish I knew a man to take the place of superintendent of the Institute. It seems to me to be the largest thing I have ever undertaken, and that it is going to accomplish more than anything I have yet been permitted to do."[14] Williams said Torrey might be ideal for the post. After an interview with Moody, Torrey became superintendent on October 1, 1889, the opening day. He was only thirty-three years of age. Four years later he became, in addition, the pastor of the Moody Church, where he remained until 1906.

During the Chicago World's Fair in 1893, Moody conducted a widespread campaign designed to reach the visitors from around the world. Torrey assisted Moody in all aspects of the campaign. In November 1899, when Moody suffered a heart attack in the midst of a campaign in Kansas City, he telegraphed Torrey, asking him to rush there and take over the meetings—which Torrey did. Then in 1901, prayer meetings for a world-wide awakening began at the Moody Institute. These resulted in Torrey undertaking a worldwide evangelistic tour.

Travels Abroad with Alexander

Torrey chose as his soloist and associate evangelist a winsome young man, Charles M. Alexander, who was soon lauded as "the twentieth-century Ira Sankey." Beginning in Melbourne, Australia, in April 1902, Torrey and Alexander conducted one month of meetings. For the first two weeks meetings were held in fifty different centers by fifty different evangelists. Then Torrey took over, and in his opening message stated, "I believe that a world-wide revival has begun. I know of 5,000 people outside of Australia who are praying for the success of this mission." Heavily dependent upon the musical ministry of Alexander and the choirs, Torrey continued to tour Australia for another six months, holding meetings in a number of cities. By the time they left Australia, more than twenty thousand converts had registered decisions for Christ. Then he (with Alexander) went on to Tasmania, New Zealand, China, Japan, and India, preaching as he went.

In London, a great welcoming meeting in Exeter Hall had been arranged by cablegram while the evangelists were still in Bombay. Britain's notable figures there included Lord Kinnaird, Lord Radstock, and F. B. Meyer. In his welcoming address Lord Kinnaird said, "We have been looking forward to your presence. We have heard what you have been doing in Australia and in other parts of the world, and we pray our Heavenly Father that through you there may be such an outpouring of the Holy Spirit as we have not seen for years."[15]

In Wales, Torrey surveyed the astonishing Welsh Revival that was to have world impact under such leaders as Evan Roberts and Seth Joshua. For three years Torrey and Alexander went to the major cities of the British Isles—Glasgow, Edinburgh, Aberdeen, Dundee, Dublin, Belfast, Liverpool, Manchester, Cardiff, Bolton, London, and elsewhere. In each city the largest halls were unable to accommodate the thousands who came to hear the men who were known as the successors of Moody and Sankey. The statistics of converts were impressive: Birmingham, 7,700; Belfast, 4,000; Manchester, 4,000; Cardiff, 3,750; Bolton, 3,600; Dublin, 3,000; London, 17,000. Altogether, the number of converts of the round-the-world tour was more than 100,000.

The climax of the tour was a five-month campaign in London in Royal Albert Hall and in a large tabernacle in South London. Lord Kinnaird and W. G. Bradshaw, a London banker, headed the executive committee. Here Torrey used effectively something he had pioneered in Ballarat, Australia: a small white card bearing upon its face only four words, "Get Right With God." In Australia workers gave out these cards by the tens of thousands, and hundreds of thousands were distributed in England. Torrey reported that he had received an incredible number of accounts of how the cards had brought someone face to face with the gospel.

Torrey was an extremely sincere man of high principles, and he was disturbed by the charges of commercialism leveled against him and others. He let it be known at the Bible Institute that the offerings and collections in the British Isles were not large. His superintendent's salary continued during the world tour, and he turned over to the Institute all moneys received. In 1904 he wrote from Liverpool to A. P. Fitt, secretary of the Institute,

> Many of the evangelists are being ruined by commercialism that has entered in evangelistic work. A good deal of commercialism has been creeping into our work, and more and more machinery and, I fear, less dependence upon God. I am going to have a talk with Alexander about it. . . . I want to eliminate the financial element from my work as much as possible and am disposed to accept no set figure from anyone, but take what the Lord shall send me from time to time.[16]

Torrey also expressed concern about Alexander, because of the marked difference between the two men. Torrey was dignified, with a pointed white beard. He used few gestures while preaching and entirely lacked the humor, persuasiveness, and rough-hewn humanity that had made Moody so beloved. To many, Torrey personified the passing age. In contrast, Alexander had a mild Southern drawl and folksy humor, embodied a freer spirit, and appealed to the audiences because he was informal, warm, energetic, and magnetic. Setting the pattern for a number of song leaders after him, Alexander believed his task was to "warm up" the congregation with rousing singing, buoyant good will, and brisk choir music before Torrey appeared on the platform. He was extremely good at this, and audiences loved him. The contrast with Torrey was often noted, and many came to the meetings simply to hear Alexander. Torrey was annoyed that Alexander had published his own hymnbook for use at the campaigns, and that he made so much money from its sale. Although Alexander donated part of the proceeds to the Institute, Torrey complained that his co-worker kept too much for himself.

After returning from this successful round-the-world tour, Torrey held campaigns in most of the large cities in America from 1905 to 1911. He then retired from evangelism to become dean of the Bible Institute of Los Angeles. By that time another evangelist, J. Wilbur Chapman, had become enormously popular, and in 1908 Alexander became his soloist and song leader. They worked together harmoniously.

Chapman—"The Greatest Evangelist"

In 1895 Moody designated J. Wilbur Chapman (1859–1918) "the greatest evangelist in the country." As a student at Lake Forest College in Illinois, he had attended a campaign and had been led to Christ by Moody himself. During two periods (1890–92 and 1895–99) he was pastor of the large Bethany Presbyterian Church in Philadelphia, which had been founded by the merchant John Wanamaker. From 1892 to 1895 Chapman worked as a full-time evangelist, assisting Moody and conducting campaigns of his own.

Chapman was of average height, with thinning black hair and a pair of pince-nez glasses on his nose. In many ways he was unlike either Torrey or Jones. He was friendly, and never berated his audiences as Jones did; nor did he lecture to them as Torrey did. Like Moody, he used stories and illustrations in his preaching, was gracious and persuasive in his evangelistic appeal, and exhibited a "wooing note" and "winsome style." In 1901 the Presbyterian Church in the U.S.A. General Assembly appointed Chapman secretary of the Committee on Evangelism, and he devoted several years to this.

Chapman's greatest contribution to evangelism—the "simultaneous evangelistic campaign"—developed logically from evangelistic practices of the previous forty years. Chapman's organizers would divide a city into zones and hold simultaneous meetings conducted by teams of evangelists. Chapman and Alexander would conduct the main meetings in a large, central meeting place downtown. It efficiently maximized impact upon a large metropolitan area. This system required a number of co-evangelists, and Chapman brought together younger men who in time became important evangelists in their own right, including William Bell Riley, William E. Biederwolf, James M. Gray, George T. B. Davis, James O. Buswell, and Billy Sunday.

The simultaneous campaign in Philadelphia in 1908 divided the city into forty-two areas. Chapman and Alexander, and twenty-one other pairs of co-evangelists and song leaders, conducted meetings at various locations for three weeks over one-half of the city. Then they covered the other one-half for a similar period. While the local meetings were in progress, Chapman and Alexander conducted services for three weeks at Bethany Presbyterian Church in South Philadelphia, and then changed

222

to the equally large Baptist Temple in the northern part of the city. Approximately four hundred churches cooperated, including Episcopalians, Lutherans, Quakers, and other groups not always sympathetic to mass evangelism. This is evidence of Chapman's broad appeal. The total attendance for all meetings was 1.47 million. In Boston in 1909, Chapman's team conducted their most successful evangelistic campaign using the same method.

The Churches' Many Challenges

In the years following the Civil War, forces had been at work in America that challenged the basic values upon which the nation had been founded. Each of these forces directly or indirectly attacked the assumptions of the Christian faith. These forces bore names like atheism, evolutionary theory, liberalism, materialism, secularism, and cynicism. By the 1920s the very survival of the church seemed in doubt. Doubly disturbing was the fact that much of the attack came from inside the church, from clergy who no longer believed orthodox Christian doctrines. They set out to modify the Protestant denominations, and especially to insert their theologies in the theological seminaries. As a result many schools were never the same again. Their legacy was the gradual weakening, liberalizing, and trivializing of mainline Protestant groups.

To adequately describe the story of twentieth-century evangelism it is necessary to mention a few key opponents of historic Christian faith. Besides Nietzsche's 1888 proclamation that "God is dead," unquestionably the most far-reaching challenge was Charles Darwin's publication in 1859 of *The Origin of Species,* and in 1871 of *The Descent of Man.* While the arguments in *The Origin of Species* were subtle enough to allow religious people to overlook some of their implications, *The Descent of Man* attacked the belief in the divine creation of humanity as well as the supernatural inspiration and authority of the Bible. This attack could not be ignored. Had humans evolved from lower animals or had they been created by God as Genesis stated?

While evolutionary thinking was influencing the study of biblical literature, "higher criticism" of the Bible was beginning to spread through educational circles and to embroil Christian leaders in bitter debate. Higher criticism and theological liberalism seemed to undermine nearly every accepted belief based on Scripture's truth and authority, including the historicity of the patriarchs, Mosaic authorship of the Pentateuch, traditional authorship of the Gospels and Epistles, and the virgin birth and resurrection of Jesus. Christians wondered what was left after the liberals had finished their work. Was the Jesus of Western Christianity still God and Savior? Some felt that the new ideas could somehow be reconciled with the Christian faith. Others, such as Charles Hodge (1797–1878) of Princeton Seminary, refused to accept the idea that God's truth is relative and changing, and sought to defend against the implications arising from this teaching.

The twentieth century brought more difficulties. The first was concern over the social gospel, particularly as developed in America by Washington Gladden and Walter Rauschenbusch. Most churches assumed that Christians had a responsibility to help those who were suffering under massive social problems, especially as these problems manifested themselves in the cities. America had changed rapidly after the Industrial Revolution; it was no longer a homogeneous nation. Churches that had known a secure niche in the leisurely tempo of rural and small-town America were suddenly confronted with a new industrial order, including the enormous problems of massive immigration (mostly Roman Catholic), unemployment, slum housing, extreme poverty, shifting populations, and the general fragmentation of life as new attractions competed for time. But the social gospel made material needs the beginning and end of the church's business.

Next came the Fundamentalist-Modernist controversy, with roots in Enlightenment philosophy, romanticism, German theology, and anti-supernatural materialism. The controversy had gained notoriety through heresy trials and the struggles of the 1880s and 1890s. Horace Bushnell (1802–1876), "the father of American religious liberalism," and Henry Ward Beecher had prepared the way for such movements. Since Beecher was persuaded that doctrines divided people, he never preached on Jesus' death on the cross. Softening Christology made Jesus into a wonderful example, the King of love, and a beautiful unseen Friend. The harsh realities of life? Beecher avoided them. Creeds were of no help. He wrote, "The creeds of the future will begin where the old ones ended: upon the nature of man, his conditions on earth, his spiritual nature, its range, possibilities." And what of God and Christ? Beecher regarded such things as mere matters of opinion.

Such trivializing of Christian teaching took a lowest-common-denominator approach. By eschewing or minimizing doctrine, and regarding humans as essentially good and without serious sin, such men as Beecher, Lyman Abbott, Theodore T. Munger, and Newman Smyth reduced the gospel to a watery concoction of self-help Pelagianism. Sydney Ahlstrom described it as, "a benign and genteel form of religious humanism."[17] Of such liberals Ahlstrom writes, "Often incredibly naive in their evaluations of man, society, and the national destiny, they did little to prepare Americans for the brutal assaults of the twentieth century. In this respect they laid the groundwork for tragedy and disillusion."[18] H. Richard

Niebuhr remarked: "The renovation of which [liberalism] spoke was not so much the restoration of health to a diseased body as the clearing out of the accumulated rubbish of traditional beliefs or customs. . . . A God without wrath brought men without sin into a kingdom without judgment through the ministrations of a Christ without a cross."[19]

Doctrinal battles intensified in a number of denominations after 1870. In 1910 the Presbyterian Church (U.S.A.) General Assembly, in a determined attempt to safeguard the denomination's orthodoxy, ruled that certain articles of faith must be held by anyone seeking ordination: the inerrancy of the Scriptures, the virgin birth of Jesus, the miracles of Jesus, his substitutionary atonement, and his resurrection. In the same year two wealthy men in Los Angeles financed the free distribution of 3 million copies of a series of booklets entitled *The Fundamentals*. The editors brought together the best conservative scholars to highlight and defend six essential Christian beliefs, much as had the Presbyterians. The term *fundamentalist* was derived from this series of books and referred to those concerned with the defense of the essentials of the faith. The term has since taken on a variety of other meanings. *Modernism* likewise described the system of thought opposed to orthodox Christianity. Modernism reinterpreted Christian beliefs to make them compatible with current thinking, and placed the authority of modern historical and scientific knowledge over that of Scripture.

In general, Americans tossed aside old values, including those of Christianity, around the time of the First World War. A moral sag normally follows war, but the years after 1918 were more demoralized than usual. The nation had embraced President Woodrow Wilson's vision and ideal—to end war and the threat to democracy. But the heroic sacrifices in the war had yielded only disappointment and cynicism. An atmosphere of skepticism came on with the crazy years of the "Jazz Age" and the "Roaring Twenties." Materialism was the unlovely offspring of cynicism. These were some of the challenges Billy Sunday faced when he came upon the evangelistic scene in the last years of the nineteenth century.

Sunday—Muscular Christianity

William Ashley Sunday was born on November 19, 1862, in a small log cabin near Ames, Iowa.[20] He never saw his father, who had enlisted as a private in the Union Army and died of disease within a few months. His mother reared a fatherless family of three boys in a home plagued by dire poverty. When Sunday was twelve he was sent to an orphanage for two years. He went to school intermittently, managing to get to high school. At fourteen he worked as a school janitor, getting up at 2 A.M. to stoke the

Billy Sunday shows his athletic preaching form in a studio portrait.
(Courtesy of the Billy Graham Center Museum)

stoves and keep up on his studies. Reflecting on this difficult early period he later remarked, "I know all about the dark and seamy side of life, and if ever a man fought hard, I have fought hard for everything I have gained."

When he was twenty, a player for the Chicago White Sox chanced to see Sunday playing baseball in Marshallton, Iowa. His base-running had made him a local celebrity, and under the Chicago player's guidance he qualified to play outfield for the Chicago White Sox. Soon Sunday was the champion sprinter of the National Baseball League. Although he was never a great hitter, he became the speediest base-runner and the most daring base-stealer in all of major league baseball. He was the first man in the history of baseball to round the bases in fourteen seconds.

One day in 1886, Sunday and some teammates were having a few drinks in a downtown Chicago bar. They went outside and sat on a curbstone to listen to the music and testimonies of a band of workers from a rescue mission. Sunday related:

> Across the street a company of men and women were playing on instruments—horns, flutes, and slide trombones—and the others were singing the gospel hymns that I used to hear my mother sing back in the log cabin in Iowa and back in the old church where I used to go to Sunday school. . . . I sobbed and sobbed and a young man stepped out and said, "We are going down to the Pacific Garden Mission. Won't you come down to the mission? I am sure you will enjoy it."
>
> I arose and said to the boys, "I'm through, I am going to Jesus Christ. We've come to the parting of the ways," and I turned my back on them. Some of them laughed and some of them mocked me; one of them gave me encouragement; others never said a word. . . . I walked to the mission and fell on my knees and staggered out of sin and into the arms of the Saviour.
>
> The next day I had to get out to the ball park and practice. Every morning at ten o'clock we had to be out there. I never slept that night. I was afraid of the horselaugh that gang would give me because I had taken my stand for Jesus Christ. I walked up to the old ball grounds. I will never forget it. Up came Mike Kelly; he said, "Bill, I'm proud of you! Religion is not my long suit, but I'll help you all I can." Up came Anson, the best ball player that ever played the game; Pfeffer, Clarkson, Flint, McCormick . . . there wasn't a fellow in that gang who knocked; every fellow had a word of encouragement for me.[21]

After his conversion, Sunday gave up drinking, the theater, and betting. He continued his baseball career but refused to play on Sundays. Soon he became interested in Helen Thompson, the daughter of a dairy owner. The family did not approve of Sunday at first because he belonged to no church, so he joined the Jefferson Park Presbyterian Church, where the Thompsons were members. Within two years he was asked to be the superintendent of the Sunday school.

"Nell" Thompson married Sunday on September 5, 1888, and shortly after their marriage he transferred to the Pittsburgh team. While he continued to play baseball, he was growing more concerned about the Christian life. This led him to give talks to boys at the YMCAs in whatever city the team was playing. Occasionally a newspaper editor would hear of the well-known ballplayer doing this, and would publish a story on him. Here is an excerpt from one such article:

When speaking, his delivery is pleasant and grammatical. He has a ready command of the English language, and uses many poetic phrases. His knowledge of human nature and the Scriptures were clearly evident in the half-hour's address at the Young Men's Christian Association yesterday afternoon. He made no reference to the baseball profession and instead of using slang, his words were well chosen. He spoke earnestly, but at first seemed somewhat nervous. There was an attendance of about eight hundred, all young men, who were much interested in the address.[22]

Eager to improve himself, in the winter of 1887–88 Sunday took a course in rhetoric at Evanston Academy, and for the next two years he took courses in Bible at the Chicago YMCA. Increasingly he felt the call to Christian work. He often heard Moody speak at the YMCA, but Sunday did not try to become a close friend. The YMCA director urged him to work for them permanently, but he postponed any decision. In 1891 he was again offered a full-time position with the YMCA, but he had just signed a three-year contract to play for the Philadelphia team, and they were unwilling to release him. Sunday prayed for guidance, and suddenly the release from Philadelphia was granted on March 17. Hearing of the release, the Cincinnati team offered Sunday five hundred dollars per month. Since his YMCA job paid only eighty-three dollars a month, he was in a quandary. Nell told him, "There is nothing to consider; you promised God to quit." That settled it; his major league baseball career was over. It had lasted from 1883 to 1891.

After a time, Sunday's work at the YMCA was rewarded with raises, first to twelve hundred dollars a year and then fifteen hundred dollars—good money then. But in 1893 a national depression struck, and the donations on which the YMCA depended dropped sharply. Sunday's salary was often in arrears. By then Billy and Nell had two children to support, and he had also promised to send money home to his invalid mother. Providentially, it was at this time that J. Wilbur Chapman offered him forty dollars a week to work as his assistant in evangelistic campaigns. As Chapman's advance man, Sunday went to cities where campaigns were to begin in a few months. He chose sites, arranged meetings, organized choirs, trained ushers, organized prayer meetings, helped local arrangement committees, and in general tied up loose ends. When a tent was to be used he would supervise that, often erecting it himself. Meetings held in a permanent auditorium required that Sunday attend to a multitude of details. He sold song books for chorister Alexander, helped take up the offering, counseled after the meetings, and when need arose, spoke from the platform. Sunday assisted in meetings in Peoria, Illinois; Terre Haute, Evansville, and Indianapolis in Indiana; Troy, New York; and a number of other cities.

On His Own

In December 1895 Chapman felt called to return to pastoring Bethany Presbyterian Church in Philadelphia, so he gave up evangelistic work. Sunday seemed to be out of a job. Necessity pushed him onto the path that would make him a world-renowned Christian leader. As Sunday told it,

> There I was, out of work, knowing not which way to turn. I had a wife and two children to support. I could not go back to baseball. I had given up my YMCA position. I had no money. What should I do? I laid it before the Lord, and in a short while there came a telegram from a little town named Garner, out in Iowa, asking me to come out and conduct some meetings. I didn't know anybody out there, and I don't know yet why they ever asked me to hold meetings. But I went.
>
> I only had eight sermons, so could not run more than ten days, and that only by taking Saturdays off. That was the beginning of my independent work; but from that day to this I have never had to seek a call to do evangelistic work. I have just gone along, entering the doors that the Lord has opened one after another. Now I have about a hundred sermons and invitations for more than two years in advance.[23]

Garner was located in north central Iowa, west of Mason City, and had a population of roughly two thousand. The three Protestant churches had united for meetings and had rented the local opera house for a week beginning January 9, 1896. At the end of the meetings one newspaper reported that there had been nearly one hundred conversions. Sunday's career had begun; he had received an invitation to conduct meetings in Sigourney (a town of two thousand near Ottumwa) even before he arrived at Garner. Four churches in Sigourney had united, and Sunday was genuinely surprised at the attendances. The local paper stated, "He has had larger audiences than any minister that ever visited our city. . . . One great trouble is there is no house in the city large enough to hold the crowds. . . . A great many are in from the country every night."[24]

Sunday was thirty-four years old and had a wealth of experience as a major league baseball player, railroad man, YMCA worker, and advance man for Chapman. He was of medium height, with a muscular build, and a pleasant but not overly handsome face. He had blue eyes, and light brown hair parted in the middle to hide the small bald spot at the top. During the first years of his new evangelistic career, he cast about to find his own particular style of speaking. It was to change dramatically from the dignified style he affected at first.

Although the Sundays lived in Chicago from 1888 to 1910, Billy deliberately assumed the attitudes and stance of rural America, befitting his Iowa background. He adopted the customs and values of the countryside, recognizing that his audiences, even in large cities, would more quickly identify with a person "of the people" and "down home." At first Sunday centered his campaigns in the Midwest. This region of the nation was quick to appreciate Sunday's character and message. He often called himself "a rube of the rubes," and "a graduate of the university of poverty."

After a few years and many campaigns, he was invited to conduct meetings in Burlington, Iowa, a city known for its numerous saloons and liquor trade. When he arrived, the antagonism toward him was widespread. Five weeks later, to the astonishment of all, public opinion had done an abrupt about-face. While there were still plenty of saloons in town, their business had been greatly weakened, and it gave Sunday enormous prestige when papers across Iowa carried headlines such as "Burlington Is Dry: Billy Sunday Has Made Graveyard Out Of Once Fast Town." The Burlington *Hawk-eye* stated:

> Rev. W. A. Sunday's labors of five weeks closed in Burlington amid a scene of wild enthusiasm. A half acre of fluttering handkerchiefs and cheers from six thousand throats, shouting in a delirium of feeling, after twenty-five hundred persons had been added to the membership of Burlington churches, with hundreds more giving notice of their coming a little later. After this staid old city, firm in the conservatism of a one-time capital of Iowa, had been faced about and given such an uplift of moral standard that the observer within its gates who saw its intense antagonism six weeks ago, is overwhelmed with amazement at the change. . . .
>
> The coming of the three hundred and forty converts of the last day was a scene worthy of better description than it will ever have. . . . Perhaps the loudest applause was when there came down a side aisle, and across the space in front of the platform, a man with a mass of silver-gray hair, topping a very strong face, a high forehead and a large head with many cranial curves suggestive of Robert E. Lee—a man whose head and features would attract attention anywhere, and who seemed to be specially the object of regard here in Burlington, where he has been a school principal for many years.[25]

Sunday had been critical of clergymen for years and often pilloried or kidded them when he spoke, suggesting they were not doing their job. Perhaps the fact that he was not ordained disturbed him, and he may have teased them in order to give himself a greater sense of dignity and standing among the ministers with whom he daily came in contact. In 1903 he decided to appeal to the Presbytery of Chicago for ordination. The presbytery was agreeable to the suggestion, since by this time Sunday was well known. Although he did not have a seminary degree, the examining committee decided that his experience and preeminence among Christian workers made him a very special case. In his examination before the committee, he was asked theological questions for an hour. "He answered their questions to their entire satisfaction," one biographer writes, "and his orthodoxy was pronounced sound in every particular. He created an excellent impression by his frank, honest manner, and the rapidity with which he gave his answers."[26] One member of the committee said, "God has used him to win more souls to Christ than all of us combined, and must have ordained him long before we ever thought of it." Chapman preached the ordination sermon.

At first, Sunday had imitated Chapman's ways in the pulpit and borrowed his sermons—for he had none of his own. He admired the nationally-famous and experienced older man. Chapman's style was much in line with the somewhat flowery orators of the day, such as Robert G. Ingersoll and William Jennings Bryan—men who during the era of the Chautauqua camp meetings were revered by many as superb rhetoricians. At first Sunday dressed like Chapman, wearing a cutaway coat, wing collar, and bow tie. By 1900, however, he realized that this did not suit him, and gradually he adopted more natural mannerisms. While retaining the good grammar he had been taught, Sunday discovered that he preferred the folksy stories of Jones and the persuasive skill of Moody. He mastered the art of using colorful word pictures to describe anything, and captivated his audience with powerful oratory. During his 1901 meetings in Perry, Iowa, the local newspaper stated, "From the first sermon it was evident that Mr. Sunday was a man of great natural ability and liberal culture, a fine orator, with an extensive vocabulary, intensely in earnest, and before the end of the week all knew that we had an expert in evangelistic work. The sermons were all good, without a single exception. Full of sentiment, pathos, argument, good logic, word pictures, impersonation, etc., all used to illustrate and drive home gospel truths."[27] As a result, he filled the auditorium night after night.

Rapid-Fire Oratory and Athleticism

It took Sunday several years, however, to arrive at his inimitable trademark style: energetic, athletic, and acrobatic movements with a rapid-fire, humorous, and slangy delivery that kept the audience—whether a thousand in a Midwestern city or fifteen thousand in a metropolis—in the palm of his hand. He learned most from Milan B. Williams, with whom he had worked in campaigns from 1893 through 1896. One of Williams' habits while preaching was to doff his coat, roll up his sleeves, pull off his tie, and use athletic and energetic motions. Eventually Sunday incorporated all of this, doing it far more

Billy and Nell lead a Sunday school parade of 22,000 through downtown Wilkes-Barre, Pennsylvania. (Courtesy of the Billy Graham Center Museum)

convincingly than Williams. He learned early that this approach imme-diately convinced crowds that they were not about to hear some dry, hum-drum speech. With a large admixture of exciting entertainment, his message would carry them along for an hour. Punctuating a mes-sage delivered at breakneck speed (trained stenographers said three hundred words a minute), he would do handstands, dash across the platform, hang precipitously over its edge while pointing, stand on chairs, and whirl about. At the climax of one story he used occa-sionally, he would pretend to be a ball player sliding into home plate, diving across the platform on his stomach. It was sensationalism, and it drew crowds.

None of this is to suggest that Sunday would tolerate emotionalism among his audiences, or even supportive "Amens!" He warned often that he had no time for that. William McLoughlin, who has studied Sunday extensively, wrote that his revivals "were thoroughly orderly and respectable affairs. . . . models of controlled mass response in which there was no place for idiosyncratic individual reactions."[28] All atten-tion was focused on Sunday; he had become America's top public speaker because he was superb at controlling and moving audiences.

Perhaps the highest praise ever given him was from Heywood Broun, drama critic of the *New York Tribune.* In 1915 Broun reviewed a new play from George M. Cohan in which Cohan parodied Sunday, and Broun wrote,

> George Cohan has forced a comparison between himself and his greatest rival in the use of dramatic slang, and strange as it may seem, it is George and not Billy who cracks under the strain. . . . George Cohan has neither the punch nor the pace of Billy Sunday. . . . It is true that Cohan waved the flag first, but Billy Sunday has waved it harder. . . . It is in language that the superiority of Sunday is most evident. . . . All in all we believe that Sunday has more of the dramatic instinct than Cohan.[29]

Though some complained of Sunday's sensationalism, crowds were packing the wooden tabernacles that, after 1905, he required to be built in cities where his campaigns were to be held. Even though the tabernacles seated thousands, they usually proved too small, and hundreds of people were turned away each meeting. In most cities, every seat was filled for three meetings on Sundays and two meetings each weekday. This pace put terrific demands on the evangelist. In the Philadelphia campaign of 1915, people began entering the tabernacle hours before the meeting, as soon as the doors were opened, to be sure of getting a seat. McLoughlin has written,

> Even in a tabernacle crowded with twenty thousand people, Sunday managed to establish an intimacy with each individual which observers could only describe as "magnetic." . . . Even such a self-possessed and hostile critic as H. L. Mencken admitted after hearing Sunday that "many persons in that crowd, I dare say, came away with a certain respect for the whirling doctor's earnestness, and a keen sense of his personal charm—as I did myself."[30]

Billy and Rody

In 1900 Sunday hired Fred Fischer as his chorister. Fischer was tall and had a walrus mustache. He did well as the singer, but was somewhat stiff. After Fischer left him in 1910, Homer A. Rodeheaver joined Sunday's growing staff. Finally the evangelist had found a chorister who matched his style. "Rody," as he was called by everyone, was born in Ohio in 1880 and reared in Tennessee. Before joining Sunday, he had been the chorister for evangelist William E. Biederwolf for five years. Rodeheaver used all of the techniques developed by Alexander, but under his direction music played a greater and more powerful part than ever before in evangelistic meetings. The choirs were larger, sometimes com-

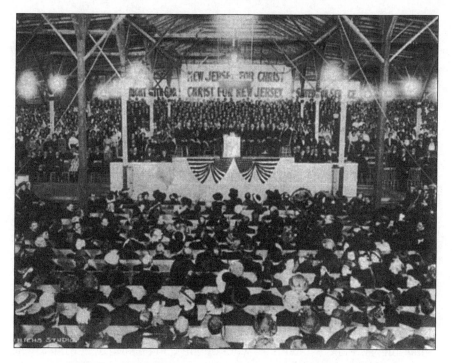

*Dedication of a "Billy Sunday Tabernacle" erected for a 1915 crusade
in Paterson, New Jersey (Courtesy of the Billy Graham Center Museum)*

prising two thousand singers. Rodeheaver played the trombone and
directed these large choirs skillfully. He had dark wavy hair and handsome features, with a warm, outgoing personality that charmed audiences. He and Sunday soon grew into a smooth-working team. Rody's
task was to greet a crowd at the beginning of a meeting and lead them in
the spirited singing of gospel songs and choruses, interspersed with jokes
and short stories. He always added a good amount of politeness and
charm with his mild Southern accent and smooth manner. Favorite
hymns he used constantly were: "One Day," "Jesus, What a Friend for
Sinners" (both by J. Wilbur Chapman), "Since Jesus Came Into My Heart,"
"More Like the Master," "The Old Rugged Cross," "I Walk With the King,
Hallelujah," and "Brighten the Corner Where You Are." Rodeheaver
trained the choirs so well that, when suddenly called upon during the
meeting, he could announce the number of a hymn and have the choir
singing it lustily within seconds.

An anecdote from their revival in Providence, Rhode Island, during
World War I illustrates the smooth management of the meetings. Sunday asked the vast crowd for contributions to defray expenses, and had

those signify who would contribute fifty dollars, twenty-five, ten, and five dollars (large amounts in those days). When he asked for those who would at least give one dollar to stand up, the two pianists on the platform suddenly began pounding out "The Star-Spangled Banner" as loud as possible—thus forcing everyone to stand out of respect. The *Providence Journal* wrote, "No need of telling what happened. Everybody stood up and broke into a roar of laughter and it was noticeable that when the dishpans came back greenbacks were more in evidence than silver."[31]

"Sunday Gets Results"

It was difficult to dislike Sunday. Some spoke of his "vulgarity and coarseness," but for each of those, probably ten said he was hilarious and emotionally moving. Some clergymen condemned him for lowering the dignity of the pulpit, but even they usually supported his campaigns. They had to admit, "Sunday gets results." Many pastors who at first reluctantly agreed to invite him to their city, later confessed how much their churches had benefited. When Pearse Pinch, a minister in Fairfield, Iowa, was asked about Sunday, he responded, "The man has trampled all over me and my theology. . . . He has outraged every ideal

Leading Revival Campaigns of Billy Sunday

Date	City	Conversions
1912–1913	Columbus	18,137
1914	Pittsburgh	25,797
1915	Philadelphia	41,724
1915	Syracuse	21,155
1916	Trenton	19,640
1916	Baltimore	23,085
1916	Kansas City, Mo.	25,646
1916	Detroit	27,109
1916–1917	Boston	64,484
1917	Buffalo	38,853
1917	New York City	98,264
1918	Chicago	49,165
1920	Norfolk	20,000

Source: *Statistics from William G. McLoughlin, Jr.,* Billy Sunday Was His Real Name *(Chicago, 1955), 45 ff.*

I have had regarding my sacred profession. But what does that count against the results he has accomplished? My congregation will be increased by hundreds."[32]

Though some may have thought him uncouth, *America Magazine* polled its readers in 1914 on the question, "Who is the greatest man in the United States?" and Sunday came in eighth. The only other clergyman named was Methodist bishop John H. Vincent, co-founder of the Chautauqua camp meeting movement.

Over a period of forty years Sunday conducted almost three hundred evangelistic campaigns. The preceding table shows something of both his rapid pace and incredible results. From his twenty most successful campaigns, including those listed in the table, a total of more than 593,000 people claimed to be converted. During his lifetime—in the days before public address systems, radios, and electronic amplification—he spoke to more than 100 million people, with conversions numbering probably more than 1 million.[33]

The years 1908–20 were the peak of his career. During those years, Sunday had to bypass the smaller Midwestern cities and towns where he had been so successful, turning instead to America's metropolises. After a forty-nine-day crusade in Columbus, Ohio, at the end of 1912, followed by campaigns in Pittsburgh and other large cities, attendance and the number of converts began to skyrocket. Coincidentally, the period from 1908 to 1920 was also a boom period for industrial production, farm prices, and wages in general.

However, urbanization brought profound changes that threatened Sunday and the nation's Christians. As people flowed into the cities, crime soared, literacy declined, slums multiplied, and dangers increased. Like most Americans brought up before World War I, Sunday saw a troubled nation, and preached messages that sought to reinforce important values. He emphasized that America had been built on work, patriotism, concern for one another, rugged individualism, and Christian faith. When World War I came and these virtues were much needed, Sunday was at the pinnacle of his fame. Even skeptics had to admit that he stressed all the right things.

After the 1918 Chicago campaign, Sunday began visiting the smaller cities once again. By 1920, however, he faced a number of problems.[34] The country was changing and, it seemed, beginning to tire of Billy. Radio and movies were strong attractions now, and crowds were harder to get at rallies. In addition, Billy and Nell Sunday had problems with their children. Although their daughter Helen was never difficult, all three sons grieved Sunday and his wife. Their son George committed suicide in 1933.

Billy Sunday died of a heart attack on November 6, 1935, in Chicago. In reflecting on the career of this gifted evangelist, a noted historian of revivals observes:

> The printed reports of Sunday's meetings portrayed his talents only imperfectly, but the phonograph, the motion pictures, and ultimately, in his last years, the talking pictures caught the excitement of the evangelist in action and preserved for posterity a record of the genius and skill and personality which combined to make Billy Sunday what he was. He was considerably more than the sum of his parts, yet it is possible only to describe these parts. The whole must be left to speak for itself.[35]

Graham, Palau, and Modern Revival Movements

For some years before the death of Billy Sunday in 1935, mass evangelism suffered a decline in vitality. Sunday's own campaigns peaked from 1908 to 1920, and then tapered off. He and Homer Rodeheaver could not maintain their dazzling pace indefinitely, but other reasons inspired the decline. World War I brought about profound national changes. After most wars a moral let down loosens behavior, but during the "Jazz Age" religion suffered a reversal that lasted about twenty years. Critics of Christianity thought, or fervently hoped, that this decline would be permanent. They failed to recognize, however, that Christianity had gone through many cycles over its nineteen-hundred-year history, always rebounding with a new vigor.

238

Unadorned earnest preaching, simple gestures, and content that sticks close to Scripture have marked Billy Graham's preaching. (Billy Graham Evangelistic Association)

The Roaring Twenties

Doughboys who returned from Europe after World War I had tasted European morality. As a result America lost much of its innocence. Materialism and cynicism set in as Americans cut loose from what Sigmund Freud termed their "inhibitions." The twenties was a decade of enthusiasm for get-rich-quick schemes. The virtues of hard work and cautious saving were commonly ridiculed. Grabbing superficial tidbits of Freud's theories, many believed sexual repressions had caused a multitude of societal wrongs, so skirts rose and semi-nudity became fashionable. "Flaming youth" traded in the demure young lady that James

Montgomery Flagg had drawn so enchantingly in 1910, replacing her with the 1920s "flapper." The new model of womanhood had bobbed tresses and dresses, low-cut necklines, painted lips, rouged cheeks, and a dangling cigarette.

This generation viewed churches, especially rural ones, as dreary and old-fashioned. Young people in the frenzied 1920s, with their gin-filled hip-flasks, were glued together in the syncopated embrace of wild new dances. Prohibition inevitably fed the moral decay. Authorized in 1919 by the Eighteenth Amendment as implemented by the Volstead Act, prohibition arrived at just the wrong time and naïvely set an impossible burden of enforcement on local government. While the Midwest and South largely supported the abolition of alcohol, Easterners hated it, especially immigrants from cultures with strong drinking habits. "Speakeasies" replaced the corner saloons, with women increasingly frequenting these places. Both sexes considered it the height of sophistication to flout laws they disliked. "Bathtub gin" and "home brew" became popular as many wallowed in booze.

The New "Freedom"

Meanwhile, churches declined in intellectual leadership. The prophets of the moral revolt were literary. F. Scott Fitzgerald, Theodore Dreiser, George Jean Nathan, Joseph Wood Krutch, and others attacked America's "Puritanism" and any interference with the new freedom. They dismissed Christianity as a blend of cant, prudery, and sanctimony from which moderns must emancipate themselves or be smothered. Krutch declared that "love," "righteousness," and "sin" were "shadows, as essentially unreal as some of the theological dogmas which have been completely forgotten."[1]

Notable among the new novelists, Sinclair Lewis produced enormously popular satires of small-town life and hypocrisies. One of his most vicious was *Elmer Gantry,* portraying a felonious clergyman who fooled a host of assorted boobs. Another defiant modern, Henry L. Mencken—"the Bad Boy of Baltimore"—used his intellectual pulpit in the *Baltimore Sun* and the *American Mercury* to castigate everything that met with his disapproval. His targets included marriage, patriotism, the "booboisie" (a combination of "boob" and "bourgeoisie") of the Bible Belt, and religion. "Protestantism is down with a wasting disease," he chortled. "Every day a new Catholic church goes up; every day another Methodist or Presbyterian church is turned into a garage."[2]

The raucous discord of the Fundamentalist-Modernist controversy even spilled over into the public schools. Christian parents claimed the teaching of Darwinian evolution undermined faith in God and a belief in the divine creation of humankind. But theirs was an uphill struggle, doomed in the climate of antagonism toward anything "religious."[3] Winthrop Hudson writes,

> Curiously enough, during the very decades when Protestantism was reaching the peak of its prestige and apparent influence, the nerve which had impelled two centuries of advance was being cut. A long process of theological erosion had opened the way to a rather complete assimilation of Protestantism to the model of the world. With its basic theological insights largely emasculated, Protestantism was robbed of any independently grounded vision of life and became more and more the creature of American culture rather than its creator.[4]

Great numbers of church members recognized that their denominations were sliding into doctrinal compromise with modernism.

As for mass evangelism and revivals, the liberal attitude was expressed by Harvard Divinity School's dean, Willard L. Sperry:

> Billy Sunday seems to have been, for the present at least, the last of this particular succession. . . . [Sunday] discredited the tradition in which he stood. He represents the final degeneration of what had been one of our major religious institutions. . . . We are tired of religious revivals as we have known them in the last half century. Their theology was often incredible; their applied psychology was filled with emotional dangers; their influence was too ephemeral; their permanent residue was too meagre; their mechanism too obvious, too well oiled; and their commercial instinct much too highly developed.[5]

Two Religions

In its giddiness, the nation edged closer to the Great Depression of the 1930s. The speculative bubble of the stock market continued to spiral upward—a fool's paradise of paper profits. On "Black Tuesday," October 29, 1929, multitudes lost everything. More than five thousand banks collapsed by 1932; 13 million workers were jobless that year. Despairing, hungry men tramped streets looking for nonexistent jobs. Bread lines and soup kitchens appeared, and honest, hard-working men often could find no better job than selling apples on the street corner. At its depth, the depression reduced respectable people to fighting over the contents of garbage cans or living in shantytowns called "Hoovervilles." The gloom and misery seemed like an endless national nightmare throughout the 1930s.

The Great Depression changed church life. With so many out of work, offerings fell, and benevolent works had to be curtailed at a time when they were most needed. Foreign missions budgets were slashed. Some churches closed their doors. In 1937 Samuel C. Kincheloe of the Chicago Theological Seminary published a *Research Memo on Religion in the Depression* for the Social Science Council. He stated that "many looked for the depression to bring revivalism back," but there was no evidence of this. He believed secularization so pervaded society that a widespread revival of religion was impossible.[6] In retrospect, William G. McLoughlin offers quite a different perspective:

> What Kincheloe missed, as Sperry did, was the fact that there was a revival of religion going on among those citizens who had not become secularized but who, for that very reason, were not frequenters of the churches of the respectable denominations which Kincheloe and Sperry looked upon as the only significant repositories of American religious life. . . . America had by the mid-1930s two national Protestant religions.[7]

The first of these two religions was liberal Protestantism; the second a blend of groups loosely called *fundamentalist, pietist, conservative, orthodox,* and (later) *evangelical.* It is wrong to label all of these people "pietist," "holiness," or "Pentecostal." Most of the conservative camp came out of mainline Protestant denominations and simply wanted to return to what the Methodists, Presbyterians, Baptists, and others had previously stood for. Only one wing of the vast conservative camp identified with holiness groups.

The Pentecostal Revival

The remarkable work of Phoebe Palmer in furthering the doctrines of holiness and preparing the way for the Revival of 1858 was noted in chapter 8. Her "Tuesday meetings for the Promotion of Holiness," begun in about 1835, played an important role in stressing the experience of entire sanctification in Methodist circles. Many held the Wesleyan doctrine of Christian perfection, but Palmer popularized terms such as "baptism of the Holy Ghost" that have since been used by the Pentecostal-Holiness movement. After Palmer, came a number of holiness leaders including Charles Parham of Topeka, Kansas; Charles Cullis of Boston; A. B. Simpson; and John Alexander Dowie. New denominations arose. In 1895, J. P. Widney and Phineas Bresee of Los Angeles organized the first congregation of the Church of the Nazarene, which, after merging with other groups in 1908 and 1914, became the largest holiness denomination.

In 1904 and 1905, Christians around the world were stirred by news of the Welsh Revival. A layman, Evan Roberts, provided the central focus for this spontaneous awakening throughout Wales. In some measure the proliferation of the holiness movement in the early years of the twentieth century grew from the impact of the Welsh experience. Beginning in April 1906, William J. Seymour, a black holiness preacher, led prayer meetings in a Los Angeles home. Crowds began to congregate at the home, and the meetings relocated to a run-down former Methodist church on Azusa Street. During three years of continuous meetings, thousands—black and white—claimed to have received "the second blessing." Ministers from around the country visited Azusa Street, carrying the Pentecostal revival to such cities as Indianapolis, Akron, Winnipeg, Dallas, Cleveland, San Francisco, and Nyack, New York.

In Nyack, A. B. Simpson had founded the Christian and Missionary Alliance (CMA) Missionary Training Institute. Two of its instructors, W. C. Stevens and G. P. Pardington, taught that the church would soon receive the "latter rain" outpouring of the Holy Spirit. The evidence of this last days blessing would be Christians speaking in tongues. Simpson himself never endorsed the tongues movement as the only proof of the Spirit's baptism, and the CMA divided over the issue.

The holiness movement achieved fame during the 1920s through the ministry of Aimee Semple McPherson (1890–1944). Converted under the ministry of Robert Semple in 1907, she later married him. Together they went as missionaries to Hong Kong in 1910, where he died. After marrying Harold McPherson she began holding camp meetings on the eastern seaboard of the United States, and later settled in Los Angeles. In 1927 Mrs. McPherson founded the International Church of the Foursquare Gospel. The declaration of faith accepted by its members (about ninety thousand in the early 1990s) stresses Pentecostal distinctives. With her masterful fund-raising methods, she built the $1.5 million Angelus Temple in Los Angeles and carried on a sensational ministry for several years.

Within Pentecostalism two parallel movements arose after World War II—the Healing and Latter Rain revivals. Evangelists associated with the Healing revival included Oral Roberts, William M. Branham, Jack Coe, A. A. Allen, and T. L. Osborn. Roberts, originally a Methodist minister, had the longest and best-known career, largely by virtue of television. Branham said that Roberts' command over demons, sin, and disease was the most amazing he had seen. Roberts began a magazine, *Healing Waters*, in 1947, and by 1953 the circulation had increased to 260,000. He later founded Oral Roberts University in Tulsa, which grew to a $125 million campus on five hundred rolling acres. A two hundred-foot prayer tower at the heart of the campus became a chief attraction in Tulsa.

Splintered Denominations

During the 1920s, 1930s, and 1940s, schisms troubled several denominations. The American (Northern) Baptists, for example, divided in 1932, with a large number of churches withdrawing to form the General Association of Regular Baptists (GARB). In 1947 another major segment broke away to constitute the Conservative Baptist Association of America. The loss of a sizable number of churches, including some of its healthiest, greatly weakened the American Baptist Convention. Although numerically not so large as the Baptist defections, break-off groups of Presbyterians tended to include leading intellectuals of the conservative Princeton tradition. After Princeton Seminary reorganized with a policy of greater theological openness, J. Gresham Machen left in 1929 to begin Westminster Theological Seminary and, a decade later, the Orthodox Presbyterian Church (OPC). Some of these groups called themselves *fundamentalists*; others thought the term connoted extremist tendencies and preferred to be thought of as *evangelical, conservative,* or *orthodox.*

Members of the Interdenominational Association of Evangelists (IAE) found it more difficult to find cities or churches willing to sponsor evangelistic campaigns in the hard economic times. Hundreds of members still gathered for annual IAE conventions in Winona Lake, Indiana, but many notable Bible teachers and evangelists either took important pulpits in major cities or founded their own churches. William E. Biederwolf, who had conducted his own campaigns since leaving J. Wilbur Chapman's evangelistic team in 1909, accepted the pulpit of the Royal Poinciana Chapel in Palm Beach, Florida; Paul Rader founded the Chicago Gospel Tabernacle in 1922; Theodore H. Elsner founded the Philadelphia Gospel Tabernacle; Harry D. Clarke went to the Billy Sunday Memorial Tabernacle in Sioux City, Iowa; Edward J. Rolling founded the Detroit Metropolitan Tabernacle; and Dewitt Johnson accepted the pulpit of the People's Gospel Tabernacle in Fort Wayne, Indiana.

The Parachurch Movement

The new, large, nondenominational churches promoted an impressive array of programs, including year-round Bible conferences for youth and adults, radio programs (and even a radio station), preaching in prisons and rescue missions, and various publications. In addition, most of these institutional churches maintained close relations with nearby Bible schools or institutes, with well-known pastors serving on their faculties and boards. During the first four decades of the twentieth century, at least twenty-five Bible colleges and Bible schools were organized across the nation, many with substantial facilities and student bodies. Their paradigm was Moody Bible Institute of Chicago, begun in 1886.

With the major denominations cool or even antagonistic to these ventures, many Christian leaders in the 1930s and 1940s saw the need for new techniques and institutions. Traditional evangelistic methods no longer worked as effectively. One answer, the parachurch organization, came into prominence at this time. Unaffiliated Christian agencies had proliferated in the volunteer movement of the nineteenth century. Between 1810 and 1830 many "benevolent societies" like the American Bible Society had sprung up. The new organizations differed in one important respect from those early societies: the older ones were compatible with the theology and aims of the denominations, whereas the twentieth-century organizations grew mostly out of a reaction to the liberal drift of Protestant denominations. Conservatives hoped that the new agencies would fill in areas of ministry that lacked a strong biblical influence.

At first the parachurch movement grew at a slow rate, but in the late 1930s, and especially after World War II, it expanded rapidly. In time, independently supported ecumenical agencies came to occupy every conceivable ministry niche including publishing houses, television and radio programs, radio stations (more than a thousand), home and foreign mission operations, Bible societies, evangelistic agencies, periodicals, theological seminaries, colleges, Bible institutes, day schools, women's ministries, men's ministries, youth ministries, prison ministries, summer conferences and camps, professional societies, avocational societies, charismatic groups, and Bible study groups. In the last half of the twentieth century, parachurch agencies took over many functions traditionally served only by denominations. In addition, they invented entirely new areas of religious activity. This meant the denominations lost millions of dollars as Christians shifted their confidence and contributions to organizations outside the institutional church. All of this set the scene for a dramatic innovation in American Christianity: an explicitly nondenominational version of evangelical faith. By 1970, "evangelicalism" was the fastest-growing and most dynamic Protestantism in America—indeed throughout the world.

The National Association of Evangelicals

The founding of the National Association of Evangelicals for United Action, in 1942, gave the greatest impetus to the emerging nonsectarian evangelical consensus. The leaders who contributed vision and energy to launch the NAE had the voice of authority, since they occupied important pulpits or positions with educational institutions, periodicals, and mission boards. Their number included Harold J. Ockenga of Boston's Park Street Church, first president of the NAE; Carl F. H. Henry of Fuller Seminary, founding editor of *Christianity Today*; Donald Grey Barnhouse of Philadelphia's Tenth Presbyterian Church; William Ward Ayer of New York's Calvary Baptist Church; Charles E. Fuller of "The Old Fashioned Revival Hour" radio broadcast; and V. Raymond Edman of Wheaton College. Other important leaders were John W. Bradbury, R. T. Davis, Rutherford L. Decker, Howard W. Ferrin, W. H. Houghton, Torrey M. Johnson, L. R. Marston, James deForest Murch, J. Edwin Orr, Stephen W. Paine, Paul S. Rees, Charles Templeton, and J. Elwin Wright. These were the intellectual elite of the emerging evangelical movement, respected by millions of church members. Murch, editor of *United Evangelical Action* (semiofficial organ of the NAE), declared early, "The very heart of this movement is evangelism."[8]

By 1950 the NAE represented at least 10 million Christians and thirty evangelical denominations or organizations. Evangelicals came from every major tradition: Reformed, Baptist, Arminian, holiness, and Pentecostal. The NAE's constitution made clear the purpose for its founding. A vast number of Christians wanted to be loyal to the gospel and to Jesus Christ. While their theologies might differ in nonessentials, they were in agreement concerning salvation by grace through faith and an authoritative Scripture. These people and churches needed organizational unity, because "in many areas of Christian endeavor the organizations which now purport to be the representatives of Protestant Christianity have departed from the faith of Jesus Christ."[9]

As first president of the NAE, Ockenga summed up their hopes for the future in a news release on December 8, 1957:

The New Evangelicalism has changed its strategy from one of separation to one of infiltration. Instead of static front battles the new theological war is one of movement. The results have been phenomenal. . . . Since I first coined the phrase 'The New Evangelicalism' ten years ago, the evangelical forces have been welded into an organizational front. First, there is the National Association of Evangelicals which provides articulation for the movement on the denominational level; second, there is the World Evangelical Fellowship which binds together these individual national associations of some twenty-six countries into a world organization; third, there is the new apologetic literature stating this point of view which is now flowing from the presses of the great publishers, including Macmillans and Harpers; fourth, there is the existence of Fuller Theological Seminary and other evangelical seminaries which are fully committed to orthodox Christianity and a resultant social philosophy; fifth, there is the establishment of *Christianity Today*, a bi-weekly publication, to articulate the convictions of the movement; sixth, there is the appearance of an evangelist, Billy Graham, who on the mass level is the spokesman of the convictions and ideas of the New Evangelicalism. The strength of this movement is recognized by the *Christian Century,* America's leading theologically liberal magazine, by its expression of fear that this movement may challenge the religious scene and change the religious climate in this nation.

The Renewal of Religious Interest

It took the Second World War to pull the United States from the Great Depression. By the conclusion of the war in 1945, the nation was again prosperous and able to turn its attention to peacetime concerns. It was in many ways a different nation than that of the 1920s and 1930s. Sobered by the Depression and war, it seemed willing to give Christianity another hearing. Suddenly, when Dwight D. Eisenhower became president in 1953, it was again popular to belong to a church, and his personal example set the tone. As Winthrop Hudson has written,

> By the 1950s it was evident that the United States was in the midst of a religious revival. Critical voices became muted, and religion was riding the crest of a wave of popularity. Church attendance soared, contributions mounted, and unprecedented sums were spent on new church buildings. Publishers discovered that religious books were profitable, and the more popular volumes dominated the best-seller lists for extended periods of time. Seldom had religion been held in greater public esteem.[10]

The religious revival of the 1950s was formless and unstructured, reinforcing all religions indiscriminately. While Christian churches benefited enormously from the new atmosphere, and church rolls burgeoned, other faiths prospered as well.

In the midst of all the popularity of religion in the 1950s, much of it superficial, American evangelicalism began to transcend its own fragmentation and sectarianism. A new consensus of vital "mere Christianity" expressed itself. Beginning with the 1948 World Congress on Evangelism, and receiving additional impetus from the 1966 Berlin Congress on Evangelism, evangelicals developed a worldwide Christian outlook. The result was an era characterized by large-scale international evangelical conferences, consultations, councils, and caucuses that gathered delegates and experts on Christian action and evangelism from around the world. A number of important evangelists and theologians emerged to command international respect and attention. Some were founders of the NAE, others rose to prominence later. Among these were well-known names like Billy Graham, Luis Palau, John Stott, J. I. Packer, and Bill Bright.

Graham—Statesman Evangelist

A worldwide evangelistic movement was born from the work of a fiery evangelist named Mordecai F. Ham. Ham began eleven weeks of evangelistic meetings in a large "tabernacle" of pine boards erected on a city block in Charlotte, North Carolina. The year was 1934, and the meetings began somewhat slowly. Ham, despite his Southern courtesy, criticized the city's ministers, and they responded by opposing his meetings. Local newspapers attacked him. Undaunted, Ham continued, and the attendance grew. Ham was an old-fashioned, hellfire-and-brimstone evangelist who pulled no punches. Walter Ramsey was his song leader. Ham heard that a few students at Charlotte's Central High School were guilty of fornication, and he announced this to the city. It caused a sensation, the papers picked it up, infuriated students marched on Ham's meetings, revival attendance soared, and the city was agog. One sixteen-year-old student decided to attend one of the meetings to see what might happen next, and his family also began to attend.

This popular high school basketball and baseball player was tall, with wavy blond hair, blue eyes, and tanned skin. He had no interest in church, but went to the meeting with a friend and sat at the back of the largest crowd he had ever seen. The crowd—more than five thousand—filled every seat; others were sitting on benches, chairs, and boxes beyond the board walls. When Ramsey led the congregation and choir in "Hallelujah, What a Savior!" the tabernacle fairly shook, and then the white-haired Ham began to preach. The student was "spellbound," he wrote thirty years later, "each listener became deeply involved with the evangelist, who had an almost embarrassing way of describing your sins and shortcomings and of demanding, on pain of divine judgment, that you mend your ways. As I listened, I began to have thoughts I had never known before."[11]

That night in his room he stared through the window at the full moon and felt "a kind of stirring in my breast that was both pleasant and scary. Next night all my father's mules and horses could not have kept me away from the meetings." Over several weeks the young man came under great conviction. One night Ham, halfway through the sermon, pointed a finger straight at him and thundered, "You're a sinner!" The student ducked behind the hat of a woman in front of him. He then applied for a place in the choir, although he could not carry a tune, in order to escape the preacher by being behind him.

Several more evenings followed until one night Ham stated, "There's a great sinner in this place tonight." The student said to himself, "Mother has been telling him about me." Finally Ham gave the invitation and the choir sang "Just As I Am." As people gathered down by the pulpit, the student stayed put. Then the choir began, "Almost Persuaded, Christ to

Believe." When he could stand it no longer, he turned to his friend Grady Wilson and said, "Let's go." He and his friend made their way down to the altar. There were no tears, no overwhelming emotions, no visions; but he later declared, "Right there I made my decision for Christ. It was a simple as that—and as conclusive." His father came down to him, threw his arms around him, and thanked God for his decision. The student, William Franklin Graham, had committed his life to Jesus.[12]

Graham was born near Charlotte, North Carolina, on November 7, 1918. His father, Frank Graham, was strong in character, six feet two inches tall, and a life-long farmer. In 1916 he had married Morrow Coffee of Steele Creek near Charlotte, and their first son, William, was born in the frame farmhouse on their prosperous three hundred-acre dairy farm. In time, three more children were born—Catherine, Melvin, and Jean. Baseball became Billy's consuming interest, although he barely made the Sharon High School team as first baseman. While not an outstanding student, he developed a love for history, and by the time he was fifteen he had read more than one hundred history books.

The Grahams worked hard all week long, but there were generous doses of fun for the kids. The Sunday Sabbath was strictly observed, and its highlight was the five-mile drive by car to the small Associate Reformed Presbyterian Church in Charlotte. This denomination remained staunchly faithful to Scottish Presbyterian traditions. Only the metrical psalms were sung, and children were disciplined strictly. Billy, with all the others, learned the Westminster Shorter Catechism, but he was not interested in religion and "thought it all hogwash." His consuming interest was racing his father's car against other boys on the deserted back roads, turning curves on two wheels, and trying to get all the speed he could. A high school senior at the time of his conversion, Billy still hoped to play baseball. Slowly his plans changed, possibly because he knew his parents were praying for their tall, gangly son. His father said years later, "When I was converted I felt immediately a desire to preach. But never once was there the slightest encouragement from God. My heart burned and I wondered why God did not answer my prayer. Now I feel I have the answer. I believe my part was to raise a son to be a preacher."[13] Billy's mother set aside a time each day to pray for him, a practice she continued for many years. Another influence was his friend Grady Wilson, who made up his mind almost immediately to preach.

After graduation, Billy wanted to enter college. His parents' first choice was Bob Jones College (then at Cleveland, Tennessee) because they admired several graduates of that school. After a summer in which Billy and Grady worked as Fuller Brush salesmen—with Billy's sales at the top of the list—the two entered Bob Jones College in the fall of 1936. One biographer describes the experience: "In his uncertain frame of mind he found the religious rigidity of the place oppressive. Dr. Jones was a difficult taskmaster. There were rules and regulations galore; a too regimented social life; no intercollegiate sports. . . . He left at the end of the first semester."[14] But the words of the president, Bob Jones, rang in his ears as he departed: "Billy, if you leave and throw your life away at a little country Bible school, the chances are you'll never be heard of. At best all you could amount to would be a poor country Baptist preacher somewhere out in the sticks."[15]

Florida Bible Institute

Billy felt more at home at the Florida Bible Institute (now Trinity College) near Tampa. The Institute was housed in a country club that had gone bankrupt and was purchased cheaply by founder W. T. Watson. It had forty women and thirty men students, who were housed in the rooms of the large building. The rest of the building served as a Bible conference hotel and guest quarters. In Tampa, Billy could watch major league ball teams at spring training.

Graham stood out with his broad smile, cheerful disposition, height, and good looks. He wore bright bow ties, and suits that were regularly sent to the cleaners. But underneath, he was still unsure of himself and lacked any real motivation for serious study. However, Dean John Minder saw his potential and took Graham to preach at a country church during the Easter vacation of 1937. The song leader led off the service with rousing hymns, pausing occasionally to spit tobacco juice into a spittoon. Young Graham was sweating as he prepared to speak, and after Dean Minder introduced him he began fast and loud. He thought he had enough material to last an hour, but Graham raced through it in eight minutes. Yet, overall, Minder was pleased; the young man showed promise. Next, Minder asked Graham to speak to the young people at Tampa Gospel Tabernacle where he pastored. Graham went through agonies of self-doubt, and early Sunday morning he went out on the empty golf course to practice on the lizards and birds. By evening when it was time to speak he was forceful and dynamic and the young people soon asked him to be their leader.

While a lack of confidence still plagued him, things began to occur that affected him deeply. Graham listened to prominent evangelical leaders who spoke in the Tampa area while on vacation. A vision of the wider world of Christian influence was unfolded before him. In 1937 the Depression hung heavy over America, and he heard of the decline of Christianity in the nation, sagging church budgets, dropping memberships, and demoralized preachers. America must be brought back to God, they called. Fresh leaders must do it.

On all sides, it seemed, people were encouraging him to sense God's call. An Institute secretary would often say, "Billy, God has called you to preach." He took walks by himself where he wrestled with these matters. If indeed God was calling him into the ministry, it would be an irrevocable choice, to be entered into with the greatest gravity. If he accepted, Graham determined, he would have no other ambition or occupation but the proclamation of the gospel to as many people as he could reach during his lifetime.

At this time, several Christians he admired were suddenly accused of serious moral lapses. This shook Billy, for no one close to him had ever undergone such accusations. He decided that he must keep his life clean and free of sinful entanglements. He was also courting Emily Cavanaugh, one of the Institute's most vivacious and admired young ladies. During the summer vacation of 1937 he proposed by letter, and a few months later Emily accepted. They set the marriage date for three or more years away, but then she developed an interest in Charles Massey, a senior, and informed Billy that she was going to marry Massey instead. Years later he commented, "One of two things can happen in a time like that. You can resist and become bitter, or you can let God break you. And I determined to let God have his way."[16] His parents saw in each letter he sent home that his heart was broken.

Increasing Opportunities

Invitations to preach increased and Billy became a popular speaker. By the summer of 1939 he was asked to perform all the pastoral duties at the Tampa Gospel Tabernacle while Minder was in California for six weeks. That responsibility gave him valuable experience and helped mature him. With his parents' approval he joined the Southern Baptist denomination and was ordained by the St. John's Association in 1940.

After graduating from Florida Bible Institute in May 1940, Graham sought further study at Wheaton College in Illinois. Once enrolled, he and another student formed a plan to make money by using a truck to perform odd jobs. He took anthropology as his major, and in time became the part-time pastor of the United Gospel Tabernacle of Wheaton and Glen Ellyn, a small church attended by many college faculty members and students.

After the bombing of Pearl Harbor, Graham offered himself as an Army chaplain, but the draft board suggested that he finish college, since he had neither the required training nor experience. He had more success with his introduction to Ruth Bell, the daughter of a prominent Presbyterian medical missionary to Northern China. In 1943 Billy graduated from Wheaton College with a B.A. degree, and that August 13 he and

Ruth Bell were married. After a short honeymoon they returned to Western Springs, Illinois, near Wheaton, where he took over the pastorate of a struggling Baptist church. It seemed that he would spend the rest of his life as a Baptist pastor, serving in churches of various sizes in different parts of the nation.

That future began to change in October 1943 with a phone call from Torrey M. Johnson, a Wheaton graduate, pastor of a large church, professor of New Testament Greek, and one of the founders of the new National Association of Evangelicals.[17] Famous for his radio broadcasts, Johnson asked Billy if his small church could take over the Sunday evening radio broadcast, "Songs in the Night," which emanated from one of Chicago's most powerful stations. Graham was elated at the opportunity, and his church was willing to underwrite the costs. He immediately sought out a well-known bass baritone, George Beverly Shea, who had written a popular new song, "I'd Rather Have Jesus." Graham was persuasive, and Shea joined the program as soloist.

With the radio broadcasts going well, Johnson offered another opportunity. In 1944, as the war continued, Johnson was concerned about the thousands of servicemen who roamed Chicago each weekend on leave, looking for amusement, alcohol, sex, or whatever. In response, he had organized "Chicagoland's Youth for Christ," and rented three thousand-seat Orchestra Hall next to the USO center for twenty-one Saturday evenings. It seemed like a foolish venture.

Youth for Christ

Although nationally-known speakers were available, Johnson chose Graham to preach for the first meeting. He wanted a speaker who had an instinctive grasp of the needs and aspirations of that generation, and he felt no one could exceed Graham in that understanding. On Saturday, May 20, 1944, a number of leaders including Graham and Johnson went on the stage of Orchestra Hall, not knowing what to expect. Billy had "the worst stage fright of my life." To their astonishment they saw that the lower floor was full of people, and so was the lower balcony, as well as the upper balcony. Only the third balcony was rather skimpy. Most were servicemen, just as Johnson had hoped. After the opening program of lively music, Graham preached. As he did so his nerves relaxed and the message flowed. Graham gave an invitation and was astonished to see forty-two people come down the aisles.

In October 1944 Graham was commissioned as an Army chaplain with the rank of second lieutenant and was told to wait for orders to proceed to chaplains' training. He then contracted a virulent form of mumps, with high temperatures, and at one point Ruth feared for his life. After six weeks in bed, Billy recovered but had lost much weight. Johnson's plans concerning Youth for Christ involved large youth rallies on weekends across the nation. The war was winding down, and Johnson approached Billy about becoming the first evangelist and field representative for the movement, at a salary of seventy-five dollars a week. With his convalescence, the Army would only assign him to a desk. When Johnson asked him to resign his chaplain's commission and his church pastorate, Graham accepted.[18]

During 1945 Billy Graham traversed Canada and the United States, organizing Youth for Christ rallies and local staffs. Ruth and he made their home in Montreat, North Carolina, and their first child, Virginia, was born in September 1945. But Graham was not able to be home much. The slogan of Youth for Christ was "Geared to the Times, Anchored to the Rock," and the staff was determined, in a time of vacillating theology, to present Christ fearlessly. They were convinced that young people would still respond to a forthright presentation of the gospel. As he traveled, Graham gained experience in speaking before crowds of up to fifteen thousand. He made contacts and met important leaders and evangelists. By the end of 1945 he had traveled nearly two hundred thousand miles by plane, had spoken in forty-seven states, and seven thousand young people had made decisions for Christ under his ministry.

Graham added a second member to his team. At a rally in North Carolina the regular song leader failed to appear. Someone suggested a young man in the audience who had some experience as a song leader. Graham was reluctant to try an amateur, and the young man was also reluctant, but there was nothing else to do, and he was put in front of the audience. After he led several hymns, Graham was impressed and found that Cliff Barrows, an athletic twenty-two-year-old Californian, was on his honeymoon with his wife Billie. Barrows had a good voice, a likable disposition, the ability to play the trombone well, and a lovely wife who was an excellent pianist. Barrows had been ordained to the Baptist ministry and had served nearly a year as an assistant pastor in Minnesota. Graham immediately invited Cliff and Billie Barrows to join him, and they accepted. Barrows soon became more important to Graham than Ira Sankey had been to Moody or Homer Rodeheaver to Billy Sunday. He was the song leader and master of ceremonies, but he also became Graham's chief advisor, working more closely with Graham than any other member of the team. Graham later said of Barrows, "He comes near to being the indispensable man."[19]

The British Isles

In March 1946 Graham, Johnson, and others held Youth for Christ rallies throughout England, Ireland, and Scotland. Graham grew to love Britain and wished to return. During the summer of 1946 he raised money in the United States, and in October he was back in Britain with Cliff and Billie Barrows. Graham had raised enough money for six months in Britain, provided they were frugal. But their sights were set high: they asked God for a thousand converts a month and for a thousand young people to answer the challenge of the mission field. The tour began in a small Welsh town named Gorseinon. All told, Graham spoke at 360 meetings in twenty-seven cities and towns between October 1946 and March 1947. Often they met opposition and disinterest, for Britain was war-weary and religion was at a low ebb.

In 1946, over 90 percent of the 1 million citizens of Birmingham never attended church, and the local clergy firmly opposed Youth for Christ. The clergy induced the city council to withdraw permission for use of the city auditorium that had been reserved. When the meetings began, the attendance was tiny. Graham got a list of the clergy most opposed to him and began calling on them one by one. Stanley Baker, one of the ministers who had refused to cooperate, said of Graham, "He wasn't bitter, he didn't chide me; he hadn't one word of a lecture; he merely wondered. . . . Within an hour I sat in Billy's hotel room. . . . His was the nearest spirit to my Lord's I have ever met." Baker at once began phoning pastors, and soon a large number had lined up behind Graham. More came each night. They secured the city auditorium for a packed Saturday and Sunday, and scores came forward, young and old. The Lord Mayor hastily reissued a canceled invitation to tea. The liberal Bishop of Birmingham, Ernest Barnes, asked Graham to address a diocesan gathering on "Evangelism in the Twentieth Century."[20]

By 1947 Graham had permanently added George Beverly Shea as soloist and Grady Wilson as "associate evangelist." The list of cities hosting Graham team crusades grew: Grand Rapids, Michigan; Charlotte, North Carolina; Des Moines, Iowa; Augusta, Georgia; Modesto, California; Miami, Florida; Baltimore, Maryland; and Altoona, Pennsylvania. But 1949, the year of his great breakthrough, was still to come.

The 1949 Los Angeles Campaign

The Christian Businessmen's Committee of Los Angeles invited Graham to preach at their annual three-week evangelistic campaign. A huge tent holding six thousand was placed on an empty downtown lot, and massive publicity spread over the city. Wilson confessed later, "We weren't sure but that in Los Angeles we'd tackled something too big for us. Perhaps our faith wasn't geared up to it."[21] For the first two weeks, the meetings ran the usual course: good crowds, but not up to capacity, and offerings adequate to meet expenses. As the scheduled closing date drew nearer, members of the committee did not know whether to extend the meetings another week, or to close. Graham had never extended a campaign. One thing, however, made these meetings different—in Los Angeles, for the first time, organized prayer meetings began weeks in advance of the crusade, and more than a thousand prayer groups were at work. Prayer-chains operated around the clock. Graham and Barrows decided to "put out the fleece," like Gideon in the Book of Judges, to see if they might receive a sign from the Lord.

Late at night a phone call came from Stuart Hamblen, a large cowboy and Southern California's best-known radio personality. Although he was the son of a minister and ran a children's program called "Cowboy Church of the Air," Hamblen had drifted far from the faith. His wife, Suzy, who had prayed for Hamblen for sixteen years, had introduced Graham to her husband. Hamblen liked the fellow Southerner and interviewed him on his radio talk show. Then he began to attend the meetings. The preaching so convicted Hamblen that he decided to leave town, but later he returned and sat in the front row. He then became so angry that he stormed out in the middle of the message. He went from bar to bar before returning home. At 2 A.M. he phoned Graham, who invited him to come right over to his hotel. Several hours later Hamblen accepted Christ. On his radio show that day he announced, "I've quit smoking and I've quit drinking. Tonight at the end of Billy's invitation, I'm going to hit the sawdust trail." Because of Hamblen's popularity, this news sent shock waves all over California. The big tent suddenly became crowded and the crusade was extended. They understood this to be the sign that they were seeking.

When the team arrived early at the tent, they found it overflowing with reporters and photographers. Flashbulbs were going off everywhere. Even after the meeting began, Graham had to ask a photographer to come down from a ladder he had placed directly in front of the platform. The next morning the Los Angeles *Herald Express* and *Examiner* had banner headlines about the crusade. The aging William Randolph Hearst had sent a two-word telegram to the editors of the Hearst newspapers: "Puff Graham." The nation now heard of the thirty-one-year-old evangelist and his famous convert. They watched to see what would happen next. The crusade became the talk of Los Angeles, and thousands arrived early to get seats for every meeting.

The tent was enlarged to nine thousand seats, and other well-known personalities came to Christ. Each time that happened the headlines screamed it. Louis Zamperini, Olympic miler and one of America's foremost war heroes, had turned to drink after the war, but his wife continued to pray for him. After hearing Graham he accepted Christ. Most startling was the conversion of twice-convicted felon Jim Vaus, wiretapper and crony of the notorious racketeer Mickey Cohen. All three of these conversions proved to be sincere; Zamperini opened a Christian boys camp, Vaus went into full-time Christian work as an evangelist, and Hamblen sold his stable of race horses and began composing such songs as "It Is No Secret What God Can Do."

Sunday, November 20 was the campaign's closing day, and crowds stood far outside the jammed tent. More than four thousand conversions had been recorded, and such magazines as *Life, Time,* and *Newsweek* covered "the rising young evangelist." Graham recalled later, "We had gone to Los Angeles unheralded. When we left we knew that the Spirit of God had moved on that California city as never before." An unprecedented career lay before the evangelist.

The Hour of Decision

Of the many impressive things that have happened during his ministry since, a few deserve particular mention. One of the most important was Graham's entrance into broadcasting. After the Los Angeles crusade, invitations to hold meetings came from an ever-increasing number of important cities, and Graham frequently was exhausted by the demands. In 1950 a prominent Philadelphia pastor, Dr. Theodore Elsner, who was president of the National Religious Broadcasters, was concerned about the death of Walter A. Maier, a radio preacher beloved across America. Elsner became convinced that Graham was the person to replace Maier on a national network, and he told the evangelist so. Graham responded that he was already overloaded. A radio ministry would take too many hours each week.[22]

A month later Elsner sent Walter Bennett and Fred Dienert, advertising executives who had managed a number of religious programs, to see Graham. They announced that a choice time slot on Sunday afternoons would soon be available on ABC radio coast-to-coast. A thirteen week contract would cost ninety-two thousand dollars. Graham was aghast; he could not raise such money. That seemed the end of it. All that month the executives persistently called and wired him, explaining that each week would cost about seven thousand dollars. If he raised twenty-five thousand dollars, the network would put him on the air, and contributions from the radio audience would cover the remainder of the cost. Graham again refused; he was overburdened already. When some well-to-do Christians started a radio fund by contributing two thousand dollars, Graham said that the final decision was "not mine, but the Lord's." The three knelt and Graham prayed—"The kind of prayer I have never prayed before or since."[23] He prayed that he might do what he did in Los Angeles—put out the "fleece" like Gideon, and let the Lord indicate his will. If, by midnight that night, twenty-five thousand dollars could be collected, that would be decisive.

Over Billy Graham's career the technology of evangelism has progressed from radio to satellite networks. (Billy Graham Evangelistic Association)

Until then, the largest single gift Graham had received had been five hundred dollars. The two men left, feeling that it would be impossible to raise so much money in such a short time. This was July 1950, and Graham was in Portland, Oregon, in the midst of his most successful crusade thus far. Eighteen thousand crowded into a specially-built tabernacle night after night. Before his message that evening, he explained to the overflow audience the possibility of a nationwide radio broadcast, of his repeated refusals so far because of the cost, and of his desire to settle the matter according to God's will. "But if any of you folks would like to have a part, I'll be in the office back here at the close of the service tonight," he announced.[24]

After the service, Grady Wilson stood at the back office with an old shoe box, collecting money and pledges. An Idaho lumberman put in a pledge for twenty-five hundred dollars. People dropped in bills of various denominations. Pledges were scribbled on scraps of paper. An Oregon teacher pledged a thousand dollars, his entire savings, for he "could think of no better investment." When counted, the total was $23,500. Everyone exclaimed, "It's a miracle!" But Graham stood firm, saying, "No, it's not a miracle. The Devil could send us $23,500. It's all or nothing."[25]

Later, back at their hotel, Wilson picked up the mail at the desk. There were three letters for Graham; one contained a check for $1,000, two held checks for $250. Total: $25,000. "Now," said Graham, "I'll grant it's a miracle."[26]

257

Increasingly, Graham's crusades have been broadcast to wide geographical areas by satellite, as in this example from Germany. (Billy Graham Evangelistic Association)

On Sunday, November 5, 1950, *The Hour of Decision* was broadcast for the first time over 150 radio stations on the ABC network. It emanated from Ponce De Leon Park in Atlanta, Georgia, where a crusade was being held. Barrows led the crusade choir, Shea sang, Wilson read Scripture, and Graham preached. In a short time the program received the highest audience rating ever given a religious broadcast. His voice became familiar to millions of listeners who had never seen Graham in person. *The Hour of Decision* influenced Graham's development as a speaker. In crusades he could repeat sermons from time to time, but the radio program required him to produce new messages constantly. This drove him to a renewed study of theology and the Bible, and he deeply probed world affairs so that he might give expert comment. In the years since, television has been used extensively, but not on a weekly basis. Instead, each crusade produced its own series of TV programs aired within a week or two afterwards across the nation.

The 1954 London Crusade

Graham came to world attention in 1954 with the Greater London Crusade. Great Britain had not been more challenged since the revivals of Dwight L. Moody in the nineteenth century, or the eighteenth century Evangelical Awakening of Whitefield and the Wesleys. Although it was the best prepared of all crusades up to that time, there were major impediments. The obstacles came mainly from the British secular press, ever alert to a headline-grabbing scandal, or what it perceived to be scandalous. While the United States was enjoying an upsurge in spiritual concern in the 1950s, religious life in Britain was at its nadir. With church membership in the United States over 60 percent and climbing, in Britain membership was only 5 to 15 percent, and church attendance was minuscule.[27] In addition to a hostile press, the churches were apathetic toward "revivalism"—especially its American version. More than one thousand London churches, two-thirds of them Church of England, sponsored the crusade, but many cooperated only reluctantly.

The worst yellow journalism of his career greeted Graham's arrival. The papers seemed to vie for the most biased headlines: "Billy's Theology 100 Years Out of Date"; "Silly Billy"; "Hot Gospeller Holds Religious Circus at Harringay"; "All the Tricks of the Modern Demagogue." Much of this was started by Hanon Swoffat, a columnist for the socialist *Daily Herald* and a spiritist. He pilloried "the wild fanaticism of Billy Graham's evangelism" even before he arrived and told him in blazing headlines to "stay away!"[28] Taking their cue from Swoffat, the British press was in an uproar, believing and printing the wildest nonsense. The scorn, bigotry, abuse, inaccuracies, and injustice of the accusations sickened many. But Graham also found strong support from both religious and secular leaders, among whom was Dr. H. R. Gough, the Anglican Bishop of Barking, who said, "Well, Billy. If you are to be a fool for Christ's sake, I'll be a fool with you."[29]

Despite the opposition, the meetings went over well. Harringay Arena—a twelve thousand-capacity, barn-like sports complex—was filled six nights a week for twelve weeks, from March through May 1954. Two and sometimes three services each evening were held to take care of the overflow crowds. Over a network of communication wires, the services were sent to capacity crowds in four hundred cities and towns throughout England, Wales, and Scotland. The press, still attempting to connect Graham with "hysterical snake-handling fundamentalists," were baffled by his dignity and genuineness. They became increasingly aware that they had made fools of themselves, and the tone of their reporting began to change.

By the third week, opposition was melting. One British editor wrote, "The Archbishop of Canterbury became enthusiastic; the Prime Minister [Winston Churchill] sent for Dr. Graham; the First Sea Lord got up in public and went to the Inquiry Room. So likewise did many thousands from all walks of life—many being persons of leading rank or high in the learned professions and big business. . . . This remarkable occurrence is of first historic importance."[30] On the afternoon of the last day of the crusade, 65,000 filled White City (an outdoor stadium), and that evening 120,000 filled Wembley Stadium—more than were drawn there by the 1948 Olympics. With the Archbishop of Canterbury at his side, Graham gave the invitation and more than 2,000 stood in the rain before the platform to make decisions. Cassandra, the *Daily Mirror* columnist who had previously declared Graham "unwelcome" in Britain, interviewed him and now wrote, "he has been welcomed with an exuberance that almost makes us blush behind our precious Anglo-Saxon reserve. I never thought that friendliness had such a sharp cutting edge. I never thought that simplicity could cudgel us sinners so damned hard."[31] Altogether, nearly 2 million heard Graham preach, and 40,000 decisions were made.

A Series of Triumphs

Since 1954, Graham has held hundreds of crusades. Among the most outstanding was the New York Crusade of 1957, when Graham accepted an invitation from the Protestant Council of New York City (representing seventeen hundred churches of all denominations) to hold meetings in the old Madison Square Garden for six weeks. Opposition again was strong, but again the results were spectacular: a total attendance of more than 2 million, and sixty thousand decisions made. In 1959, the Graham team toured major cities in Australia, plus New Zealand. Yet one of the most spectacular, in terms of numbers, was the crusade in Seoul, Korea, in 1973, where three hundred thousand gathered for the first service. At the Lausanne Congress on World Evangelism in 1974, Graham began a world ministry on a wider scale than ever before. Here four thousand Christian leaders from 150 nations gathered to plan for the future. "Lausanne 1974 had become a date in Billy Graham's life comparable to 1949 and 1954," according to John Pollock. "The Los

Left: *In Moscow in 1982 Graham meets Mikhail Gorbachev, whose openness to religion in the USSR paved the way for evangelistic tours.*
Above: *Graham is greeted by Soviet leader Boris Yeltsin in 1991.*
Below: *Graham preaching through an interpreter in Moscow.*
(Billy Graham Evangelistic Association)

Graham presents his book Peace with God *to Kim Il Sung, president of North Korea, and preaches to an overflow crowd of North Koreans in Bongsu Protestant Church. (Billy Graham Evangelistic Association)*

Angeles campaign . . . in 1949 had made him a national figure. Five years later the Greater London Crusade of 1954 had brought him world fame. Twenty years after London, Lausanne showed him to be far more than an evangelist: he was a world Christian statesman, a catalyst who could bring individuals and movements to a fusion that set them on a new path for the glory of God."[32]

In 1977, after five years of patient diplomacy, Graham was invited to hold meetings in Hungary, and in 1978 he conducted a ten day series of meetings in Poland, a Roman Catholic nation. The Catholics opened their churches to him in an unprecedented way, however, and Cardinal Wojtyla of Krakow strongly supported Graham's coming. This same cardinal was soon to be elected Pope John Paul II. In 1980 Graham held meetings throughout Japan, and in 1981 the Mexico City meetings opened an entire new future for the few Protestants in Mexico. It was a difficult decision when the Russian Orthodox Church invited him to Moscow in 1982, for criticisms abounded. Some feared that he would be used by the Communists, that he was naive, and that he would bring respectability to the Kremlin's religious policies. Graham went, and the criticisms proved groundless. He made further inroads into Russia in 1984, 1988, and in 1992, when he returned to Moscow and held meetings that were broadcast to cities across the former Soviet Union. In 1983 came the International Conference of Itinerant Evangelists, or "Amsterdam 1983," where four thousand Christian leaders from around the world came together for ten days. He also held major crusades in London again in 1989; the cities of Scotland in 1991; and Philadelphia, Portland (Oregon), and Moscow in 1992.

Graham instituted a counseling and follow-up program for converts, constantly improving it over the decades. The workshops used to train counselors before the meetings drew praise as early as 1961 when *The Sunday Telegraph* of London stated, "As far as the churches are concerned, this is almost the most important part of the Crusade. The great benefit of the training classes is the corps of trained laypeople they leave behind."[33]

Attempting to deride evangelists, one critic wrote,

> The improved efficiency of the media made Graham's rise to fame more rapid than that of former professional evangelists but for that same reason, interest in his career might drop more rapidly. By the middle of 1957 newspaper coverage of his meetings had lost their attitude of respect. Finney, Moody, Sam Jones, and Billy Sunday kept their popularity for only about ten years. Graham's decline might be gradual, like that of Finney, Moody or Jones, or it might be rapid, like that of Sunday.[34]

The statement, made in the 1950s, assumed that Graham could not possibly be around much longer. Yet Graham's long career has gone from

Graham meeting young girls in mainland China
(Billy Graham Evangelistic Association)

strength to strength, each period building upon its predecessors. Having written sixteen best-selling books and conducted nearly four hundred crusades in every part of the world, he has become the foremost Christian statesman of our time, and for four decades has topped the list of those most admired by Americans.

Through his crusades, Graham has been seen in person by more people (an estimated 180 million) than any other human throughout history. Through television and radio he has spoken to far more people than has any other person, and has influenced more people to accept the Christian gospel than any other evangelist.

In March 1995, Graham was televised by satellite from San Juan, Puerto Rico, to 165 countries worldwide. Through this transmission he was able to preach to more people at one time than he had reached in all his previous years of ministry—a potential audience of one billion people. The telecast was translated into more than forty languages, with over half a million Christian workers stationed at hundreds of viewing sites around the globe to counsel those who responded to Graham's message. [35]

Palau—Evangelist for the Next Generation

The notion that all evangelists of the past two hundred years have had short careers is also contradicted by another dynamic man with a worldwide outreach—Luis Palau. Palau's ministry stretches back more than three decades to 1963. That there could be two evangelists of this stature at the same time winning such large numbers of converts around the world, and that these men should be independent and yet supportive of each another, is indeed amazing. Yet there is a precedent for this in two other outstanding leaders working at an earlier time—Whitefield and Wesley. Both had long careers as evangelists, were close friends, and supported one another.[36]

Palau was born on November 27, 1934, in the province of Buenos Aires, Argentina. His father was a successful businessman of Spanish ancestry, and his mother was half French and half Scottish. Both of them had been converted by Christian Brethren missionaries from Britain. When Luis was eight he was sent to Quilmes Preparatory School, about forty miles from his home. Two years later he was called home, because his father was dying. Although Luis had been close to his father, he was comforted after his death by the knowledge that his father was with the Lord. "That has affected my ministry and my whole adult life," he says. His mother told the boy of her husband's dying hours: "'He was struggling to breathe, but suddenly he sat up and began to sing [a hymn].' It was such a contrast to the typical South American scene, in which the dying person cries out in fear of going to hell. It thrilled me that my father was sure of his salvation."[37] Growing up without his father, however, made life difficult.

At eleven Palau entered St. Alban's College, a British boarding school near Buenos Aires that was part of the Cambridge University Overseas Program. Then in 1947 he went to a summer camp and accepted Christ as Savior. In 1951 Palau rededicated his life to Christ. He finished the equivalent of a junior college degree, but his precarious financial situation did not allow for study toward a bachelor's degree. He took a position with the Bank of London in Buenos Aires and heard Billy Graham for the first time on radio. What Palau heard excited him, and he prayed that God might help him to become an evangelist. When he was eighteen, he began speaking at street-corner meetings, developed a short radio broadcast, and helped in his local church. As the years went by he became increasingly involved in evangelistic work in Argentina, and thought seriously of leaving the bank.

The turning point came for Palau in 1959, when he began work for SEPAL, the Latin American division of Overseas Crusades. Equally at ease in Spanish and English, his first job was translating for a Christian magazine. In 1960 he joined a church-planting ministry. Shortly thereafter he received an offer from Ray Stedman (a pastor from Palo Alto, California) and some Christian businessmen to finance his studies in the United States. Palau attended Multnomah Biblical Seminary in Portland, Oregon, for a one-year graduate course in theology. There he met and

Luis Palau addresses a rally in 1991 celebrating a century of Protestant missions in Costa Rica. (Luis Palau Evangelistic Association, photo by Sam Friesen)

eventually married Patricia Scofield, another student, and after graduation joined OC (Overseas Crusades) International.

After further training—including work with Billy Graham's 1962 crusade team in Fresno, California—Palau was sent by OC to Guatemala in 1964. There he made friends and contacts that proved beneficial when he later returned for evangelistic crusades. Palau says that he still feels "more welcome in Guatemala than in any other country I have ever preached in." The growth of the Guatemalan evangelical church has brought perhaps one-third of the country's population into the evangelical camp.

It was in Colombia in 1964 that Palau began to realize his dreams of mass evangelism. The city of Cali, with 1 million people, seemed to be more receptive than any other municipality, so they set up headquarters there. Palau began a daily radio program over HCJB in Quito, Ecuador, which is still heard all over Latin America by an estimated audience of 20 million. In 1965 he began the TV counseling program *Responde*, where people were invited to call in to talk with Palau about the gospel and their problems. Both programs were immediately successful, and were especially timed to air in conjunction with crusades in order to prepare people to understand the gospel. The TV viewers were invited to the crusade meetings, and the audiences at the meetings were invited to tune

Along with his work in the Americas, Palau has been active in Europe. Here he speaks in Constanta, Romania, where 16,300 registered decisions for Christ. (Luis Palau Evangelistic Association, photo by David L. Jones)

in to the program later. They were broadcast on a large number of stations, gave superb coverage for the campaigns, and helped build the base for future crusades across Latin America.

In 1966, Palau spoke to his first huge crowd (twenty thousand) in the Presidential Plaza in Bogota, Colombia. It was the opening day of his first large-scale evangelistic drive in Latin America. Three hundred responded to his invitation, indicating that they wanted to trust Christ as Savior, and during meetings over the next four nights, several hundred more made the same decision. The great success inspired him to begin forming the Luis Palau Evangelistic Team and to frame the team's objectives: to win people to Christ, to stimulate and mobilize the church to effective evangelism, to see many enter the ministry, and to plant local churches.

More Triumphs

In 1966 Palau attended the World Congress on Evangelism in Berlin. There he conferred with several Overseas Crusades board members, who told him, "Begin to set your sights on Mexico. You'll be field director for Mexico, with your headquarters there." This was both an exciting and difficult challenge. Mexico was a country with huge potential, but also a country where evangelicals had been persecuted. In mid-1968 Palau and his team arrived in Mexico, and by 1969 they were organized for action. In Monterrey more than thirty thousand attended meetings over nine days and two thousand made decisions, but progress was difficult. Palau explained,

> The gigantic crusade we planned for and promoted at a baseball park in Mexico City was canceled at the last minute by the government. We were discouraged—all of us. . . . The next year, 1970, we heard that another religious group had drawn a big crowd to a convention, so we called our crusade a convention, too, and drew more than 106,000 people in ten days, doing very little advertising other than by word-of-mouth. In many ways, that crusade was the catalyst that began to focus the attention of many on what God was doing in Latin America.[38]

Some 6,670 made decisions in Mexico City, a breakthrough for religious freedom in Mexico. The team followed-up on converts, and a number of new churches were begun.

Over the next few years Palau concentrated his attention on Paraguay, Venezuela, Honduras, Guatemala, Peru, and other Latin American countries. Large crowds attended the rallies. A sign of his expanding appeal, in 1974 Palau conducted his first European crusade in Seville, Spain, and in 1980 he spoke to campaigns in ten British cities, six Scottish cities, and six South American cities. In 1978 he incorporated the Luis Palau Evangelistic Association as an independent organization, while continuing friendly relations with Overseas Crusades.

Greater things came: nearly 200,000 attended the Glasgow, Scotland crusade in 1981, and on November 28, 1982, an estimated 700,000 attended one meeting in Guatemala City. Palau's longest crusade, ninety-one days in London in 1983 and 1984, had an aggregate attendance of 528,000 with 28,000 decisions for Christ. In 1986, roughly 337,000 attended his first Asian crusade, in Singapore, where Palau's messages reached across Asia in eight languages on mission radio stations.

The Greatest Response in History

In May 1990—after crusades in Hong Kong, Denmark, India, Wales, the Soviet Union, and Thailand—some amazing things began to happen in Romania. Two days after the nation held its first free election in over 50 years, Palau preached across the nation, and an estimated 46,100 made decisions for Christ. This was the largest response ever in his twenty-four years of mass evangelism. Recognizing the incredible spiritual hunger of Eastern Europe, in 1991 Palau returned to Romania at the invitation of the Evangelical Alliance of Romania and held crusades in five

Palau addresses a crowded stadium during his 1987 Hong Kong crusade.
(Luis Palau Evangelistic Association, photo by David L. Jones)

cities. On June 4, 1991, he invited his audience of 10,500 in Constanta's stadium to come to the platform if they would accept Christ. More than 8,100 made a public declaration of faith in Christ—nearly 80 percent of the audience! The previous night in the same stadium, 8,120 people among the crowd of 14,000 made commitments to Christ—nearly 60 percent. These may be the highest response percentages in the history of mass evangelism. Of the 125,000 people who attended the meetings, 39,446 (31 percent) made commitments to Christ. Later in 1991, in the first evangelistic campaign in Sofia, Bulgaria in more than 50 years, 5,900 of the 16,200 who attended the three meetings in Academic Stadium made decisions for Christ. That 36 percent response rate for a single campaign is the highest in the Palau team's history, and may also be an all-time record in the history of mass evangelism.

In 1992 Palau returned to Mexico, where evangelicals were experiencing increased opportunities for growth. He conducted a three-week campaign in Mexico City and also greeted 425,000 evangelicals who had rallied in support of Mexican President Salinas' proposal for religious freedom for all churches. Altogether, the statistics of Palau's ministry are extremely impressive: more than three hundred campaigns and rallies over thirty years, with 560,000 known decisions for Christ. More than

11 million people in sixty nations have seen Palau in person over that period, and his estimated daily radio audience is 22 million. His newest radio program, "Luis Palau Responds," is broadcast in English on more than 170 stations nationwide.

At this writing, Palau expresses optimism about the future of mass evangelism throughout the world, and especially in Latin America: "As I see it, we're in a last surge of evangelism, in which many hundreds of thousands of new Christians are being added to the fold every day. Just look how many millions have been converted in just the last fifty years! There are more Christians today than ever in history. . . . I believe we're soon going to see perhaps three nations in Latin America that will have a majority of evangelical Christians, professing biblical ethics and a love for Jesus Christ."[39]

Palau also has hopes for the United States, his adopted country, although he believes Christians must update their evangelistic methods to speak to an increasingly secular society. When he first came to the United States to study in Portland during the social unrest of the 1960s, he doubted many could be won to Christ. "It seemed like America was truly headed for hell," he recalls. "It seemed like all the demons had broken loose on the States." He now has more hope that Americans can be evangelized, but it must be with contemporary means. The United States is a racially divided country driven by greed and money, making it an even harder place to evangelize, he says. "America is not the bottom of the pit; don't get me wrong—there are worse places. But there is a selfishness that has come in." An Associated Press story on Palau reported:

> The fight against the violence and hopelessness in America must be fought with more contemporary weapons, Palau says. So he incorporates modern devices into his crusades. Christian rap music occasionally replaces the traditional hymns at some events, and in-person or big-screen video shots of Christian athletes giving testimonies at sporting events are used to attract younger audiences.
>
> "I think we need to adapt rather than fight it," he says.[40]

In an interview for *National & International Religion Report*, Palau stressed that this doesn't mean watering down the gospel. Rather, it means turning the focus of Christian ministry from "good advice" aimed at the saved to good news aimed at the lost.

> Almost all Christian radio and television programs are geared exclusively to a Christian population, or to a population that thinks it's Christian and doesn't know the difference. . . . I try to demonstrate the relevance of Christ for everyone, from the upper classes, the wealthy, and leaders to the humblest and least educated. . . . I try to be intelligent about the gospel, but I

use simple language so no one can misunderstand what I'm saying. It's not shallow thinking; it's deep thinking in basic language.[41]

High praise for Palau came from one close observer of the world of evangelism. William Martin, a Rice University sociologist who wrote a biography of Graham, said, "I think Palau is extraordinarily good. He has about as good results as you would find among contemporary evangelists."[42]

In addition to Graham and Palau, the last several decades of the twentieth century brought forth a number of successful evangelists with national or international ministries: Ralph Bell, Akbar Haqq, John Wesley White, Ron Hutchcraft, Robert Cunville, and others. All of these cooperate with each other, recognizing that the job of world evangelism is big enough to engage all whom the Lord calls. Mass evangelism is serving the spiritual, moral, and, ultimately, the physical needs of humans as never before. The spiritual hunger of millions and the opportunities to spread the Christian faith over wide areas are greater than ever.

Conclusion

Christians in the United States, Great Britain, and other countries that God has blessed with mighty awakenings, may be awed by the awakenings occurring in other places. But will it ever happen again in the West? Has the industrialized, highly technological world become too cynical, materialistic, secular, and humanistic, and the church become too cold?

The 1990s continued as a time of spiritual deadness throughout much of the nominally Christian West. While many churches in Europe and America thrived, others struggled for survival as the world unraveled around them. Millions, especially among the young, saw no reason not to descend into sexual obsession, hedonism, cynicism, violence, and alienation. Many openly expressed their hatred for "institutional religion."

The situation in contemporary Europe provides a harrowing example of cultural change toward fierce secularism. The United Kingdom, in the 18th and 19th centuries, was the bastion of vital Christianity, largely because of the Evangelical Awakening stemming from Whitefield and the Wesleys. Throughout the 19th century, so many of the great biblical scholars and preachers in the world were Englishmen. But then a rapid change set in. A pastor in the UK recently estimated the percentage of converted Christians there at no more than 3 to 4 percent. In 2005 the author attended a service in London's Westminster Abbey, and was shocked when an Anglican priest in the sermon preached on ecology—saving the trees—and never mentioned God or Jesus! England's severe spiritual decline in the last century clearly shows what happens when there is no vital evangelism. Britain now lacks the aspects of what a strong ministry requires.

Most of Europe now demonstrates its radical shift away from Christian values. This is doubly sad because the Reformation began there. The January 16, 2000 issue of the *London Times* carried the headline "Europeans Are a Vanishing Species." Patrick Buchanan, in his book *Death of the West,* states that of the 20 countries in the world that have zero or negative population growth, 18 are in Europe. Two factors—abortion and euthanasia—are largely responsible for this decline. Abortion is taking on bubonic plague-like numbers. Consider this sampling of abortion rates across Europe as a percentage of live births: Albania, 45.2 percent; the Czech Republic, 44 percent; Romania, 110 percent. In 1999 in Romania 234,600 babies were born, while 259,888 babies were aborted.

At the same time there are hopeful signs in many other parts of the world. Frequently, those seeking for meaning discovered religion to be the best source of help. In a Gallup poll of American high school students, one-half said faith was important to them. One-third of Americans identified themselves as "born-again" Christians, especially those in the "baby boom" generation. Evangelicals included in their number many from the generation that rebelled in the 1960s and 1970s. The evangelical resurgence after World War II was enormous, spawning new ministries, new schools, new publications, and new churches that were independent of the older mainline denominations.

"Megachurches" are now common across the United States, such as the Willow Creek Community Church in the suburbs of Chicago, with 18,000 attending six services each Sunday. California teems with megachurches, the outstanding example being Saddleback Church and its well-known pastor Rick Warren and his best-selling book, *The Purpose-Driven Church.* On its 120-acre campus thousands of pastors, over 4,000 each year, flock to the church's Purpose-Driven Ministries conferences to learn Warren's techniques for church growth. In 2003, pastors from all 50 states and 30 countries came, many with stories of explosive growth in their churches.

In the U.S., television ministries are influential and popular. D. James Kennedy of the Coral Ridge Presbyterian Church in Florida has a TV ministry on hundreds of stations, as do David Jeremiah, Pat Robertson, and many other pastors. With over one billion people around the world on the internet, this too has become a medium for evangelism. Almost immediately after the beginning of the Toronto Blessing in 1994 and the Pensacola Revival in 1995, email and the internet brought news of the awakenings everywhere, and both cities became pilgrimage centers for charismatic Christians. The Global Day of Prayer, originating in one city and spreading to 160 countries in less than five years, illustrates the vast potential of internet technology.

In fact, the future of world Christianity has never looked brighter. Astounding things are happening. In 1900 about 558 million claimed to be Christian. Today over 2 billion Christians cover the globe. Christians are in every inhabited country on earth. In two-thirds of the countries Christians form the majority. Christianity has become accepted as the faith of developing countries of the Third World, especially in the continent of Africa.

In Africa 10 million converts in 1900 grew to 315 million by 2000. The net increase in the 1990s was 7 million new believers a year, almost twenty thousand a day. In 1995 the United Nations reported that the Sudan was experiencing the world's worst famine, with 1.8 million starving and another 3 million at risk. Intense fighting during the civil war displaced 2 million Sudanese, creating a horrendous refugee problem. Yet, during this time the Sudan has also experienced a startling Christian revival. Bill Lowery of the Association of Christian Relief Organizations Serving Sudan said that the expansion of the church in Sudan probably now leads the world. "There is a great deal of coming out of tribal religions and animism, and a lot of liberation from the forces of evil. There is a very powerful movement of the Spirit of God." Civil wars and dictatorships continue to plague Africa, but people are coming to Christ in ever-increasing numbers.

Latin America provides an equally positive example. Missionaries have penetrated into remote areas of every nation there for decades, often by airplanes. Brazil has become especially fruitful. It is considered the largest Roman Catholic country in the world, but millions have joined other churches. In Brazil's northeast, an area four times larger than Texas, evangelicals are scattered among the 45 million people. Gildario Nevez, the young pastor of a Missionary Baptist Church, has never gone to school. "Jesus taught me how to read!" he says. Nevez hosts a radio broadcast on a local station. Radio is the only way church members can regularly hear him preach. Otherwise, many must walk 20 miles to church.

Among Brazil's 175 million citizens, there are an estimated 3.1 million Baptists, 800,000 Lutherans, and nearly every other Protestant group, altogether about 8.2 million non-charismatic evangelicals. According to the Brazilian Institute of Geography and Statistics, Protestants have gone from 9 percent of the population in 1991 to 16 percent in 2001. By far the largest Protestant group are the estimated 17 to 20 million Brazilians who belong to Pentecostal churches, making Pentecostalism the most prominent feature of the Brazilian Protestant profile. *The Atlas of World Christianity* estimates that the number of Pentecostal churches across South America grew 500 percent between 1960 and 1980. Growth has slowed since then, but still, today South America has "the strongest Christian community in the world," the *Atlas* declares. Religious statistician David Barrett has estimated that there are at least 523 million charismatics and Pentecostals throughout the world.

In Brazil, much of the growth surge has come from a year-round focus on evangelism and church planting. For example, in Campinas, a city of 1 million in southern Brazil, young people from a 3,500 member Nazarene church spend each weekend in evangelistic outreach, distributing tracts, speaking in public, and performing with puppets in a large market area. The church leaders set a goal of 1,000 professions of faith in one year, which was met.

Among Baptists in one Brazilian state, 900 relatively new congregations are looking for new ways to extend their outreach. While more than 130 million Roman Catholics are organized into about 25,000 parish churches, the nation's Protestants have an estimated 165,000 congregations to choose from. Developing new Protestant leaders, lay and ordained, has understandably become an enormous problem. One Southern Baptist missionary has said, "The Assemblies of God, with 9 million members, have a church in every neighborhood. As soon as they can, they will get a man out there. He might not have much training, but he will be there trying to start a church." Of course, with such exponential growth, there are problems.

The gospel of God's gracious love holds a great attraction for many in the world who daily face oppression, injustice, violence, poverty, and hatred. In China particularly, despite government persecutions and communist propaganda, the church has undergone phenomenal growth in the last twenty to thirty years. In 1948, when missionaries were expelled, the communists took over, and the country closed almost totally to the West, estimates of actual believers ranged from under 1 million to perhaps 3 million. In a recent article entitled "Christianity is Booming in China Despite Rifts," the *New York Times* spoke of "the boldness and strength of the underground church, which is booming as never before. One of the paradoxes of modern China is that Christianity may well be growing at a more rapid rate today under a repressive communist government, than it ever did early in the last century when missionaries were free to evangelize at will . . . . Unofficial estimates of church organizations run as high as 90 million Christians throughout the country."

By anyone's estimate, Christianity has exploded in China during 50 years of the worst imaginable repression and persecution. And this despite the known facts that many of its pastors and leaders have been martyred, imprisoned for years, and brutally tortured, and that most of the underground churches have few if any Bibles or other materials. If the ancient saying has ever been true, it is true in China: "The blood of the martyrs is the seed of the church."

With the collapse of Russian communism in 1989, new opportunities for growth presented themselves throughout the former Soviet Union. For decades, Christianity had experienced massive losses in the USSR, from 83.6 percent of the population in 1900 to 36.1 percent in 1980. Christians in the West anticipated communism's final collapse and immediately mounted strenuous efforts to establish churches, Bible schools, seminaries, print ministries, and to put on radio and TV programs. So many Christian workers of every stripe entered Russia that soon, laws were passed to restrict them, and the Russian Orthodox Church was alarmed and sought to protect itself. As is always the case in situations where a new territory is opened up, the worst problem was the lack of indigenous leaders and the time needed to train them to take over the new projects.

Throughout the 1990s, Protestants—mostly Baptist, Pentecostal, Presbyterians, and Seventh-day Adventists—grew rapidly and now represent about 1.2 million of Russia's 148 million people. Roman Catholics also grew, and now have about 1 million adherents. In the early 1990s, American Christians significantly influenced the emergent Russian Protestant churches, focusing on planting new congregations, crusade evangelism, and establishing better theological education. But since then, questions have been raised whether Russia's newest churches are mature enough to stand on their own two feet without outside help. Igor Nikitin, a pastor in St. Petersburg and president of the Association of Christian Churches of Russia (ACCR), believes that a great opportunity for Russian evangelicals lies in pairing social ministry with gospel outreach. ACCR has been doing fine work in overcrowded prisons. Russia's largest prison, in the city of Kommunar, was built for 1,000 but now houses 15,000 inmates. Prisoners sleep in shifts. The ACCR has done much to alleviate these conditions in prisons, and they are much appreciated by officials in the cities.

Much more could be written of advances for the gospel in India, Nepal, and elsewhere, especially in the "10–40 corridor" of Third World countries, where people are desperate for hope. There have been many conversions to Christ in South Asia (450,000 a year) and East Asia (370,000 a year). Truly, Christ's Church is moving forward magnificently!

Notes

Introduction

1. D. Martyn Lloyd-Jones, foreword to *Lectures on Revivals of Religion,* by William B. Sprague (Edinburgh, 1958), v.

2. From the hymn "There Is a Green Hill Far Away," by Cecil F. Alexander.

3. Irenaeus, *Adversus Haereses,* 4.20.6.

4. Williston Walker, *A History of the Christian Church,* 3d ed. rev. (New York, 1970), 302.

5. Georgia Harkness, *John Calvin: The Man and His Ethics* (New York, 1931), 73–74.

6. John Calvin, *Institutes of the Christian Religion* (Grand Rapids, 1953), 3.14.9.

7. John T. McNeill, *The History and Character of Calvinism* (New York, 1967), 234.

8. Nathan O. Hatch, "Can Evangelicalism Survive Its Success?" *Christianity Today* (5 October 1992): 22.

9. Willard L. Sperry, *Religion in America* (New York, 1946), 159–61.

10. Luis Palau, *Luis Palau: Calling the Nations to Christ* (Chicago, 1983), 200.

11. *Philadelphia Inquirer,* 11 April 1993, D5.

12. *Christianity Today* (20 November 1992): 64.

13. David B. Barrett, ed., *World Christian Encyclopedia* (Nairobi, 1982), 796–97.

14. Ibid., 19.

Chapter 1: The Beginnings of Modern Mass Evangelism

1. John T. McNeill, *The History and Character of Calvinism* (New York, 1967), 337.

2. William Bradford, "History of Plimoth Plantation," cited in Perry Miller and Thomas H. Johnson, *The Puritans* (New York, 1963), 1.100–101.

3. Quoted in H. S. Smith, R. T. Handy, and L. A. Loetscher, *American Christianity: An Historical Interpretation with Representative Documents* (New York, 1960), 1.136.

4. Samuel Torrey, "A Plea for the Life of Dying Religion," in Thomas Prince, Jr., ed., *The Christian History, Containing Accounts of the Revival and Propagation of Religion in Great Britain, America, &c.* (Boston, 1743), no. 13, May 28, 1743.

5. Cited in W. W. Sweet, *The Story of Religion in America* (New York, 1950), 2.

6. Cited in Prince, *Christian History,* no. 13, May 28, 1743.

7. Smith, Handy, and Loetscher, *American Christianity,* 1.204–16.

8. Cited in Prince, *Christian History,* no. 13, May 28, 1743.

9. Thomas McCrie, *Sketches of Scottish Church History* (London, 1846), 1.190–93.

10. Ibid., 1.193–94.

11. Ibid., 1.194, 196.

12. Jonathan Edwards, *A Faithful Narrative of the Surprising Work of God in the Conversion of Many Hundred Souls in Northampton and the Neighboring Towns and Villages* (Boston, 1737), 12.

13. John Calvin, *Commentary upon the Acts of the Apostles* (Edinburgh, 1844), 2.84.

14. J. R. Trumbull, *A History of Northampton* (Northampton, Mass., 1898).

15. Perry Miller, "Solomon Stoddard," *Harvard Theological Review* 34 (1941): 277–320.

16. Perry Miller, *The New England Mind: From Colony to Province* (Boston, 1953), 228.

17. Paul R. Lucas, "An Appeal to the Learned: The Mind of Solomon Stoddard," *William and Mary Quarterly* 30 (1943): 257–92.

18. Miller, *New England Mind*, 228.

19. Solomon Stoddard, *The Doctrine of Instituted Churches Explained, and Proved from the Word of God* (London, 1700), 6.

20. Miller, "Solomon Stoddard," 298.

21. Increase Mather, *A Dissertation Concerning the Strange Doctrine of Mr. Stoddard* (Boston, 1708), 1, 20–21.

22. Solomon Stoddard, *The Inexcusableness of Neglecting the Worship of God, Under a Pretense of Being in an Unconverted Condition* (Boston, 1708), preface.

23. Miller, "Solomon Stoddard," 316–17.

24. Solomon Stoddard, *The Defects of Preachers Reproved in a Sermon Preached at Northampton, May 19, 1723* (New London, Conn., 1724), 20–21.

25. Ibid., 26.

26. Ibid., 27.

27. Ibid., 18.

28. Ibid., 20.

29. Ibid., 11–12.

30. Ibid., 13–14.

31. Solomon Stoddard, *A Guide to Christ* (Boston, 1714), 39.

32. Solomon Stoddard, *The Presence of Christ with the Ministers of the Gospel* (Boston, 1718), 27–28.

33. Miller, *New England Mind*, 282.

34. Solomon Stoddard, *The Safety of Appearing at the Day of Judgment, in the Righteousness of Christ* (Boston, 1689), 277.

35. Solomon Stoddard, *The Efficacy of the Fear of Hell* (Boston, 1713), 194. This is the seventh sermon, with no title, on the subject: "There are some special seasons wherein God doth in a remarkable manner revive religion among His people." It was preached in 1712.

36. Stoddard, *Safety of Appearing*, 277.

37. Ibid., 279.

38. Ibid., 343.

39. Stoddard, *Efficacy*, 187–89.

40. Ibid., 186.

41. See Thomas A. Schafer, "Solomon Stoddard and the Theology of the Revival," in Stuart C. Henry, ed., *A Miscellany of American Christianity* (Durham, N.C., 1963), 328–61.

Chapter 2: Frelinghuysen: Pietist Evangelist

1. The preceding conversation is taken almost verbatim from *Ecclesiastical Records [of the] State of New York* (Albany, 1902), 3.2197–2200.

2. James Tanis, *Dutch Calvinistic Pietism in the Middle Colonies: A Study in the Life of Theodorus Jacobus Frelinghuysen* (The Hague, 1967), 2. For excellent discussions of Pietism see this book and F. Ernest Stoeffler, *The Rise of Evangelical Pietism* (Leiden, 1965). Both of these fine studies uncover previously unknown sources of pietism in the Reformed tradition, and make necessary distinctions between Lutheran and Reformed Pietism.

3. Theodore J. Frelinghuysen, *Sermons* (New York, 1856), 25–36.

4 Ibid., 43–47.

5. Ibid., 7.

6. Ibid., 23–24.

7. *Ecclesiastical Records*, 3.2201–2.

8. Ibid., 3.2202.

9. Frelinghuysen, *Sermons*, 142–43.

10. *Ecclesiastical Records*, 3.2638–39, 3.2652–58.

11. Charles H. Maxson, *The Great Awakening in the Middle Colonies* (Chicago, 1920), 19.

12. George Whitefield, *Journals* (London, 1960), 351–52.

13. C. C. Goen, ed., *The Great Awakening,* in *The Works of Jonathan Edwards* (New Haven, Conn., 1972), 4.155–56.

14. Marilyn J. Westerkamp, *Triumph of the Laity: Scots-Irish Piety and the Great Awakening,* 1625–1760 (New York, 1988), 167.

15. Leonard J. Trinterud, *The Forming of an American Tradition: A Re-examination of Colonial Presbyterianism* (Philadelphia, 1949), 35, 53. The entire story of the Presbyterian thrust in evangelism is well told in Trinterud, *Forming,* 53–108, and Westerkamp, *Triumph,* 165–213.

16. Maxson, *Great Awakening,* 25–30; Trinterud, *Forming,* 53.

17. *Ecclesiastical Records,* 4.2557.

18. Thomas Prince, Jr., *The Christian History* (Boston, 1743–1744), 2.293.

19. Westerkamp, *Triumph,* 167–77.

20. *Ecclesiastical Records,* 4.2556–57, 2567–69.

21. This is not a misspelling by Tennent, but an approximation of the Dutch pronunciation.

22. Prince, *Christian History,* 2.292–93.

23. Trinterud, *Forming,* 53–57.

24. Peter H. B. Frelinghuysen, Jr., *Theodorus Jacobus Frelinghuysen* (Princeton, 1938), 37.

25. Maxson, *Great Awakening,* 16. A revisionist article by Herman Harmelink III, "Another Look at Frelinghuysen and His 'Awakening,'" *Church History* 37.4 (December 1968): 423–38, examines available evidence and evaluates Frelinghuysen's life and labors. No evidence supports a large scale awakening.

26. Sydney E. Ahlstrom, *A Religious History of the American People* (New Haven, Conn., 1972), 269.

Chapter 3: Edwards: America's Greatest Theologian

1. Sydney E. Ahlstrom, *A Religious History of the American People* (New Haven, Conn., 1972), 298.

2. C. C. Goen, ed., *The Great Awakening,* in *The Works of Jonathan Edwards* (New Haven, Conn., 1972), 4.146.

3. Ibid., 4.149.

4. Ibid., 4.151.

5. Ibid., 4.158.

6. Ibid., 4.159.

7. Jonathan Edwards, "Pressing Into the Kingdom of God," in *Puritan Sage,* ed. Vergilius Ferm (New York, 1953), 290.

8. Jonathan Edwards, *Some Thoughts Concerning the Present Revival of Religion in New England* (Boston, 1742), 6–7.

9. Jonathan Edwards, *A Divine and Supernatural Light, Immediately Imparted to the Soul by the Spirit of God, Shown to be both a Scriptural, and Rational Doctrine* (Boston, 1734), 15–16.

10. Edwin S. Gaustad, *The Great Awakening in New England* (New York, 1957), 25.

11. Joseph Tracy, *The Great Awakening: A History of the Revival of Religion in the Time of Edwards and Whitefield* (Boston, 1842), 83.

12. *News-Letter* (Boston) 20 September 1740.

13. Luke Tyerman, *Life of George Whitefield* (London, 1890), 2.127.

14. Perry Miller, *Jonathan Edwards* (New York, 1949), 51.

15. Jonathan Edwards, *Sinners in the Hands of an Angry God: A Sermon Preached at Enfield, July 8, 1741* (Boston, 1741), 9, 16.

16. Ahlstrom, *Religious History,* 301.

17. Edwards, "The Justice of God in the Damnation of Sinners," in *Puritan Sage,* 298–99, 316, 324.

18. Miller, *Edwards,* 110.

19. Charles Chauncy, *Seasonable Thoughts on the State of Religion in New England* (Boston, 1743), 50–51.

Chapter 4: Whitefield: Catalyst of Evangelism

1. George Whitefield, *Journals* (London, 1960), 40. For a definitive biography of Whitefield see Harry S. Stout, *The Divine Dramatist: George Whitefield and the Rise of Modern Evangelicalism* (Grand Rapids, 1991). See also Arnold Dallimore, *George Whitefield: The Life and Times of the Great Evangelist of the Eighteenth-Century Revival* (Westchester, Ill., 1980).

2. Henry Fielding, *Enquiry Into the Late Increase of Robbers* (London, 1751), 19.

3. See Sir George Romilly, *Observations on the Criminal Code* (London, 1810).

4. R. H. Tawney, *Religion and the Rise of Capitalism* (New York, 1926), 188–89.

5. Sir Leslie Stephen, *English Thought in the Eighteenth Century* (New York, 1949), 2.337.

6. A. D. Belden, *George Whitefield, The Awakener* (Nashville, 1930), 56.

7. C. J. Abbey and J. H. Overton, *The English Church in the Eighteenth Century* (London, 1878), 2.37.

8. J. C. Ryle, *A Sketch of the Life and Labors of George Whitefield* (Edinburgh, 1850), 12.

9. Whitefield, *Journals,* 44–45.

10. George Whitefield, "Sermon 9: The Folly and Danger of Being Not Righteous Enough," *Works of Whitefield* (London, 1954), 5.129.

11. Belden, *George Whitefield,* 17.

12. Whitefield, *Journals,* 46–47.

13. Ibid., 53.

14. Joseph Tracy, *The Great Awakening: A History of the Revival of Religion in the Time of Edwards and Whitefield* (Boston, 1842), 44.

15. Luke Tyerman, *Life of George Whitefield* (London, 1890), 1.51.

16. Whitefield, *Journals,* 77.

17. Ibid., 88–89.

18. Tracy, *Great Awakening,* 48.

19. Ibid.

20. Ibid., 48–49. See also Stout, *Divine Dramatist,* 66–76.

21. Ryle, *Sketch,* 33.

22. Ibid., 49–51; Tyerman, *Life,* 1.307–11.

23. Tyerman, *Life,* 1.323. Stout (*Divine Dramatist,* 87–89) believes Whitefield developed a clearly defined plan of action for his American tour that was "set in motion from the moment he stepped on American shores." This plan involved "an international, interconnected revival" with Whitefield at the center.

24. Benjamin Franklin, "Autobiography," in *A Benjamin Franklin Reader,* ed. Nathan Goodman (New York, 1945), 140.

25. Tracy, *Great Awakening,* 52.

26. Whitefield, *Journals,* 347–48.

27. Ibid., 351–52.

28. Ibid., 354.

29. Franklin, "Autobiography," 141.

30. Belden, *George Whitefield,* 110–11.

31. Ryle, *Sketch,* 52.

32. Belden, *George Whitefield,* 155.

33. Ibid., 233–34.

34. Ezra Stiles, *A Discourse on the Christian Union* (Boston, 1760), quoted in Edwin S. Gaustad, *The Great Awakening in New England* (New York, 1957), 114.

35. Sydney E. Ahlstrom, *A Religious History of the American People* (New Haven, Conn., 1972), 287–88.

36. See W. DeLoss Love, *Samson Occum and the Christian Indians of New England* (Boston, 1899), 176–87.

37. Louis F. Benson, "President Davies as a Hymn Writer," *Journal of the Presbyterian Historical Society* 2 (1903): 277–86, 343–73.

38. Guy S. Klett, *Presbyterians in Colonial Pennsylvania* (Philadelphia, 1937), 204–5; Archibald Alexander, *Biographical Sketches of the Founder and Principal Alumni of the Log College* (Philadelphia, 1851); Thomas C. Pears and Guy S. Klett, eds., *Documentary History of William Tennent and the Log College* (Philadelphia, 1940).

Chapter 5: The Second Great Awakening in the East

1. Sydney E. Ahlstrom, *A Religious History of the American People* (New Haven, 1972), 287. Because of poor record keeping, it is impossible to arrive at an exact figure; only estimates can be given.

2. Richard J. Purcell, *Connecticut in Transition: 1775–1818* (Middletown, Conn., 1963), 8–9.

3. Timothy Dwight, *Travels in New-England and New-York* (Cambridge, Mass., 1969), 4.259. In this work Dwight gives a fine description of events in New England from the Revolutionary period to his death in 1817, essential reading for any student of the period.

4. Ibid., 4.261.

5. Peter Gay, *Deism: An Anthology* (Princeton, N.J., 1968), 171–72.

6. Ashbel Green, *A Sermon Delivered . . . on the 19th of February, 1795* (Philadelphia, 1795), 19.

7. Gay, *Deism,* 153.

8. Ethan Allen, *Reason the Only Oracle of Man, or a Compendious System of Natural Religion* (Bennington, Vt., 1784), 352, 356.

9. Elihu Palmer, *Principles of Nature; or, A Development of the Moral Causes of Happiness and Misery among the Human Species* (London, 1823), 112.

10. Ibid., 25.

11. Ibid., 23.

12. *New York Evening Post*, 8 December 1802.

13. Dwight, *Travels*, 4.266–267.

14. Daniel Dorchester, *Christianity in the United States* (New York, 1895), 316.

15. William B. Sprague, *Lectures on Revivals of Religion* (Edinburgh, 1958), 131.

16. Lyman Beecher, *Autobiography*, ed. Barbara Cross (Cambridge, Mass., 1961), 1.27.

17. Frank G. Beardsley, *A History of American Revivals* (New York, 1912), 80.

18. James D. Richardson, ed., *A Compilation of the Messages and Papers of the Presidents, 1789–1904* (New York, 1904), 1.285.

19. Dorchester, *Christianity*, 348.

20. William M. Engles, ed., *Minutes of the General Assembly of the Presbyterian Church, 1789–1820* (Philadelphia, 1847), 152–53.

21. Ibid., 177.

22. Ibid., 209.

23. E. H. Gillett, *History of the Presbyterian Church in the United States of America* (Philadelphia, 1864), 1.299.

24. W. M. Gewehr, *The Great Awakening in Virginia, 1740–1790* (Gloucester, Mass., 1965), 230.

25. Sprague, *Revivals*, 151–52.

26. Ibid., 269–73.

27. Cited in E. E. Beardsley, *History of the Episcopal Church in Connecticut* (Boston, 1883), 2.212.

28. Cited in Charles E. Cuningham, *Timothy Dwight, 1752–1817* (New York, 1942), 178–79.

29. Ibid., 181.

30. Beecher, *Autobiography*, 1.27.

31. Chauncey A. Goodrich, "Narrative of Revivals of Religion in Yale College," *American Quarterly Register* 10 (1838): 295–96.

32. Cuningham, *Timothy Dwight*, 329.

33. Charles R. Keller, *The Second Great Awakening in Connecticut* (New Haven, Conn., 1942), 42.

34. Cuningham, *Timothy Dwight*, 334.

35. A good discussion of these three parties appears in Ahlstrom, *Religious History*, 403f.

36. Timothy Dwight, *Theology: Explained and Defended* (Middletown, Conn., 1818–19), 4.43, 58, 60.

37. Sidney Earl Mead, *Nathaniel William Taylor, 1786–1858: A Connecticut Liberal* (Chicago, 1942), 101.

38. Jesse Lee, *History of the Methodists* (Baltimore, 1810), 24.

39. Abel Stevens, *History of the Methodist Episcopal Church* (New York, 1864–67), 2.60.

40. Ezra S. Tipple, *Francis Asbury, The Prophet of the Long Road* (New York, 1916), 67.

41. William Warren Sweet, *Religion on the American Frontier: The Methodists* (Chicago, 1946), 4.6.

42. Winthrop S. Hudson, *Religion in America* (New York, 1981), 122–23.

43. Ahlstrom, *Religious History*, 371.

44. Ibid., 438.

45. Francis Asbury, *The Journal and Letters of Francis Asbury* (Nashville, 1958), 2.576.

46. Ibid., 1.368.

47. Sweet, *Religion on the American Frontier*, 4.134ff.; Ahlstrom, *Religious History*, 436–37.

48. Herbert Asbury, *A Methodist Saint: The Life of Bishop Asbury* (New York, 1927), 41.

49. Ahlstrom, *Religious History*, 372.

Chapter 6: The Second Great Awakening in the West

1. Ray A. Billington, *Westward Expansion* (New York, 1949), 246.

2. Wood Furman, ed., *A History of the Charleston Association of Baptist Churches* (Charleston, S.C., 1811), 145.

3. Francis Asbury, *The Journal and Letters of Francis Asbury* (Nashville, 1958), 2.125.

4. John Rippon, *The Baptist Annual Register* (London, n.d.), 2.201.

5. Steiner and Schweinitz, *Report of the Journey of the Brethren* (n.p., n.d.), 513.

6. Jesse Mercer, *A History of the Georgia Baptist Association* (Washington, Ga., 1838), 145–46.

7. Cited in Perry Miller and Thomas Johnson, eds., *The Puritans* (New York, 1963), 1.143–45.

8. Cited in Peter G. Mode, *Source Book and Bibliographical Guide for American Church History* (Menasha, Wis., 1921), 430–32.

9. Barton W. Stone, "A Short History of the Life of Barton W. Stone," in James R. Rogers, *The Cane Ridge Meeting-House* (Cincinnati, 1910), 121. For a thorough study of the beginnings of the awakening in the West see Paul K. Conkin, *Cane Ridge: America's Pentecost* (Madison, Wis., 1990).

10. Peter Cartwright, *Autobiography of Peter Cartwright* (London, 1856), 5.

11. Franceway R. Cossit, *The Life and Times of Rev. Finis Ewing* (Louisville, 1853), 44; Conkin, *Cane Ridge*, 55–58.

12. John McGee to Thomas L. Douglas, in *Methodist Magazine* (London, 1821), 4.190; Conkin, *Cane Ridge*, 59–60.

13. John Rankin, "Autobiographical Sketch, Written in 1845," cited in J. P. McLean, "The Kentucky Revival and Its Influence on the Miami Valley," *Ohio Archeological and Historical Publications* 12 (April 1903): 280.

14. Charles A. Johnson, *The Frontier Camp Meeting: Religion's Harvest Time* (Dallas, 1955), 36. This work, Conkin's, and John B. Boles, *The Great Revival: 1787–1805* (Lexington, Ky., 1972) provide the finest studies available on the camp meeting and the Kentucky revival.

15. James McGready, "A Short Narrative of the Revival of Religion in Logan County, in the State of Kentucky, and the Adjacent Settlements in the State of Tennessee, from May 1797, until September 1800," *New York Missionary Magazine* 4 (New York, 1803): 193.

16. Rogers, *Cane Ridge*, 165.

17. Cited in William W. Woodward, *Surprising Accounts of the Revival of Religion in the United States of America* (Philadelphia, 1802), 225–26.

18. Boles, *Great Revival*, 68.

19. Bernard A. Weisberger, *They Gathered at the River* (Boston, 1958), 35.

20. Cartwright, *Autobiography*, 18.

21. Ibid., 17–18.

22. *Methodist Magazine* 26 (1803): 93.

23. Cartwright, *Autobiography*, 5.

24. Ibid.

25. Boles, *Great Revival*, 45–46.

26. Cartwright, *Autobiography*, 6.

27. Ibid., 10.

28. Ibid., 11.

29. Ibid., 243.

30. Ibid., 41.

31. Ibid., 64–65.

Chapter 7: Finney: Developer of Planned Mass Evangelism

1. William C. Cochran, *Charles Grandison Finney* (Philadelphia, 1908), 13. For an in-depth biography of Finney see Keith J. Hardman, *Charles Grandison Finney, 1792–1875: Revivalist and Reformer* (Syracuse, 1987; reprint, paperback edition, Grand Rapids, 1990).

2. Charles G. Finney, *Memoirs of Rev. Charles G. Finney* (New York, 1876), 13.

3. Ibid., 19.

4. Ibid., 24.

5. Garth M. Rosell, *Charles Grandison Finney and the Rise of the Benevolence Empire* (Ann Arbor, Mich., 1971), 23.

6. Perry Miller, *The Life of the Mind in America: From the Revolution to the Civil War* (New York, 1965), 9, 22–24.

7. Finney, *Memoirs* (1876), 4.

8. Cochran, *Charles Grandison Finney*, 17–18.

9. Finney, *Memoirs* (1876), 7–8.

10. Ibid., 11.

11. Ibid., 14.

12. *New York Evangelist*, 23 May 1850. For a fuller description of Finney's ancestry and early life see Hardman, *Charles Grandison Finney*, 3–58.

13. Finney, *Memoirs* (1876), 45–46.

14. Ibid., 80–81.

15. Cochran, *Charles Grandison Finney*, 13.

16. George F. Wright, *Charles Grandison Finney* (New York, 1891), 71–74.

17. Finney, *Memoirs* (1876), 84.

18. Bernard A. Weisberger, *They Gathered at the River* (Boston, 1958), 108. An excellent treatment of the situation is given in Whitney R. Cross, *The Burned-over District* (Ithaca, N.Y., 1950).

19. Samuel C. Aikin, *A Narrative of the Revival of Religion in the County of Oneida, Particularly in the Bounds of the Presbytery of Oneida, in the Year 1826* (Utica, N.Y., 1826), 23–24.

20. See Hardman, *Charles Grandison Finney*, 84–85, 134–48.

21. Thomas Seward, *Address: A Memorial of the Semi-Centennial of the Founding of the Sunday School of the First Presbyterian Church, Utica, New York* (Utica, 1867), 126–27.

22. A. B. Johnson to Charles G. Finney, 5 December 1826, Finney Papers, Oberlin (Ohio) College Library.

23. Rosell, *Charles Grandison Finney*, 36. This was preceded by the shaky coalition of pro-revival pastors and evangelists pieced together by Lyman Beecher, which made up the New England contingent at the New Lebanon Conference. But those, with the exception of Asahel Nettleton, were settled clergymen not itinerant evangelists, and they received salaries from the churches they pastored. The members of the Oneida Association, on the other hand, were paid for the revivals they conducted in various places.

24. Lyman Beecher to Nathan S. S. Beman, January 1827, in Lyman Beecher and Asahel Nettleton, *Letters on "New Measures" in Conducting Revivals of Religion* (New York, 1828), 81.

25. Hardman, *Charles Grandison Finney*, 136.

26. Howard A. Morrison, "The Finney Takeover of the Second Great Awakening During the Oneida Revivals of 1825–1827," *New York History* 59.1 (January 1978): 47.

27. Lyman Beecher, in *Autobiography*, ed. Barbara Cross (Cambridge, Mass., 1961), claimed that he said to Finney during the convention, "I know your plan, and you know I do. You mean to come into Connecticut, and carry a streak of fire to Boston. But if you attempt it, as the Lord liveth, I'll meet you at the state line, and call out all the artillery-men, and fight every inch of the way to Boston, and I'll fight you there" (2.75). Finney had no recollection of such a thing being said, and it is doubtful.

28. Charles G. Finney, *Lectures on Revivals of Religion*, ed. W. G. McLoughlin, Jr. (Cambridge, Mass., 1960), 13.

29. Finney, *Memoirs* (1876), 235–36.

30. David L. Dodge to Finney, 25 February 1828, Finney Papers, Oberlin College Library.

31. Z. Platt to Finney, 10 March 1828, Finney Papers, Oberlin College Library.

32. William G. McLoughlin, Jr., *Modern Revivalism: Charles Grandison Finney to Billy Graham* (New York, 1959), 54–55.

33. Cross, *Burned-over District*, 155–156.

34. McLoughlin, *Modern Revivalism*, 57.

35. Rosell, *Charles Grandison Finney*, 132. For works dealing with the "Benevolence Empire" see Clifford S. Griffin, *Their Brothers' Keepers: Moral Stewardship in the United States, 1800–1865* (New Brunswick, N.J., 1960); Miller, *Life of the Mind*, 78–84; Cross, *Burned-over District*; and Charles I. Foster, *An Errand of Mercy: The Evangelical United Front, 1790–1837* (Chapel Hill, N.C., 1960).

36. Charles G. Finney, *Sermons on Various Subjects* (New York, 1835), 96–103.

37. For a full treatment of Finney's theology and the development of "Oberlin Perfectionism," see Hardman, *Charles Grandison Finney*, 275–92, 324–49.

38. Miller, *Life of the Mind*, 9.

39. The standard study of William Wilberforce is R. Coupland, *Wilberforce*, 2d ed. (Oxford, 1945).

40. Thomas A. Bailey, *The American Pageant: A History of the Republic* (Boston, 1961), 368. It has been a difficult task for historians to achieve a balanced view of Garrison and his achievements. A brilliant reevaluation of Garrison, not so negative as Barnes, is John L. Thomas, *The Liberator* (New York, 1963).

41. Gilbert H. Barnes, *The Antislavery Impulse, 1830–1844* (Gloucester, Mass., 1964), 107.

42. Edmund Burke, *Reflections on the Revolution in France . . .* , 9th ed. (London, n.d.), 134–36.

43. Foster, *Errand*, 23.

44. Lyman Beecher, *Address of the Charitable Society for the Education of Indigent Pious Young Men for the Ministry of the Gospel* (Concord, Mass., 1820), 20.

45. *Panoplist and Missionary Magazine* 10 (1814): 1.

46. Donald G. Mathews, "The Second Great Awakening as an Organizing Process, 1780–1830: An Hypothesis," *American Quarterly* 21.1 (Spring 1969): 30–31.

47. The term Benevolence (or Benevolent) Empire, refers to the united evangelical crusade to bring in the kingdom of God in America through revivals and social reform. Many Christians in the first half of the nineteenth century were confident that the task of establishing God's kingdom could be accomplished through reform causes and the conversion of individuals. See the works under note 35, above.

48. Sir James Stephens, *Essays in Ecclesiastical Biography* (London, 1849), 1.382.

49. *First Annual Report of the American Bible Society* (New York, 1816), 1.12.

50. Stephens, *Ecclesiastical Biography*, 1.384.

51. For information on "the Great Eight," see Charles Cole, *The Social Ideas of the Northern Evangelists, 1826–1860* (New York, 1954); Oliver Elsbree, *The Rise of the Missionary Spirit in America* (Williamsport, Pa., 1928); Colin Goodykootz, *Home Missions on the American Frontier* (Caldwell, Idaho, 1939), and works cited in note 35.

52. For the life and work of Mills see Thomas C. Richards, *Samuel J. Mills: Missionary Pathfinder, Pioneer, and Promoter* (Boston, 1906). For a study of one of the first missionaries ordained by the American Board of Commissioners, Adoniram Judson, see Courtney Anderson, *To the Golden Shore* (Grand Rapids, 1972).

53. Robert Baird, *Religion in America* (New York, 1970), 251.

54. In major archives such as the Presbyterian Historical Society in Philadelphia, the author has examined church records from the early 1830s from across the settled part of the nation. Time and again such records indicate a relatively large influx of new members to the churches around that time, particularly in 1831. A number of churches referred to revivals in their area, far from Finney's ministry, indicating a "ripple effect" from the center in Rochester.

Chapter 8: The Third Great Awakening and the Civil War

1. Charles Finney's "Holy Band" has been the subject of some discussion over the years. For a full treatment see Keith J. Hardman, *Charles Grandison Finney, 1792–1875: Revivalist and Reformer* (Syracuse, 1987; reprint, paperback edition, Grand Rapids, 1990), 92, 460 n. 40.

2. "Review on the Employment of Evangelists in Our Older Settlements," *Quarterly Christian Spectator* 1 (September 1829): 425ff.

3. Charles G. Finney, *Lectures on Revivals of Religion*, ed. W. G. McLoughlin, Jr. (Cambridge, Mass., 1960), 176.

4. W. F. P. Noble, *A Century of Gospel Work* (Philadelphia, 1876), 399–400.

5. For an extended treatment of evangelistic work in the pre–Civil War period see Timothy L. Smith, *Revivalism and Social Reform: American Protestantism on the Eve of the Civil War* (New York, 1957).

6. Whitney R. Cross, *The Burned-over District: The Social and Intellectual History of Enthusiastic Religion in Western New York, 1800–1850* (Ithaca, N.Y., 1950), 287.

7. Ibid., 307.

8. Ibid., 308.

9. J. Schoulder, *History of the United States under the Constitution* (New York, 1922), 5.384.

10. H. U. Faulkner, *American Economic History* (New York, 1938), 235.

11. Warren A. Candler, *Great Revivals and the Great Republic* (Nashville, 1904), 190.

12. Robert Baird, *Religion in America* (New York, 1970), 242.

13. Smith, *Revivalism*, 46.

14. Ibid., 67–68, 81–82, 116–17, 122–27, 140–46, 169–71.

15. *The Revival*, 17 September 1859 and 1 October 1859. The definitive biography of Phoebe Palmer is Charles E. White, *The Beauty of Holiness: Phoebe Palmer as Theologian, Revivalist, Feminist, and Humanitarian* (Grand Rapids, 1986).

16. T. W. Chambers, *The Noon Prayer Meeting of the North Dutch Church* (New York, 1858), 33–44.

17. J. Edwin Orr, *The Second Evangelical Awakening in America* (London, 1952), 25–26.

18. *New York Christian Advocate and Journal*, 13 May 1858, 1.

19. Ibid., 28 January 1858, 2.

20. *New York Daily Tribune*, 10 February 1858, 1.

21. *Washington National Intelligencer*, 2 March 1858, 1.

22. Ibid., 11 March 1858, 3.

23. *New York Herald*, 26 February 1858, 1.

24. *New York Times*, 20 March 1858, 2.

25. *The Watchman and Reflector*, a Baptist paper in Boston, gave weekly reports with statistics showing the growth in the prayer meetings in Philadelphia, Baltimore, Providence, Boston, and Portland, Maine. See issues of February 18, 25, March 4, 11, 18, and 25, 1858.

26. Chambers, *Noon Prayer Meeting*, 125.

27. Smith, *Revivalism*, 64.

28. James W. Alexander, *Forty Years Familiar Letters of James W. Alexander*, ed. John Hall (New York, 1860), 2.275–77.

29. *Washington National Intelligencer*, 23 March 1858, 4.

30. *The Presbyterian* (June 1858): 2.

31. Charles G. Finney, *The Memoirs of Charles G. Finney*, ed. Garth M. Rosell and Richard A. G. Dupuis (Grand Rapids, 1989), 563.

32. Smith, *Revivalism*, 67.

33. *Cincinnati Daily Commercial*, 2 April 1858, 1.

34. William C. Conant, *Narratives of Remarkable Conversions and Revival Incidents* . . . (New York, 1858), 373.

35. Samuel I. Prime, *The Power of Prayer* (New York, 1859), 171.

36. Charles P. McIlvaine, *Bishop McIlvaine on the Revival of Religion* . . . (Philadelphia, 1858), 22.

37. Conant, *Narratives*, 433.

38. Ibid., 432.

39. John Shaw, *Twelve Years in America* (London, 1867), 182–84.

40. *New York Christian Advocate and Journal*, 13 May 1858, 2.

41. Ibid., 12 October 1857 and 24 December 1857.

42. Shaw, *Twelve Years*, 182–84.

43. *The Presbyterian* (June 1858), 1.

44. *Western Christian Advocate*, 10 March 1858, 1.

45. *New York Daily Tribune*, 17 February 1858, 4.

46. *Chicago Daily Press*, 27 March 1858, 2.

47. Noble, *Century*, 421.

48. *New York Christian Advocate and Journal*, 6 May 1858, 1.

49. Prime, *Power of Prayer*, 46, 287–91; Noble, *Century*, 422.

50. *Washington National Intelligencer*, 20 March 1858 and 23 March 1858.

51. Conant, *Narratives*, 376.

52. Candler, *Great Revivals*, 194.

53. Ibid., 195.

54. Frank G. Beardsley, *A History of American Revivals* (New York, 1912), 236.

55. Finney, *Memoirs* (1989), 565.

56. J. Edwin Orr, *The Second Evangelical Awakening in Britain* (London, 1949), 36–37. See Candler, *Great Revivals*, 193.

57. *The Congregational Quarterly* (January 1859), 6; (April 1859), 3, 5; (October 1859), 3, 5; (January 1860), 4; Candler, *Great Revivals*, 194.

58. J. William Jones, *Christ in the Camp; or, Religion in the Confederate Army* (Richmond, Va., 1904; reprint, Harrisonburg, Va., 1986), 542. Other invaluable sources describing the revivals include: William W. Bennett, *A Narrative of the Great Revival Which Prevailed in the Southern Armies* (Philadelphia, 1877); and *Christ in the Army; A Selection of Sketches of the Work of the U.S. Christian Commission* (Philadelphia, 1865). See also Gardiner H. Shattuck, Jr., *A Shield and Hiding Place: The Religious Life of the Civil War Armies* (Macon, Ga., 1987).

59. Jones, *Christ in the Camp*, 540.

60. Ibid., 557.

61. Ibid., 556.

62. Ibid., 95–96.

63. Ibid., 58.

64. Ibid., 161.

65. Ibid., 187.

66. Bennett, *Narrative*, 64.

67. Jones, *Christ in the Camp*, 583.

68. Ibid., 618.

69. Ibid., 398–99.

70. Ibid., 399.

71. Bennett, *Narrative*, 413.

72. Jones, *Christ in the Camp*, 391.

Chapter 9: Moody: Perfecter of Urban Evangelism

1. William R. Moody, *The Life of Dwight L. Moody* (New York, 1900), 281. This is the "official authorized edition" of the life of Moody by his son, published soon after Moody's death. It is filled with anecdotes, as is the revised edition of 1930. Another excellent work by a friend of Moody's is William H. Daniels, *D. L. Moody and His Work* (Hartford, 1876).

2. Moody, *Life*, 57.

3. Ibid., 56–57.

4. Ibid., 83.

5. Ibid., 74.

6. Stanley N. Gundry, *Love Them In: The Proclamation Theology of D. L. Moody* (Chicago, 1976), 18. This is a fine scholarly work that corrects numerous mistakes of previous writers on Moody.

7. Moody, *Life*, 41.

8. James F. Findlay, Jr., *Dwight L. Moody, American Evangelist 1837–1899* (Chicago, 1969), 52, gives the various reasons for Moody's move to Chicago. Findlay's biography is the standard recent work on Moody; it is scholarly, well-written, fair, and thorough.

9. Ibid., 56.

10. Ibid., 63.

11. Moody, *Life*, 65.

12. Findlay, *Dwight L. Moody*, 96ff., has some excellent material on Moody's family life.

13. J. Wilbur Chapman, *Dwight L. Moody* (Philadelphia, 1900), 102.

14. Moody, *Life*, 125.

15. Ibid., 126.

16. Ibid., 130.

17. For an important discussion of Moody's theological understanding of this experience, see Gundry, *Love Them In*, 46, 153–55.

18. Ibid., 46.

19. Moody, *Life*, 155.

20. Ibid., 158.

21. Findlay, *Dwight L. Moody*, 157, has a good discussion of the cross-cultural difficulties Moody and Sankey encountered in the British Isles.

22. Moody, *Life*, 187–88.

23. Ibid., 202.

24. Ibid., 206.

25. *The Congregationalist* 4 (March 1875): 138–39.

26. *New York Times*, 22 June 1875.

27. *Times* (London), 22 April 1875.

28. Moody, *Life*, 263.

29. *New York Times*, 3 March 1889.

30. Moody, *Life*, 278.

Chapter 10: Evangelism at the Beginning of the Twentieth Century

1. Warren A. Candler, *Great Revivals and the Great Republic* (Nashville, 1904), 7–12.

2. Ibid., 14.

3. Ibid., 262–66.

4. Ibid., 242.

5. Ibid., 243–44.

6. Walt Holcomb, *Sam Jones: An Ambassador of the Almighty* (Nashville, 1947), 40.

7. Ibid., 43–44.

8. Ibid., 57–59.

9. Quoted in Laura M. Jones, *The Life and Sayings of Sam P. Jones* (Atlanta, 1906), 107.

10. Holcomb, *Sam Jones*, 60–61.

11. *Chicago Tribune*, 6 March 1886, 5.

12. G. Campbell Morgan, *Lessons of the Welsh Revival* (New York, 1905), 13–14.

13. George T. B. Davis, *Torrey and Alexander: The Story of a World-Wide Revival* (New York, 1905), 37–38.

14. Ibid., 41.

15. Ibid., 92.

16. R. A. Torrey to A. P. Fitt, 29 November 1904, Moodyana Collection, Moody Bible Institute, Chicago.

17. Sydney E. Ahlstrom, *A Religious History of the American People* (New Haven, Conn., 1972), 740.

18. Ibid., 784.

19. H. Richard Niebuhr, *The Kingdom of God in America* (New York, 1937), 192–93.

20. For biographical details on Billy Sunday see Elijah P. Brown, *The Real Billy Sunday* (New York, 1914); Lyle W. Dorsett, *Billy Sunday and the Redemption of Urban America* (Grand Rapids, 1991); William T. Ellis, *"Billy" Sunday: The Man and His Message* (Philadelphia, 1914); and William G. McLoughlin, Jr., *Billy Sunday Was His Real Name* (Chicago, 1955).

21. Ellis, *"Billy" Sunday,* 41–42; Dorsett, *Billy Sunday,* 23–29.

22. Brown, *Real Billy Sunday,* 51–52.

23. Ellis, *"Billy" Sunday,* 58.

24. *Sigourney (Iowa) News,* 30 January 1896, 3, quoted in McLoughlin, *Billy Sunday,* 12.

25. Brown, *Real Billy Sunday,* 116–21.

26. Ibid., 200.

27. Ibid., 103–4.

28. McLoughlin, *Billy Sunday,* 127.

29. Quoted in McLoughlin, *Billy Sunday,* 163.

30. Ibid., 154–55.

31. Quoted in McLoughlin, *Billy Sunday,* 107. Dorsett, *Billy Sunday,* 90–91, 115–19, 139–40, has a good treatment of Sunday's concern with offerings.

32. Lindsay Denison, "The Rev. Billy Sunday and His War on the Devil," *American Magazine* 64 (September 1907): 454–55.

33. These statistics are found in McLoughlin, *Billy Sunday,* 293.

34. Dorsett, *Billy Sunday,* 117–43, presents an excellent discussion of these problems.

35. McLoughlin, *Billy Sunday,* 154–55.

Chapter 11: Graham, Palau, and Modern Revival Movements

1. Joseph Wood Krutch, *The Modern Temper: A Study and a Confession* (New York, 1929), 191–92.

2. Wilbur C. Abbott, *Prejudices,* 5th series (New York, 1926), 157.

3. For literature on the post-war religious situation see George M. Marsden, *Fundamentalism and American Culture* (New York, 1980); E. R. Sandeen, *The Roots of Fundamentalism* (Chicago, 1970); T. P. Weber, *Living in the Shadow of the Second Coming: American Premillennialism, 1875–*

1925 (New York, 1979); Robert M. Miller, *American Protestantism and Social Issues, 1919–1939* (Chapel Hill, N.C., 1958); and Donald B. Meyer, *The Protestant Search for Political Realism, 1919–1941* (Berkeley, Calif., 1960).

4. Winthrop S. Hudson, *Religion in America: An Historical Account of the Development of American Religious Life* (New York, 1981), 373.

5. Willard L. Sperry, *Religion in America* (New York, 1946), 160–61.

6. Samuel C. Kincheloe, *Research Memo on Religion in the Depression* (New York, 1937), 44–46, 95.

7. William G. McLoughlin, Jr., *Modern Revivalism: Charles Grandison Finney to Billy Graham* (New York, 1959), 464.

8. *United Evangelical Action,* 17 April 1944, 9.

9. Ibid., 3 March 1943, 7.

10. Hudson, *Religion in America,* 384.

11. John Pollock, *To All the Nations* (San Francisco, 1985), 15.

12. Ibid., 14–17. Other biographies on Graham include Stanley High, *Billy Graham* (New York, 1956); John Pollock, *Billy Graham, Evangelist to the World: An Authorized Biography* (New York, 1971); William Martin, *A Prophet with Honor: The Billy Graham Story* (New York, 1991).

13. Pollock, *To All the Nations,* 20.

14. High, *Billy Graham,* 72.

15. Pollock, *To All the Nations,* 19.

16. Ibid., 22–23.

17. High, *Billy Graham,* 138.

18. Ibid., 141.

19. Ibid., 142.

20. Pollock, *To All the Nations,* 36–37.

21. High, *Billy Graham,* 147.

22. Ibid., 161.

23. Pollock, *To All the Nations,* 53–55.

24. Ibid., 55.

25. Ibid., 56.

26. Ibid.

27. High, *Billy Graham,* 170.

28. Pollock, *To All the Nations,* 60–61.

29. Ibid., 62.

30. Quoted in High, *Billy Graham,* 169.

31. *The Daily Mirror* (London), 4 May 1954.

32. Pollock, *To All the Nations*, 124.

33. *Sunday Telegraph* (London), 28 May 1961, 20.

34. McLoughlin, *Modern Revivalism,* 473.

35. *Decision*, March 1995.

36. It is of course true that Whitefield and Wesley differed on theology, the former being a Calvinist and the latter an Arminian. While in the early years Wesley seemed to be bothered by this, Whitefield did not let it trouble him overly, and in later years their friendship flourished despite the difference.

37. Luis Palau, *Luis Palau: Calling the Nations to Christ* (Chicago, 1983), 43.

38. Ibid., 194.

39. Ibid., 200–201.

40. *Philadelphia Inquirer*, 24 October 1993, 11.

41. Harry Covert, "An Interview with Luis Palau," *National & International Religion Report* 7.17 (9 August 1993): 1–4.

$\mathcal{B}$ibliography

Abbey, C. J., and J. H. Overton. *The English Church in the Eighteenth Century*. London, 1878.

Abbott, Wilbur C. *Prejudices*. 5th series. New York, 1926.

Ahlstrom, Sydney E. *A Religious History of the American People*. New Haven, Conn., 1972.

Aikin, Samuel C. *A Narrative of the Revival of Religion in the County of Oneida, Particularly in the Bounds of the Presbytery of Oneida, in the Year 1826*. Utica, N.Y., 1826.

Alexander, Archibald. *Biographical Sketches of the Founder and Principal Alumni of the Log College*. Philadelphia, 1851.

Alexander, James W. *Forty Years Familiar Letters of James W. Alexander*. Ed. John Hall. New York, 1860.

Allen, Ethan. *Reason the Only Oracle of Man, or a Compendious System of Natural Religion*. Bennington, Vt., 1784.

Anderson, Courtney. *To the Golden Shore*. Grand Rapids, 1972.

Asbury, Francis. *The Journal and Letters of Francis Asbury*. Nashville, 1958.

Asbury, Herbert. *A Methodist Saint: The Life of Bishop Asbury*. New York, 1927.

Bailey, Thomas A. *The American Pageant: A History of the Republic*. Boston, 1961.

Baird, Robert. *Religion in America*. New York, 1970.

Barnes, Gilbert H. *The Antislavery Impulse, 1830–1844*. Gloucester, Mass., 1964.

Barrett, David B., ed. *World Christian Encyclopedia*. Nairobi, 1992.

Beardsley, E. E. *History of the Episcopal Church in Connecticut*. Boston, 1883.

Beardsley, Frank G. *A History of American Revivals*. New York, 1904.

Beecher, Lyman. *Address of the Charitable Society for the Education of Indigent Pious Young Men for the Ministry of the Gospel*. Concord, Mass., 1820.

———. *Autobiography*. Ed. Barbara Cross. Cambridge, Mass., 1961.

Beecher, Lyman, and Asahel Nettleton. *Letters on "New Measures" in Conducting Revivals of Religion*. New York, 1828.

Belden, A. D. *George Whitefield, The Awakener*. Nashville, 1930.

Bennett, William W. *A Narrative of the Great Revival Which Prevailed in the Southern Armies*. Philadelphia, 1877.

Benson, Louis F. "President Davies as a Hymn Writer." *Journal of the Presbyterian Historical Society* 2 (1903): 277–86, 343–73.

Billington, Ray A. *Westward Expansion*. New York, 1949.

Boles, John B. *The Great Revival: 1787–1805*. Lexington, Ky., 1972.

Bradford, William. "History of Plimoth Plantation." In *The Puritans,* Perry Miller and Thomas H. Johnson. New York, 1963.

Brown, Elijah P. *The Real Billy Sunday.* New York, 1914.

Burke, Edmund. *Reflections on the Revolution in France.* . . . 9th ed. London, n.d.

Calvin, John. *Commentary upon the Acts of the Apostles.* Edinburgh, 1844.

——. *Institutes of the Christian Religion.* Grand Rapids, 1953.

Candler, Warren A. *Great Revivals and the Great Republic.* Nashville, 1904.

Cartwright, Peter. *Autobiography of Peter Cartwright.* London, 1856.

Chambers, T. W. *The Noon Prayer Meeting of the North Dutch Church.* New York, 1858.

Chapman, J. Wilbur. *Dwight L. Moody.* Philadelphia, 1900.

Chauncy, Charles. *Seasonable Thoughts on the State of Religion in New England.* Boston, 1743.

Christ in the Army; A Selection of Sketches of the Work of the U.S. Christian Commission. Philadelphia, 1865.

Cochran, William C. *Charles Grandison Finney.* Philadelphia, 1908.

Cole, Charles. *The Social Ideas of the Northern Evangelists, 1826–1860.* New York, 1954.

Conant, William C. *Narratives of Remarkable Conversions and Revival Incidents.* . . . New York, 1858.

Conkin, Paul K. *Cane Ridge: America's Pentecost.* Madison, Wis., 1990.

Cossit, Franceway R. *The Life and Times of Rev. Finis Ewing.* Louisville, 1853.

Coupland, R. *Wilberforce.* 2d ed. Oxford, 1945.

Covert, Harry. "An Interview with Luis Palau." *National & International Religion Report* 7.17 (9 August 1993): 1–4.

Cross, Whitney R. *The Burned-over District: The Social and Intellectual History of Enthusiastic Religion in Western New York, 1800–1850.* Ithaca, N.Y., 1950.

Cuningham, Charles E. *Timothy Dwight, 1752–1817.* New York, 1942.

Dallimore, Arnold. *George Whitefield: The Life and Times of the Great Evangelist of the Eighteenth-Century Revival.* Westchester, Ill., 1980.

Daniels, William H. *D. L. Moody and His Work.* Hartford, 1876.

Davis, George T. B. *Torrey and Alexander: The Story of a World-Wide Revival.* New York, 1905.

Denison, Lindsay. "The Rev. Billy Sunday and His War on the Devil." *American Magazine* 64 (September 1907).

Dorchester, Daniel. *Christianity in the United States.* New York, 1895.

Dorsett, Lyle W. *Billy Sunday and the Redemption of Urban America.* Grand Rapids, 1991.

Dwight, Timothy. *Theology: Explained and Defended.* Middletown, Conn., 1818–1819.

——. *Travels in New-England and New-York.* Cambridge, Mass., 1969.

Ecclesiastical Records [of the] State of New York. Albany, 1902.

Edwards, Jonathan. *A Divine and Supernatural Light, Immediately Imparted to the Soul by the Spirit of God, Shown to be both a Scriptural, and Rational Doctrine.* Boston, 1734.

——. *A Faithful Narrative of the Surprising Work of God in the Conversion of Many Hundred Souls in Northampton and the Neighboring Towns and Villages.* Boston, 1737.

——. "The Justice of God in the Damnation of Sinners." In *Puritan Sage,* ed. Vergilius Ferm. New York, 1953.

——. "Pressing Into the Kingdom of God." In *Puritan Sage,* ed. Vergilius Ferm. New York, 1953.

——. *Sinners in the Hands of an Angry God: A Sermon Preached at Enfield, July 8, 1741.* Boston, 1741.

——. *Some Thoughts Concerning the Present Revival of Religion in New England.* Boston, 1742.

Ellis, William T. *"Billy" Sunday: The Man and His Message.* Philadelphia, 1914.

Elsbree, Oliver. *The Rise of the Missionary Spirit in America.* Williamsport, Pa., 1928.

Engles, William M., ed. *Minutes of the General Assembly of the Presbyterian Church, 1789–1820.* Philadelphia, 1847.

Faulkner, H. U. *American Economic History.* New York, 1938.

Fielding, Henry. *Enquiry Into the Late Increase of Robbers.* London, 1751.

Findlay, James F., Jr. *Dwight L. Moody, American Evangelist 1837–1899.* Chicago, 1969.

Finney Papers, Oberlin (Ohio) College Library.

Finney, Charles G. *Lectures on Revivals of Religion.* Ed. W. G. McLoughlin, Jr. Cambridge, Mass., 1960.

———. *The Memoirs of Charles G. Finney.* Ed. Garth M. Rosell and Richard A. G. Dupuis. Grand Rapids, 1989.

———. *Memoirs of Rev. Charles G. Finney.* New York, 1876.

———. *Sermons on Various Subjects.* New York, 1835.

First Annual Report of the American Bible Society. New York, 1816.

Foster, Charles I. *An Errand of Mercy: The Evangelical United Front, 1790–1837.* Chapel Hill, N.C., 1960.

Franklin, Benjamin. "Autobiography." In *A Benjamin Franklin Reader,* ed. Nathan Goodman. New York, 1945.

Frelinghuysen, Peter H. B., Jr. *Theodorus Jacobus Frelinghuysen.* Princeton, 1938.

Frelinghuysen, Theodore J. *Sermons.* New York, 1856.

Furman, Wood, ed. *A History of the Charleston Association of Baptist Churches.* Charleston, S.C., 1811.

Gaustad, Edwin S. *The Great Awakening in New England.* New York, 1957.

Gay, Peter. *Deism: An Anthology.* Princeton, N.J., 1968.

Gewehr, W. M. *The Great Awakening in Virginia, 1740–1790.* Gloucester, Mass., 1965.

Gillett, E. H. *History of the Presbyterian Church in the United States of America.* Philadelphia, 1864.

Goen, C. C., ed. *The Great Awakening.* In vol. 4 of *The Works of Jonathan Edwards.* New Haven, Conn., 1972.

Goodrich, Chauncey A. "Narrative of Revivals of Religion in Yale College." *American Quarterly Register* 10 (1838).

Goodykootz, Colin. *Home Missions on the American Frontier.* Caldwell, Idaho, 1939.

Green, Ashbel. *A Sermon Delivered . . . on the 19th of February, 1795.* Philadelphia, 1795.

Griffin, Clifford S. *Their Brothers' Keepers: Moral Stewardship in the United States, 1800–1865.* New Brunswick, N.J., 1960.

Gundry, Stanley N. *Love Them In: The Proclamation Theology of D. L. Moody.* Chicago, 1976.

Hardman, Keith J. *Charles Grandison Finney, 1792–1875: Revivalist and Reformer.* Syracuse, 1987; reprint, paperback edition, Grand Rapids, 1990.

Harkness, Georgia. *John Calvin: The Man and His Ethics.* New York, 1931.

Harmelink, Herman, III. "Another Look at Frelinghuysen and His 'Awakening.'" *Church History* 37.4 (December 1968): 423–38.

Hatch, Nathan O. "Can Evangelicalism Survive Its Success?" *Christianity Today* (5 October 1992).

High, Stanley. *Billy Graham.* New York, 1956.

Holcomb, Walt. *Sam Jones: An Ambassador of the Almighty.* Nashville, 1947.

Hudson, Winthrop S. *Religion in America: An Historical Account of the Development of American Religious Life.* New York, 1981.

Johnson, Charles A. *The Frontier Camp Meeting: Religion's Harvest Time.* Dallas, 1955.

Jones, J. William. *Christ in the Camp; or, Religion in the Confederate Army.* Richmond, Va., 1904; reprint, Harrisonburg, Va., 1986.

Jones, Laura M. *The Life and Sayings of Sam P. Jones.* Atlanta, 1906.

Keller, Charles R. *The Second Great Awakening in Connecticut.* New Haven, Conn., 1942.

Kincheloe, Samuel C. *Research Memo on Religion in the Depression.* New York, 1937.

Klett, Guy S. *Presbyterians in Colonial Pennsylvania*. Philadelphia, 1937.

Krutch, Joseph Wood. *The Modern Temper: A Study and a Confession*. New York, 1929.

Lee, Jesse. *History of the Methodists*. Baltimore, 1810.

Love, W. DeLoss. *Samson Occum and the Christian Indians of New England*. Boston, 1899.

Lucas, Paul R. "An Appeal to the Learned: The Mind of Solomon Stoddard." *William and Mary Quarterly* 30 (1943): 257–92.

Marsden, George M. *Fundamentalism and American Culture*. New York, 1980.

Martin, William. *A Prophet with Honor: The Billy Graham Story*. New York, 1991.

Mather, Increase. *A Dissertation Concerning the Strange Doctrine of Mr. Stoddard*. Boston, 1708.

Mathews, Donald G. "The Second Great Awakening as an Organizing Process, 1780–1830: An Hypothesis." *American Quarterly* 21.1 (Spring 1969).

Maxson, Charles H. *The Great Awakening in the Middle Colonies*. Chicago, 1920.

McCasland, S. V., G. E. Cairns, and D. C. Yu. *Religions of the World*. New York, 1982.

McCrie, Thomas. *Sketches of Scottish Church History*. London, 1846.

McGready, James. "A Short Narrative of the Revival of Religion in Logan County, in the State of Kentucky, and the Adjacent Settlements in the State of Tennessee, from May 1797, until September 1800." *New York Missionary Magazine* 4 (New York, 1803).

McIlvaine, Charles P. *Bishop McIlvaine on the Revival of Religion. . . .* Philadelphia, 1858.

McLean, J. P. "The Kentucky Revival and Its Influence on the Miami Valley." *Ohio Archeological and Historical Publications* 12 (April 1903).

McLoughlin, William G., Jr. *Billy Sunday Was His Real Name*. Chicago, 1955.

———. *Modern Revivalism: Charles Grandison Finney to Billy Graham*. New York, 1959.

McNeill, John T. *The History and Character of Calvinism*. New York, 1967.

Mead, Sidney Earl. *Nathaniel William Taylor, 1786–1858: A Connecticut Liberal*. Chicago, 1942.

Mercer, Jesse. *A History of the Georgia Baptist Association*. Washington, Ga., 1838.

Meyer, Donald B. *The Protestant Search for Political Realism, 1919–1941*. Berkeley, Calif., 1960.

Miller, Perry. *Jonathan Edwards*. New York, 1949.

———. *The Life of the Mind in America: From the Revolution to the Civil War*. New York, 1965.

———. *The New England Mind: From Colony to Province*. Boston, 1953.

———. "Solomon Stoddard." *Harvard Theological Review* 34 (1941): 277–320.

Miller, Perry, and Thomas Johnson, eds. *The Puritans*. New York, 1963.

Miller, Robert M. *American Protestantism and Social Issues, 1919–1939*. Chapel Hill, N.C., 1958.

Mode, Peter G. *Source Book and Bibliographical Guide for American Church History*. Menasha, Wis., 1921.

Moody, William R. *The Life of Dwight L. Moody*. New York, 1900.

Moodyana Collection, Moody Bible Institute, Chicago.

Morgan, G. Campbell. *Lessons of the Welsh Revival*. New York, 1905.

Morrison, Howard A. "The Finney Takeover of the Second Great Awakening During the Oneida Revivals of 1825–1827." *New York History* 59.1 (January 1978).

Moule, Handley C. G. *The Epistle to the Romans*. London, 1954.

Niebuhr, H. Richard. *The Kingdom of God in America*. New York, 1937.

Noble, W. F. P. *A Century of Gospel Work*. Philadelphia, 1876.

Orr, J. Edwin. *The Second Evangelical Awakening in America*. London, 1952.

———. *The Second Evangelical Awakening in Britain*. London, 1949.

Palau, Luis. *Luis Palau: Calling the Nations to Christ*. Chicago, 1983.

Palmer, Elihu. *Principles of Nature; or, A Development of the Moral Causes of*

Happiness and Misery among the Human Species. London, 1823.

Pears, Thomas C., and Guy S. Klett, eds. *Documentary History of William Tennent and the Log College.* Philadelphia, 1940.

Pollock, John. *Billy Graham, Evangelist to the World: An Authorized Biography.* New York, 1971.

———. *To All the Nations.* San Francisco, 1985.

Prime, Samuel I. *The Power of Prayer.* New York, 1859.

Purcell, Richard J. *Connecticut in Transition: 1775–1818.* Middletown, Conn., 1963.

"Review on the Employment of Evangelists in Our Older Settlements." *Quarterly Christian Spectator* 1 (September 1829).

Richards, Thomas C. *Samuel J. Mills: Missionary Pathfinder, Pioneer, and Promoter.* Boston, 1906.

Richardson, James D., ed. *A Compilation of the Messages and Papers of the Presidents, 1789–1904.* New York, 1904.

Rippon, John. *The Baptist Annual Register.* London, n.d.

Romilly, Sir George. *Observations on the Criminal Code.* London, 1810.

Rosell, Garth M. *Charles Grandison Finney and the Rise of the Benevolence Empire.* Ann Arbor, Mich., 1971.

Ryle, J. C. *A Sketch of the Life and Labors of George Whitefield.* Edinburgh, 1850.

Sandeen, E. R. *The Roots of Fundamentalism.* Chicago, 1970.

Schafer, Thomas A. "Solomon Stoddard and the Theology of the Revival." In *A Miscellany of American Christianity,* ed. Stuart C. Henry. Durham, N.C., 1963.

Schoulder, J. *History of the United States under the Constitution.* New York, 1922.

Seward, Thomas. *Address: A Memorial of the Semi-Centennial of the Founding of the Sunday School of the First Presbyterian Church, Utica, New York.* Utica, 1867.

Shattuck, Gardiner H., Jr. *A Shield and Hiding Place: The Religious Life of the Civil War Armies.* Macon, Ga., 1987.

Shaw, John. *Twelve Years in America.* London, 1867.

Smith, H. S., R. T. Handy, and L. A. Loetscher. *American Christianity: An Historical Interpretation with Representative Documents.* New York, 1960.

Smith, Timothy L. *Revivalism and Social Reform: American Protestantism on the Eve of the Civil War.* New York, 1957.

Sperry, Willard L. *Religion in America.* New York, 1946.

Sprague, William B. *Lectures on Revivals of Religion.* Edinburgh, 1958.

Steiner and Schweinitz. *Report of the Journey of the Brethren.* n.p., n.d.

Stephen, Sir Leslie. *English Thought in the Eighteenth Century.* New York, 1949.

Stephens, Sir James. *Essays in Ecclesiastical Biography.* London, 1849.

Stevens, Abel. *History of the Methodist Episcopal Church.* New York, 1864–67.

Stiles, Ezra. *A Discourse on the Christian Union.* Boston, 1760.

Stoddard, Solomon. *The Defects of Preachers Reproved in a Sermon Preached at Northampton, May 19, 1723.* New London, Conn., 1724.

———. *The Doctrine of Instituted Churches Explained, and Proved from the Word of God.* London, 1700.

———. *The Efficacy of the Fear of Hell.* Boston, 1713.

———. *A Guide to Christ.* Boston, 1714.

———. *The Inexcusableness of Neglecting the Worship of God, Under a Pretense of Being in an Unconverted Condition.* Boston, 1708.

———. *The Presence of Christ with the Ministers of the Gospel.* Boston, 1718.

———. *The Safety of Appearing at the Day of Judgment, in the Righteousness of Christ.* Boston, 1689.

Stoeffler, F. Ernest. *The Rise of Evangelical Pietism.* Leiden, 1965.

Stone, Barton W. "A Short History of the Life of Barton W. Stone." In *The Cane Ridge Meeting-House,* by James R. Rogers. Cincinnati, 1910.

Stout, Harry S. *The Divine Dramatist: George Whitefield and the Rise of Modern Evangelicalism.* Grand Rapids, 1991.

Sweet, William Warren. *Religion on the American Frontier: The Methodists.* Chicago, 1946.

——. *The Story of Religion in America.* New York, 1950.

Tanis, James. *Dutch Calvinistic Pietism in the Middle Colonies: A Study in the Life of Theodorus Jacobus Frelinghuysen.* The Hague, 1967.

Tawney, R. H. *Religion and the Rise of Capitalism.* New York, 1926.

Thomas, John L. *The Liberator.* New York, 1963.

Tipple, Ezra S. *Francis Asbury, The Prophet of the Long Road.* New York, 1916.

Torrey, Samuel. "A Plea for the Life of Dying Religion." In *The Christian History, Containing Accounts of the Revival and Propogation of Religion in Great Britain, America, &c.,* ed. Thomas Prince, Jr. Boston, 1743.

Tracy, Joseph. *The Great Awakening: A History of the Revival of Religion in the Time of Edwards and Whitefield.* Boston, 1842.

Trinterud, Leonard J. *The Forming of an American Tradition: A Re-examination of Colonial Presbyterianism.* Philadelphia, 1949.

Trumbull, J. R. *A History of Northampton.* Northampton, Mass., 1898.

Tyerman, Luke. *Life of George Whitefield.* London, 1890.

Walker, Williston. *A History of the Christian Church.* 3d ed. rev. New York, 1970.

Weber, T. P. *Living in the Shadow of the Second Coming: American Premillennialism, 1875–1925.* New York, 1979.

Weisberger, Bernard A. *They Gathered at the River.* Boston, 1958.

Westerkamp, Marilyn J. *Triumph of the Laity: Scots-Irish Piety and the Great Awakening, 1625–1760.* New York, 1988.

White, Charles E. *The Beauty of Holiness: Phoebe Palmer as Theologian, Revivalist, Feminist, and Humanitarian.* Grand Rapids, 1986.

Whitefield, George. *Journals.* London, 1960.

——. "Sermon 9: The Folly and Danger of Being Not Righteous Enough." In vol. 5 of *The Works of Whitefield.* London, 1954.

Woodward, William W. *Surprising Accounts of the Revival of Religion in the United States of America.* Philadelphia, 1802.

Wright, George F. *Charles Grandison Finney.* New York, 1891.

Index